the

writing

clinic . . .

RALPH E. LOEWE

Cuyahoga Community College

the writing clinic...

PRENTICE-HALL, INC. Englewood Cliffs, New Jersey

PRENTICE-HALL INTERNATIONAL INC., *London*
PRENTICE-HALL OF AUSTRALIA, PTY. LTD., *Sydney*
PRENTICE-HALL OF CANADA, LTD., *Toronto*
PRENTICE-HALL OF INDIA PRIVATE LIMITED, *New Delhi*
PRENTICE-HALL OF JAPAN, INC., *Tokyo*

TO THE TEACHER

THE WRITING CLINIC teaches standard English writing with a minimum of grammatical theory. Although its major emphasis is on sentence structure and development, the book introduces the student to the writing of expository paragraphs and themes, and it provides pictures, cartoons, poems, and essays for writing assignments, for reading, and for class discussion.

The book uses the following approaches:

It teaches the sentence in context. Many students who can write correctly structured sentences lose their sentence "sense" when they write paragraphs and themes.[1] To counter this tendency, THE WRITING CLINIC provides writing assignments in its first and last chapters so that the instructor can diagnose the students' sentences in context at the beginning of the course and measure their improvement at the end. Other paragraph assignments are interspersed throughout the book. This approach helps students avoid the frustration they face when they succeed in their short answer exercises only to fail in the grammatical and mechanical aspects of sentence writing when they write longer units.

It takes nothing for granted. There are many reasons why students may have gaps in their knowledge of language: some students come from overcrowded, undermanned urban schools; some come from inadequately staffed, impoverished rural schools; some students have a history of illness; others may have moved from school to school. This text, therefore, begins with the most basic sentence structures and works gradually to the more complicated.

It uses a minimum of grammatical theory and terminology. Every effort has been made to eliminate those aspects of grammar needed only for a theoretical understanding of the language (aspects which can be reserved for more

---

[1] These sentences may contain grammatical and mechanical errors, but they will have subjects and verbs, and the periods will be in the right places.

specialized courses) and to concentrate on those aspects of grammar needed directly in writing acceptable sentences at the college level.

Also eliminated are aspects of grammar that cause no problems for most students and those that can be bypassed because of the highly structured methods used by the book. Such bypassed elements include transitive, intransitive, and linking verbs, direct and indirect objects and predicate nominatives, gerunds, and many others—without avoiding any of the major problem areas.

This approach makes it possible to teach the three basic sentence types—simple, compound, and complex—using only three sentence parts: subjects, verbs, and conjunctions. Once the student has learned these, many other sentence parts fall naturally into place.

The theoretical method is implemented by a pedagogical method.   Because language is partially an automatic response, and because many nonstandard reactions have become habitual, this book uses a test and drill method to reinforce the standard responses that it teaches. Since many students with writing problems also have reading problems, there are comprehension tests as well as drill-type exercises. The comprehension tests are included to help students concentrate on their reading rather than just look at words as many of them tend to do. The tests are not included to force students to memorize rules. Vocabulary work is also part of the testing process.

Keys are provided for all self-quizzes.   To help students become more involved in the teaching-learning process, answers are given at the end of the chapter for correcting the exercises that are done in the book. Students who are not mature enough to use the keys effectively may require initial help. All students will benefit by patience, understanding, and encouragement.

The instructor's judgment cannot be programmed.   Most remedial students need the stimulation of regular class attendance, lecture, and discussion or periodic help from carefully trained tutors to help them get the most from the book. In addition, teacher-graded tests are placed throughout the book to give the student further help in evaluating his homework and the teacher periodic measures of the student's progress. All tests are to be written on separate paper and handed in for grading. The teachers' manual provides end-of-chapter tests to further aid the instructor in evaluating the student's work.

On evaluating the first writing assignments, the instructor will probably find that most students need to work with the entire sequence of chapters. However, the profusion of self-quizzes with keys plus teacher-graded tests that must be handed in will enable the instructor to be flexible with the better students and turn them loose to teach themselves.

TO THE STUDENT

The major thrust of this book is on the writing of good sentences. However, sentences are not usually written in isolation but as parts of paragraphs. For this reason THE WRITING CLINIC begins and ends with brief writing assignments, and there is a scattering of such assignments throughout the book.

Students need varying amounts of help from their instructors, but the book is designed to help you *teach yourself* to a great extent. In addition to carefully planned instructions and examples, most of the chapters contain self-quizzes to help you measure your understanding of each section. Space is provided so that you can do the quiz exercises in the book. The benefit you derive from these teach-yourself exercises will depend upon how thoughtfully you do them and especially how carefully you *correct* them against the answer keys given at the end of the chapter. The other tests are more complicated than the quizzes and require more writing. They should be written on separate paper and handed in to your instructor for grading, so that he can check your progress.

Plan of the book. The book is divided into five parts. In the first you will receive a series of writing assignments to determine your weaknesses and problems. Part II consists of six closely-knit chapters that help you to analyze and practice building sentences. In Part III you will get into special problems such as punctuation, the tenses, parts of speech—the various areas involved in polishing your writing. Part IV demonstrates how to organize and write short themes and papers. Part V consists of a final series of writing assignments designed to help measure your overall improvement.

The book and your instructor will help as much as possible to remedy your writing problems. You, the student, however, are the only one who can effect the cure.

ACKNOWLEDGMENTS

To my students, who work hard for a living and for an education.

To Cuyahoga Community College, where concern for students runs deep.

To my colleagues—especially Norman Prange and Raymond Ackley—who willingly tried the developing lessons and criticized wisely.

To professors Michael J. Cardone, Henry Ford Community College, and Donald C. Rigg, Broward Junior College; and to William F. Smith, Fullerton Junior College, who reviewed my manuscript and made helpful suggestions.

To Chuck Kramer, artist extraordinary, who drew the illustrations introducing each chapter.

To editor William Oliver for getting me started, and to Hilda Tauber, production editor, for seeing me through.

To Bess, who helped with writing, research, and patience; and to Ronnie and Debbie, who have long had to surmount the indignities of having an English teacher for a father.

CONTENTS

PART I

WRITING is one of the most complicated tasks that human beings undertake. It requires a combination of skills that we begin to learn in the cradle and continue to develop all our lives. For various reasons, many students entering college have not developed their writing skills to adequately handle college-level work. Our first job is to find out what your weaknesses are, so that proper treatment may begin. Turn the page and

check

into

the clinic...

CHAPTER 1

The
DIAGNOSIS

The assignments in this chapter are designed to give you something to write about to find how fully you express your ideas, and how well you handle the form of the language—such things as grammar, spelling, and mechanics.[1] Study the suggestions below before you start to write.

WRITING SUGGESTIONS

1. Read the directions for each assignment carefully.
2. Since all the assignments provide choices, choose those which you know most about or feel most strongly about.

[1] "Mechanics" refers to punctuation, capitalization, possession, and contraction.

3. Think over your idea carefully *before* you start writing.

4. Limit your idea so that you can do a good job in the allotted time. It is better to develop one idea in depth than to state many ideas superficially.

5. Do not try to impress the instructor with fancy language. Keep your wording simple and straightforward.

6. Plan to leave at least five minutes for editing your work. Try to read it through twice: first, to see if it makes good sense and holds together well; then to check your grammar, spelling, and mechanics.

ASSIGNMENT 1: React to Pictures

Write a paper of about 200 words in which you react to one or more of the pictures on the following pages. Review the writing suggestions above before proceeding.

Courtesy Gilbert, Felix & Scharf, Inc.

Photo by Bill Nehez

Courtesy Denver Public Library

Courtesy McDonnell, Douglas Corp.

what to write about

In reacting to one picture, you might discuss what it means to be brought up in a rubble-filled back alley, or how a poverty-stricken migratory worker's family lives. You might write about glassy offices and high-rise buildings, traffic jams, or pollution problems.

Cleveland Press Photo

In reacting to more than one picture, you might discuss the extremes of wealth and poverty in this country, rural versus urban life, the diversity of America, or whether we should spend money for missiles and space programs while there is so much need on earth.

ASSIGNMENT 2: React to Poems

Write a paper of about 200 words in which you react to one or more of the poems on the following pages. If you use more than one poem, be sure that you do not write two separate themes. Keep your work unified. Review the writing suggestions on pages 3-4 before starting to write.

CAUTION: Do not write a poem. Write a paragraph giving your reactions to the poetry you have chosen.

Lies

—YEVGENY YEVTUSHENKO

Telling lies to the young is wrong.
Proving to them that lies are true is wrong.
Telling them that God's in his heaven
and all's well with the world is wrong.
The young know what you mean. The young are people.
Tell them the difficulties can't be counted,
and let them see not only what will be
but see with clarity these present times.
Say obstacles exist they must encounter
sorrow happens, hardship happens.
The hell with it. Who never knew
the price of happiness will not be happy.
Forgive no error you recognize.
It will repeat itself, increase,
and afterwards our pupils
will not forgive in us what we forgave.

From *Selected Poems*, translated by Robin Milner-Gulland and Peter Leir, S. J. © 1962 by Robin Milner-Gulland and Peter Leir. Reprinted by permission of Penguin Books Ltd.

what to write about

1. Write about the lies that have been told to you and how they affected you.

2. Write about the necessity of telling lies at certain times.

3. Discuss Yevtushenko's poem specifically. Is he right or wrong? Support your criticisms.

Those Winter Sundays

—ROBERT HAYDEN

Sundays too my father got up early
and put his clothes on in the blueblack cold,
then with cracked hands that ached
from labor in the weekday weather made
banked fires blaze. No one ever thanked him.

I'd wake and hear the cold splintering, breaking.
When the rooms were warm, he'd call,
and slowly I would rise and dress,
fearing the chronic angers of that house.

Speaking indifferently to him,
who had driven out the cold
and polished my good shoes as well.
What did I know, what did I know
of love's austere and lonely offices?

Mother to Son

—LANGSTON HUGHES

Well, son, I'll tell you:
Life for me ain't been no crystal stair.
It's had tacks in it,
And splinters,
And boards torn up,
And places with no carpet on the floor—
Bare.
But all the time
I'se been a-climbin' on,
And reachin' landin's,
And turnin' corners,
And sometimes goin' in the dark
Where there ain't been no light.
So, boy, don't you turn back.
Don't you set down on the steps
'Cause you find it kinder hard.
Don't you fall now—
For I'se still goin', honey,
I'se still climbin',
And life for me ain't been no crystal stair.

what to write about

1. Describe a person in your life who has quietly, selflessly helped you.

2. If there has been no such person in your life, describe someone who has created problems for you.

3. Does the philosophy of "Mother to Son" affect you? Will it help you to keep on "climbin"?

4. Which poem do you like better? Why? Explain in detail.

Resistance

—CRAIG WILLIAMSON

Before I kill one man more
I will say no.
Before I die
I will see loving.
Before I war upon my man
I will say no to war lords.
Before I sleep in one more bed
I will find one more brother.
Before I break one more fast
I will know hungry others.
Before I step in one more street
I will stand up in ghettos.
Before I profit one more crime
I will know why the criming.
Before I buy one more lie
I will say no to lying.
Before I sleep the sleep of dead
I will say no to dying.
Before I kill one man more
I will say no.
Before I die
I will know loving.

From *African Wings* by Craig Williamson.
Copyright 1969 by Craig Williamson.
Reprinted by permission of Citadel Press, Inc.

what to write about

1. Discuss the title of this poem and its implications. What is the poet resisting? Why? Does he appear to be a highly moral person or an immoral one?

2. If you believe that the poet is wrong, criticize his ideas and give reasons for your criticism.

3. Discuss your moral code and how it affects your way of life. Compare it to that of the poet.

Street Window

—CARL SANDBURG

The pawn-shop man knows hunger,
And how far hunger has eaten the heart
Of one who comes with an old keepsake.
Here are wedding rings and baby bracelets,
Scarf pins and shoe buckles, jeweled garters,
Old-fashioned knives with inlaid handles,
Watches of old gold and silver,
Old coins worn with finger-marks.
They tell stories.

Incident

—COUNTEE CULLEN

Once riding in old Baltimore,
Heart-filled, head-filled with glee,
I saw a Baltimorean
Keep looking straight at me.

Now, I was eight and very small,
And he was no whit bigger,
And so I smiled, but he poked out
His tongue, and called me, "Nigger."

I saw the whole of Baltimore
From May until December;
Of all the things that happened there
That's all that I remember.

My Heart Leaps Up

—WILLIAM WORDSWORTH

My heart leaps up when I behold
A rainbow in the sky;
So was it when my life began,
So is it now I am a man,
So be it when I shall grow old,
Or let me die!

what to write about

1. Do pawnshops affect you the same way they did Carl Sandburg? If not, write a paragraph about your reactions. If so, present the same idea in your own words. Perhaps some other kind of familiar scene brings similar sad stories to mind. Describe it.

2. Describe a childhood incident that affected you deeply. It doesn't have to be an unhappy incident.

3. William Wordsworth was a nineteenth-century British poet. "My Heart Leaps Up" is quite different from the other poems in this section, mostly because it looks for the beauty in life rather than at the sad realities. Which do you prefer? Why? Discuss.

ASSIGNMENT 3: React to Cartoons

Write a paper of about 200 words in which you react to one or more of the cartoons on the following pages. No specific "what to write about" ideas are provided. If, however, you see a relationship between any of the cartoons and any of the poems or pictures in this section, you may combine your ideas into one unified theme.

Review the writing suggestions on pages 3-4 before you proceed.

Courtesy Great Northern
Nekoosa Corporation

"I give up."

ANIMAL CRACKERS   by Roger Bollen

Courtesy National Newspapers Syndicate

Drawing by CEM © 1961 The New Yorker Magazine, Inc.

"And *that* one is an *anti*-anti-missile-missile."

ASSIGNMENT 4: React to Essays

Write a paper of about 200 words in which you react to one of the essays on the following pages. Review the writing suggestions on pages 3-4 before proceeding.

The End of the World

—PETER FLEMING

The other day a great many people in Rome became suddenly and inexplicably convinced that the world was going to end at midnight on Monday; the Vatican had to issue a statement saying "there is nothing to warrant the present panic." When I read about this I began to wonder how, if the British nation knew for a fact that the world was going to end in twenty-four hours' time, it would spend those hours. I suppose that most people, including many who had not done such a thing for years, would go to church. What else would happen? Except for midwives, stockmen, B.B.C. announcers, the crews of ships at sea and keepers in zoological gardens, hardly anybody would have any reason to do any work. If the Government recommended a "business as usual" policy, would it work? There wouldn't be much point in the shops or the banks staying open, since money and goods would be valueless; and the schools (which in Rome were poorly attended on Monday) might just as well be closed. It would, on the other hand, be a pity to cancel cricket fixtures. Cricket is one of the few forms of human activity which would not be robbed, both for players and spectators, of all meaning and all interest by the fact that the world was about to end; it would still be worth hitting a six or holding a catch, when designing a cathedral or assassinating a tyrant had become completely pointless acts. But I suspect that most people would spend an anxious, frustrated and probably rather boring day, irked by remembrance of all the things they had always wanted to do and by the realization that, if it was not too late, it was either impossible or useless to do them now.

From *My Aunt's Rhinoceros* by Peter Fleming. © 1956 by Peter Fleming. Reprinted by permission of Rupert Hart-Davis Ltd.

what to write about

1. Describe in detail how the world will end.

2. What would you do if you were the only one in the world to know that it was going to explode in twenty-four hours. You could not, of course, tell others.

3. How do you feel most Americans would act if they knew that the world would end in twenty-four hours?

A Quiet Elderly Couple

—CARL SANDBURG

A quiet elderly couple had their home on the south side of Berrien west of Pearl. They had been there a year or two and we hadn't heard their name or what they lived on. When they sat on their front porch they might look at each other once in a while but they didn't speak to each other. When us kids passed by they didn't look at us. They just went on looking straight ahead at nothing in particular. They seemed to be living in a quiet world of their own. They looked quiet and acted quiet. They were so still and peaceable that we got to talking about how still and peaceable they were and we ought to do something about it. One boy said, "Let's give 'em the tin cans." It wasn't a case of hate. We didn't hate them. We were just curious about them and we thought maybe something funny would happen. Again we strung together a dozen cans on each of two ropes. We saw their light on, waited and saw their kerosene lamp go out, waited a while longer and then sent the two strings of cans slam-bang against the front door. We skipped across the street, three of us and each behind his own tree. We waited. Nothing happened. The door didn't open. Nobody came out. We waited a while wondering whether the man had gone out the back door and was circling around to surprise us. We picked up our feet and ran.

It was several months later that one of the boys went into a Main Street grocery and saw this couple. For how many bars of soap they wanted or how many pounds of butter, they held up their fingers, two fingers for two bars of soap and so on. They didn't say a word. They were deaf and dumb. When the three of us heard this we were honest with each other. We asked why we had done such a fool thing. "What the hell," said one boy as he turned his back to me and stooped, "kick me." I gave him a swift kick in the hind end, then stooped for him to kick me. Each of the three of us gave the other two a swift kick. Once later when I passed the house and saw the couple sitting quiet and peaceable on their front porch I looked straight at them and touched my hat. They didn't nod nor smile. They just went on looking ahead at nothing in particular.

From *Always the Young Stranger* by Carl Sandburg. © 1953 by Harcourt Brace Jovanovich, Inc. Reprinted by permission of the publisher.

what to write about

1. Write about a thoughtless prank that you performed, a prank that turned out to be meaner than you had planned it to be. Perhaps the victim was injured instead of just being frightened. Perhaps the person was ill or retarded and you didn't know it.

2. Tell about a situation in which you first were antagonized by someone and later became friends.

3. Tell about a thoughtless prank that was played on you.

Conformity of Young Rebels

—HOWARD PRESTON

From vantage points both in and out of town recently I had the chance to take a sideline view of hippies, the young rebels, the boys and girls who go out of their way to be history's greatest nonconformists.

And their conformity is startling.

In their zeal to do almost anything which will confound the establishment, angry young men and women—some of whom are honest in their dissent and some of whom are sheer fakes—have set up their own organization with its own set of rules.

But in the revolt against their elders and the world which they would like to remake, they have arranged a new code for themselves which calls for the very sort of strict conformity they criticize.

The key word is permissiveness, permissiveness in dress, in personal habits, in political credos if that's the right word, in attitudes. But the permissiveness has led to rigidity. The army of the non-conforming, anti-status quo people has become an army of conformists.

If one wears fringed clothing, they all wear it. If the leaders wear long hair, they all wear long hair. If vests are in, then all wear vests.

Let one member of the loosely knit clan wear a floppy felt hat, then there is a rush on floppy felt hats.

Conforming to the style of the day makes most of the hippies into followers, not leaders. If Madison Avenue has the image of the man in the gray flannel suit, then hippieland has the bearded guy in the too tight jeans and sandals.

In summer, just about all that is sloppy in the matter of personal grooming or attire has been accepted by the rebel cult. Plus bad manners. And greatly to blame, it seems to me, is their intense desire not to be caught discriminating.

In the sense of illogically determining one's companions, of choosing them or rejecting them simply because of race, color or religious belief or nonbelief, discrimination is a bad word. But in its preferred meaning, that the thoughtful, educated person of good will has enough brains not to run around with idiots, thieves, lunkheads or people of low character, the word is essential for advancing civilization.

Yet, because of the evil context of the word the young people who are antisocial with parents, friends and elders often try to make up for this by being completely nondiscriminatory in other circles. Because they are hung up on the advice to love one another, they do so with abandon instead of with selectivity.

The thousands of kids with long dirty hair, dirty feet, frayed clothing and with a bewildering lack of announced progressive goals probably would be shocked to be told that their original basic hatred, against conformity, has led them into a blah of unanimity in which almost every one has lost his own identity.

From *The Cleveland Plain Dealer*, Sept. 21, 1970. Reprinted by permission of the editor, The Cleveland Plain Dealer.

what to write about

1. If you agree with Mr. Preston, write an article supporting his viewpoint. If you disagree, write one based on your observation of hippies.

2. Describe the group with which you associate as to dress, interests, and attitudes.

3. Describe the "in" group or most dominant group in your school, neighborhood, or church.

4. Describe the most conservative group with which you come into contact.

Potter's Field

—WILLIAM STYRON

Potter's Field for New York City is on an island in the Sound, half a mile east of the Bronx and just inside the city limits. . . .

The island itself is bleak and unprepossessing. There are islands like this, serving all sorts of cheerless but necessary municipal functions, near every great city in the world—islands in the Thames and Danube and the Seine, and in the yellow waters of the Tiber. This one, perhaps because it is American, seems more than necessarily dreary. No blade of grass grows here, only weeds. On the south end of the island stands a sewage disposal plant. North of this is a city detention home, a great mass of soot-stained brick and iron bars, where derelicts and drunks and the less-involved dope addicts are "rehabilitated." Moss and flakes of pale green lichen creep along the walls. In the treeless shade of the courtyards, flowering in crannies below shuttered windows, are chickweed and ghostly dandelions. Still farther north of this jail, separated from it by a quarter mile of dusty, weed-choked rising ground, is Potter's Field. The glens and willow-groves are gone, the picnickers and the slain deer; if you stand here on the hill beneath a dead, wind-twisted cedar, the island's only tree, you can get a good view of the land—the sewage plant and the prison and the burial ground, each recipient, in its fashion, of waste and decay. . . .

To transport bodies from the morgue they once had a tugboat; painted black, a flag at half-mast on its stern, it chugged up the East River on Thursdays. When it passed, barge captains and sailors would uncover their heads, cross themselves, or murmur a prayer. Now a truck is used, and the dead no longer receive this final benediction: who would salute a truck, so green and so commonplace? The coffins are made of plain pine and these—twenty-five or thirty each week—are laid four deep in the big mass graves. There are no prayers said; city prisoners are used for the burying, and they receive a day off from their sentence for each day's work in Potter's Field. The other dead must be crowded out—those who have lain there for twenty years. Now they are bones and dust and, taking up valuable space, must be removed. Not just twice dead like the relics beneath Washington Square, they become triply annihilated: the prisoners won't let them rest, remove them—bones, rotted cerement, and rattling skull—and throw them in a smaller hole, where they take up one tenth the space they did twenty years before. The new coffins are laid in precisely, tagged and numbered; in this way many souls occupy, undisturbed, their own six feet of earth for two decades. . . .

what to write about

1. If you have ever been to a cemetery for those who can not afford private burial, try your hand at describing it.

2. Describe any cemetery that brings pictures to your mind.

3. Describe any place which evokes vivid memories—a favorite camping spot, a "haunted" house in your old neighborhood, a cave, or a farm.

PART II

SENTENCES are the basic building blocks with which paragraphs are constructed. To correct your grammatical and mechanical weaknesses diagnosed in chapter one, treatment must begin with the writing of good sentences. In the next six chapters you will analyze sentence structure, from the simplest level to compound-complex levels, as you practice

building

sentences . . .

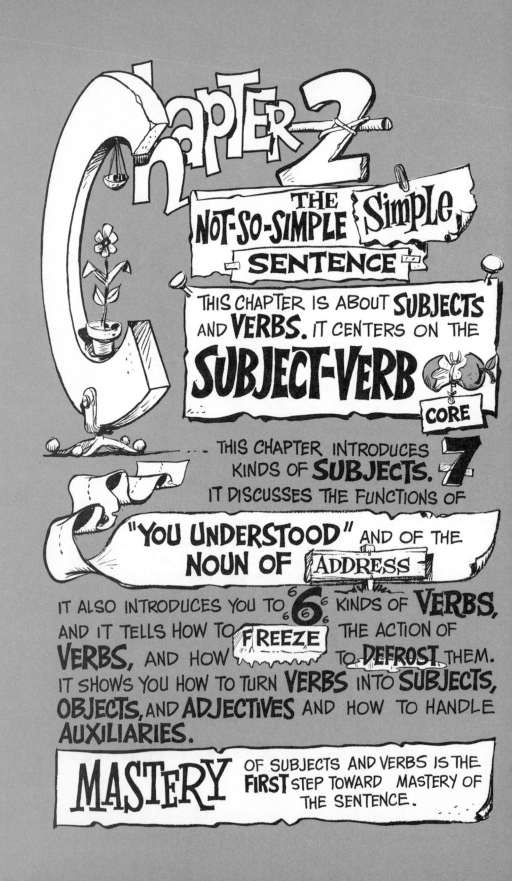

CHAPTER 2

THE NOT-SO-SIMPLE Simple SENTENCE

THIS CHAPTER IS ABOUT **SUBJECTS** AND **VERBS**. IT CENTERS ON THE

SUBJECT-VERB

CORE

... THIS CHAPTER INTRODUCES **7** KINDS OF **SUBJECTS**. IT DISCUSSES THE FUNCTIONS OF

"YOU UNDERSTOOD" AND OF THE NOUN OF **ADDRESS**

IT ALSO INTRODUCES YOU TO **6** KINDS OF **VERBS**, AND IT TELLS HOW TO **FREEZE** THE ACTION OF **VERBS**, AND HOW TO **DEFROST** THEM. IT SHOWS YOU HOW TO TURN **VERBS** INTO **SUBJECTS**, **OBJECTS**, AND **ADJECTIVES** AND HOW TO HANDLE **AUXILIARIES**.

MASTERY OF SUBJECTS AND VERBS IS THE **FIRST** STEP TOWARD MASTERY OF THE SENTENCE.

The not-so-simple
SIMPLE SENTENCE

The average college student has used his language for so many years that he takes much of it for granted. He does not realize what an ingenious method of communication his language is. Whenever he writes a sentence, he brings together a vast complex of knowledge and skills which he has acquired from babyhood on. Here are some of them: vocabulary, spelling, capitalization, punctuation, tense, person, gender, mood, number, agreement of subject and verb, agreement of pronoun and antecedent, case, possession, and contraction. At the college level the student is expected to handle these and other sentence elements correctly. Insofar as he is weak in any area, he shows gaps in his understanding of the most elementary aspects of his language.

THE SUBJECT–VERB CORE

Generally speaking, sentences are formed by the interaction between subjects and verbs. Since most sentence-writing problems seem to center upon the subject-verb relationship, this book focuses a great deal of attention on what it calls the subject-verb core. In addition, since every sentence must contain within it the basic elements of the simple sentence, we start with the simple sentence and move from it to the compound and complex structures. Once you have mastered the simple sentence you should have relatively little trouble mastering the others.

SELF-QUIZ 1

Write the answers to the questions below in the space provided.

1. The average student does not realize how ingenious a means of

   _____ his language is.

2. Sentences are formed by the interaction between what two sentence parts?

   _____

3. Every sentence must contain within it the basic elements of _____

   _____

4. (a) Explain "complex" as used on page 21.

   _____

   (b) What does "complex" mean as used in the paragraph above?

   _____

5. Why does this book place emphasis on the subject-verb core?

   _____

   _____

Correct your work.

.ıl.ıl.ıl.ıl.ıl.ıl.ıl.ıl.ıl.ıl.ıl.ıl.ıl.ıl.ıl.ıl.ıl.ıl.ıl.ıl.ıl.ıl.ıl.

how to do the quizzes

The self-quizzes in this book are intended as study aids. They are meant to help you check your comprehension and progress so that you can teach yourself as much as possible. In order to benefit from these exercises, you must do them carefully, then compare your answers with the key given at the end of the chapter, and, most important, *correct your work* before you move on.

Refer back to the text sections as often as you need, not only to get the answers right but to understand *why* they are right. No memorization is required unless specified. You are expected to look up all unfamiliar words in the dictionary; if you use a dictionary definition in one of your answers, make sure it fits in context.

Approach every quiz as a *writing* exercise. That means, your answers should be written in complete sentences (unless words alone are called for) and you should pay attention to *details*: spelling, punctuation, capitalization. A missing or incorrectly spelled word can negate a whole idea; a missing comma or period can change or obscure your intended meaning. Write thoughtfully, carefully. Proofread your work. CORRECT ALL ERRORS.

WHAT IS A SIMPLE SENTENCE?

A simple sentence has the following characteristics: (a) it must contain at least one verb and a subject which is either stated or implied (understood), and (b) it must contain a complete idea.[1]

A sentence may consist of only one word, a verb in the present tense: *Stop. Go. Hurry!* On the other hand, you may string together a thousand words which make sense in sequence, but if they do not contain a subject (either stated or understood) and a verb which interacts with the subject, you have not written a sentence.

SUBJECT: A subject is the word or words which combine with the verb to form the core of the sentence. The subject can be a person, a group, a thing, a place, a quality, an idea, or an activity.[2]

VERB: A verb is the word or words which combine with the subject to form the core of the sentence. A verb can describe an action (*run, bleed, breathe, advertise*), indicate existence (*is, has been, will be*), express feeling or sensory reactions (*smell, crave, adore, distrust*), or indicate possession (*have, keep, own*).

SELF-QUIZ 2

Answer the questions below in the allotted spaces.

1. A one-word sentence must consist of _____

2. What is the subject of a sentence? _____

_____

3. List seven kinds of subjects.

_____

_____

[1] Many authorities feel that "contain a complete idea" is not clear. You will understand better what a sentence is as we go along.

[2] This book uses the term "subject" as some books use the term "simple subject." The simple subject is the one word with which the verb must agree in number, that is, singular or plural.

4. What is the verb of a sentence? _____

_____

5. List four things that a verb can do.

_____   _____

_____   _____

Check your answers.

.ıı.ı

THE SUBJECT OF A SENTENCE

Words do not become subjects until they are *used* as subjects in sentences. To be a subject, a word (or words) must combine with a verb in a subject-verb core that makes sense.

Characteristics of Subjects

Although subjects in one sentence may differ in some ways from subjects in other sentences, all subjects have the following similarities:

1. The subjects work together with their verbs.

2. The other words in the sentence describe the subject, tell what it is doing, or say something about it.

3. If you delete the subject, you usually get a response such as "*Who* did that?" "*What's* this about?" or "*Which* one are you describing?"

Study the subjects in the sentences below. Note how they work together with their verbs. Then cover each with a finger while you read the rest of the sentence, applying the *who*, *what*, and *which* test. Subjects are underlined once; verbs are underlined twice. (This system is followed throughout the book.)

Types of Subjects

PERSON, PLACE, and THING Subjects

George was a fine person.
The North has long been highly industrialized.
The rusty, rickety, dirt-covered old car suddenly collapsed.
Each is capable of doing the job.
No one has volunteered.

GROUP Subjects

The band has arrived.
The herd of cattle will be here tomorrow.
Members of the team will speak at the rally.

All of them are here.
Everyone has promised to come.

IDEA Subjects

Democracy is the best form of government.
Religion is a comfort to many people.
His principles are not being questioned.

ACTIVITY Subjects

Running the mile[1] is a difficult feat.
To act promptly can save many lives.
To retreat at this moment would be wise.

QUALITY Subjects

Honesty may not always be profitable.
Faithfulness is considered a virtue.
"Love" has become a byword among youth groups.

"You Understood" as Subject

One of the convenient exceptions to the rule that every sentence must have a subject is the "you understood" exception. When verbs are used in the present tense as commands, directives, or strong requests, we accept the fact that the "you" is understood, and that the sentence is complete with only the verb or with the verb and its modifiers (the predicate).

The constructions below are considered sentences because each has a verb which makes sense with "you understood" as the subject.

Go! Look at her. Please do not eat the daisies. Take the pastrami sandwich with you. Demand your rights! Sign here. Keep your children in the barn. Stop!

Nouns of Address Are Not Subjects

Nouns of address are proper nouns used in direct oral communications. They can appear in various parts of the sentence and are separated from the body of the sentence by commas. On paper they look like this:

John, come here. Come here, *Stephen.* Take this, *Dolores,* to your mother.

---

[1] The phrase, "Running the mile" is actually the subject of the sentence. However, in order to master the problem of agreement of subject and verb, you must learn to recognize the single word that works with the verb. For example, in the sentence: "Running many miles is a difficult feat," the verb must agree with the word "running" (singular), not with the word "miles" (plural). Chapter 4 concentrates on the problem of subject-verb agreement.

The nouns of address (John, Stephen, Dolores) are *not* the subjects of the above sentences. The subject in each case is "you understood."

SELF-QUIZ 3

Part I : Underline the subjects in the following sentences; then check them against the key. To help you, verbs are double underlined in the first 10.

1. The girls threw eggs at the boys.
2. Some are wearing green hats.
3. The freshmen are having tryouts.
4. Do not go there.
5. The team arrived at eight.
6. His mother voted for Blodget.
7. It will cost twenty yen.
8. The gruesome-looking, three-headed thing attacked.
9. Everyone walked across campus.
10. Benjamin ate sixteen hamburgers.
11. His sincerity can be questioned.
12. The soldiers stopped the jeep abruptly.
13. John, go to the store.
14. The plane landed safely.
15. I want to go.
16. The boys threw yams at the girls.
17. Breathing is a reflex action.
18. Despair descended on them.
19. Men and women attended together.
20. Mr. President, our city needs help.

Part II : Fill in the blanks.

21. Subjects work together with their _____ .

22. When checking for subjects, try the _____, _____, or _____ test.

23. (*The same word fits all the blanks*): The other words in the sentence describe

the _____, tell what the _____ is doing, or say

something about the _____ .

24. Words do not become subjects until they are _____ as subjects.

25. To be a subject, a word (or words) must combine with a _____ in a

_____ core that makes _____ .

ᴵˑᵈ

THE VERB IN A SENTENCE

Words do not become verbs until they are *used* as verbs in sentences. To be a verb, a word (or words) must combine with a subject in a subject-verb core that makes sense. The *function* of words in each particular sentence must be ascertained before one can decide what to call them. There is no "parts-of-speech" list that can be provided for you to memorize.

In this section you will study the overall characteristics of verbs, see how they function with subjects, and learn how they can be changed to other parts of speech and back to verbs again. You will also learn how to add auxiliaries correctly.

Characteristics of Verbs

1. Verbs work with their subjects to provide the core meanings of sentences.
2. Verbs adapt to their subjects so that they can agree in *number*, one verb form being used when the subject is singular (one person or thing) and another verb form being used when the subject is plural (more than one).
3. Verbs help to set the *time* of sentences. For this reason it is necessary to know how to change each verb so that it correctly indicates the past, present, future, or the in-between times (the perfect and progressive tenses).[1]

Types of Verbs

In this text we recognize four types of verbs: (1) existence verbs, (2) possessive verbs, (3) action verbs, and (4) feeling or sensory verbs. The sentences below illustrate the four types and show how the verbs (underlined twice) work together with their subjects (underlined once).

EXISTENCE (state of being) VERBS

They are here often.
It is dead.
That was the end.
Many were there before.
The scientist will be in Kansas soon.

---

[1] Both of these problems, number and tense, will be discussed in detail later.

POSSESSIVE VERBS

The company has many subsidiaries.
They had more before the depression.
The men have stock in the company.
She owns property.
They possess many admirable qualities.

ACTION VERBS

The soldiers camouflaged their position.
He thought about it for days.
The pitchman guessed her weight.
They slept for hours.
The hen sat on its eggs.

VERBS of FEELING or SENSORY REACTIONS

The rose smelled good.
The apple tastes good.
Her appearance appeals to him.
Heat soothes sore muscles.
Everyone appears to be calm.
She loves him dearly.
He hates her bitterly.

Other texts may classify verbs somewhat differently, and you may find that some overlap in the above method of classification. The important point is that you should learn to recognize verbs by their *function* in the sentences you write. They always operate as part of a subject-verb core.

SELF-QUIZ 4

Part I: Fill in the blanks.

1. _____ work with their _____ to provide the core meanings of sentences.

2. Verbs adapt to their _____ so that they can agree in _____

_____, one verb form being used when the subject is _____,

and another verb form being used when the subject is _____.

3. Verbs help to set the _____ of sentences. For this reason it is necessary to know how to change each verb so that it correctly indicates

the _____, _____, _____, or in-between times.

4. List the four types of verbs according to this text.

_____   _____

_____   _____

5. Words used as verbs must combine with the _____ in a _____

_____ that makes sense.

Part II: Double underline each verb in the following sentences. To help you, the subjects are indicated in the first 10.

1. They ate a big meal.
2. The kitchen is pink.
3. Smoke poured from the barn.
4. The bus left early.
5. Senators give many speeches.
6. She traveled by bus, train, and plane.
7. Jim and Charley opened a restaurant.
8. A pretty girl won the "ugliest man" contest.
9. Seventy-eight men died in the mine.
10. Mine workers protested.
11. Someone tripped the burglar alarm.
12. Many policemen reported to work late.
13. The old man had diabetes.
14. To continue running is futile.
15. Clara was one of the youngest patients.
16. No one will know.
17. Enemy troops ambushed our forces.
18. The mayor spoke slowly.
19. Two holdup suspects escaped.
20. Gentle George plants tulips every spring.

How to "Freeze" an Action Verb

Words which are commonly used as verbs can often be very confusing because their function in the sentence may change completely even when their form seems to change only slightly. Two of the most common verb "freezers" are *to* and *ing*. Let's observe the effect they have on a verb of action.

Effect of "*to*"

When the preposition *to* is placed in front of an action verb like *run* or *sing*, the *to* freezes the action of the verb and the two words together (*to run*, *to sing*, etc.) are called an infinitive. An infinitive can function as subject or as direct object[1] in a sentence, but it cannot act as a verb. In the examples below, notice how the infinitive is used either as subject or as direct object (shown in brackets).

> To sing is fun.
> He loves [to sing].
> To congregate in large groups can be exciting.
> People like [to congregate] in large groups.

Remember, when you place *to* before a verb, it is no longer a verb; it is an infinitive. In such cases another word must act as a verb, or you don't have a sentence.

SELF-QUIZ 5

Double underline the verbs in the following sentences.

1. He loved to ride.
2. To ride for hours was his favorite sport.
3. The explorers tried to find the gold.
4. To betray her country was unthinkable.
5. The astronauts attempted to reach Mars.

Effect of "*ing*"

Similar to the effect of *to*, an *ing* freezes the action of verbs. You have already seen examples of *ing* words used as subjects (*Running* makes you tired). An *ing* word can also be used as an adjective, to modify or describe a noun or a pronoun (She took a *running* stitch). In the following sentences watch the verbs change to subjects and then to adjectives.

> The congressman decided to vote for the bill.
> Deciding was difficult.
> The *deciding* votes were cast by absentee ballot.

> The old lady presided at the meeting.
> Presiding at meetings was no novelty for her.
> The *presiding* officer was given a bouquet.

SELF-QUIZ 6

Double underline the verbs in the following sentences.

1. He swims all day long.
2. Swimming is exhilarating.

[1] The direct object receives the action of the verb. It answers the question *what* or *whom*. For example, I hit the *ball*. We saw the *man*.

3. He loves to swim.

4. The swimming instructor drowned.

5. To swim every day is good exercise.

6. We debated your team last year.

7. Debating makes one think carefully.

8. To dream is to aspire.

9. He dreams all the time.

10. Dreaming too much is not good.

.n.n.n.n.n.n.n.n.n.n.n.n.n.n.n.n.n.n.n.n.n.n.n.n.n.n.n.n.n.n.n.n.n.n.n.n.n.n.n.n.n.n.n

How to "Defrost" an *ing*ed Verb

To "defrost" an *ing*ed verb, you simply add a form of the verb *be*.

Below are examples of how *ing*ed verbs can be reactivated. In each group of three sentences, you can see how a word is used as a verb first, then *ing*ed into noun or adjective form, and finally reactivated into verb form again.

He kissed her.
Kissing is fun.
She is kissing him now.

The snake hissed.
The *hissing* snake struck.
The snake was hissing.

The bananas rotted in the strong sunlight.
The *rotting* bananas were covered with flies.
The bananas have been rotting there for several days.

TEST 1: Defrosting an *ing*ed Verb

Similar to the examples above, write five sets of sentences in which you use a word first (a) as a verb, then (b) as a noun or adjective, and finally (c) with an auxiliary as a verb again. Underline your subjects once and verb phrases twice. The verb phrase is the verb and its auxiliaries.

how to do the tests

The tests are more complicated than the quizzes and require more writing. No keys are provided. Write the assignment on your own paper and hand it in to your instructor for grading. Most tests are based on the material immediately preceding them. *Use the book to help you pass the tests.*

Switching Verbs into Adjectives

You have seen verbs changed by adding *to* and by adding *ing*. In the following sentences you will see another kind of change. Words commonly used as verbs are often placed so that they describe subjects or other words in the sentence. They are then no longer functioning as verbs but as adjectives, and the writer must be sure to add verbs to go with his subjects.

Watch the words below switch from verb functions to subject or adjective functions. Note that in each case another word takes up the job of the verb.

Remember that you can identify the verb by its relationship with the subject—the subject and verb working together in the subject-verb core.

The dog *hunted* for rabbits.   The soldier *fired* the rifle.
The *hunted* man escaped.   The *fired* rifle exploded.

The car was *stolen* yesterday.
The *stolen* car was stripped by the thief.

She *wrecked* the car.
The *wrecked* car is worthless.

They *programmed* the lesson carefully.
Programmed lessons can be helpful.

The black man's home was *burned.*
The *burned* home is being rebuilt.

Note that the *ed* and *en* endings are retained by the adjective forms of the switched words: hunt*ed* (verb), hunt*ed* (adjective); stol*en* (verb), stol*en* (adjective).

TEST 2: Switching Verbs into Adjectives

Using the examples above as a model, write five new pairs of sentences in which you use the same word first as a verb and then as an adjective. Underline subjects once and verbs twice. Keep your sentences simple. Don't repeat the verbs used in the examples. Pay special attention to the *ed* and *en* endings.

AUXILIARIES

There are two kinds of auxiliaries, *modal* and *regular.*

Modal Auxiliaries

There are ten modals. These are words that form verb phrases with verbs but that are not used as verbs alone. They signal the approach of a verb. Study the list of modals below and note how they are used in sentences.

can   I can go.   I can do many things.

could   He could have done that.   He could never win her love.

may   He may arrive at any moment.   He may have been injured.

might   They might have left last night.   They might never be found.

shall[1]   I shall be there on time.   I shall not have been deceived.

should   I should go.   They should remain with you.   They should be answering us soon.

---

[1] *Shall* is rarely used today. *Will* seems to have almost completely replaced it.

will	He will be stopped. They will achieve their goals.
would	She would not listen. The enemy would have stopped at nothing.
must	They must be intercepted. It must have been a very sad scene.
ought (**to**)	He ought never to have gone.[1] They ought to notify us immediately.

TEST 3: Modal Auxiliaries

Write a sentence for each of the ten modals, using them with verbs to form verb phrases. Underline subjects once and verb phrases twice. Keep the sentences simple.

Regular Auxiliaries

Regular auxiliaries are verbs in their own right which often combine with other verbs to form verb phrases. In such combinations, the other verbs are called the main verbs. The most common regular auxiliaries are:

be	**have**	**do**
being	**has**	**does**
been	**having**	**did**
am	**had**	
is		
was		
were		

In the following examples, the verbs listed above are used (a) first by themselves and (b) then as auxiliaries. Notice that as auxiliaries they sometimes combine with modals or with other regular auxiliaries to form three- and four-word phrases.

1. (a) Be kind.   He will be here on time.
   (b) He may be dying.   He can be tried for murder.
2. (a) He is being as kind as possible.   They are being pleasant this year.
   (b) He is being tested by the colonel.   They may be being fooled by the enemy.
3. (a) You have been there?   She had been a lovely woman.
   (b) The man has been fired.   They have been shot out of cannons.
4. (a) I am here.
   (b) I am being persecuted.   I am having troubles.
5. (a) She is sweet.
   (b) She is giving the men her closest attention.   She is having fun.
6. (a) He was madly in love.
   (b) The fire was burning wildly.

---

[1] Since *ought to* is considered an auxiliary, the *to* in this case does not, of course, freeze the verb. "Ought to have gone" is the verb phrase.

7. (a) They were in contempt of court.
   (b) Men were rushing to help her.

8. (a) They have money.
   (b) They have been criticized for their views.

9. (a) Mike has two wives.
   (b) Ben has taken a third wife.

10. (a) He is having fun.
    (b) They have been having many problems.

11. (a) The cat had a kitten.
    (b) It had been having six at a time for several years.

12. (a) We do rather well.
    (b) We do care about our clients.

13. (a) The management does its best.
    (b) The custodian does maintain a high quality of service.

14. (a) His boy did well in the basketball games.
    (b) The apple did fall on her head.

TEST 4: Regular Auxiliaries

Write 14 pairs of sentences using each of the regular auxiliaries (*be, being, been,* etc.) first as a verb and then as an auxiliary.

what you have learned in chapter 2

This chapter has centered on the study of subjects and verbs, because this understanding is the key to all your work with sentences. Remember that words act as subjects and verbs only when they work together in sentences as subject-verb cores.

SUBJECTS are of seven kinds: *person, place, thing, group, activity, idea,* and *quality.* You have learned to recognize "you understood" as the subject of certain sentences; you know that the "noun of address" is *not* the subject.

VERBS may be classified as *possessive, action, existence* verbs, and verbs that express *feeling* and *sensory* reactions. There are two kinds of AUXILIARIES, regular and modal.

(If you still feel "shaky" about subjects and verbs, the best medicine now is to keep going. Things will become clearer in the next two chapters.)

ıı.ıı

KEY 1

(1) communication (2) Sentences are formed by the interaction between subjects and verbs. (3) Every sentence must contain within it the basic elements of the simple sentence. (4a) "Complex" on page 21 means something composed of intricate or interconnected parts. (4b) "Complex" on page 22 refers to a sentence with one main clause and at least one subordinate clause. (5) This book places emphasis on what it calls the "subject-verb" core because most sentence-writing problems seem to center around the subject-verb relationship.

KEY 2

(1) a verb in the present tense　(2) The subject of a sentence is the word or words which combine with the verb to form the core of the sentence.　(3) Person, group, thing, place, quality, idea, activity　(4) The verb of a sentence is the word or words which combine with the subject to form the core of the sentence.　(5) Describe an action, indicate existence, express feeling or sensory reactions, indicate possession.

KEY 3

Part I:　(1) girls　(2) some　(3) freshmen　(4) "you understood"　(5) team　(6) mother　(7) it　(8) thing　(9) Everyone　(10) Benjamin　(11) sincerity　(12) soldiers　(13) "you understood"　　(14) plane　　(15) I　　(16) boys　(17) Breathing　(18) Despair　(19) Men, women　(20) city

If you missed any of the first ten subjects, read Comment A. If you got all ten correct, skip to Comment B.

Comment A:　If you selected any word after the verb, you were wrong. Most verbs follow their subjects. Don't look for any verbs to precede their subjects until we discuss *inversions.*

In number 4 the subject is *you* understood. This is explained on page 25.
In number 6 *his* didn't vote; *mother* did vote.
In number 8 *thing* did the attacking. The other words merely describe the thing.

Comment B:　To help you better understand which words are the subjects in 11–20, here are the verbs:

(11) can be questioned　　(12) stopped　　(13) go　　(14) landed　　(15) want　(16) threw　(17) is　(18) descended　(19) attended　(20) needs

Part II:　　(21) verbs　　(22) who, what, which　　(23) subject　　(24) used　(25) verb, subject-verb, sense

KEY 4

Part I:　(1) Verbs, subjects　(2) subjects, number, singular, plural　(3) tense, past, present, future　(4) existence, possessive, action, feeling or sensory reactions　(5) subject, subject-verb core

Part II:　(1) ate　(2) is　(3) poured　(4) left　(5) give　(6) traveled　(7) opened　(8) won　(9) died　(10) protested

Comment A:　If any word you chose as a verb was incorrect, check back to see if the words you selected really make sense with the subjects as a subject-verb core. Remember that verbs must work with subjects and *make sense.*

Comment B:　For a better understanding, the entire subject-verb core is given in 11–20 below. Check yourself only on your choice of verbs (italics).

(11) Someone *tripped*　(12) policemen *reported*　(13) man *had*　(14) to continue *is*　(15) Clara *was*　(16) one *will know*　(17) troops *ambushed*　(18) mayor *spoke*　(19) suspects *escaped*　(20) George *plants*

KEY 5

(1) loved　(2) was　(3) tried　(4) was　(5) attempted

KEY 6

(1) swims　(2) is　(3) loves　(4) drowned　(5) is　(6) debated　(7) makes　(8) is　(9) dreams　(10) is

In **Chapter 3**

YOU WILL **WORK** WITH THE **SUBJECT** AND **VERB**

TOGETHER

AS THEY INTERACT IN VARIOUS simple SENTENCE patterns

YOU WILL MOVE FROM THE SIMPLEST ONE WORD SENTENCE TO SENTENCES WHICH CONTAIN **MULTIPLE SUBJECTS** AND **MULTIPLE VERBS**, YET REMAIN **SIMPLE**

V
S-V
S-S-V
S-V-V
S-S-V-V-V

ALONG THE WAY YOU WILL LEARN ABOUT INVERSIONS (S-V) (V-S)

THEN, YOU WILL **EXPAND** THE SIMPLE SENTENCE PATTERN BY ADDING NEW WORDS BEFORE THE **SUBJECT** AND **VERB**, AND AFTER THE **SUBJECT**, STILL KEEPING THE SENTENCE **SIMPLE**.

YOU MUST BE **SURE** ABOUT THE STRUCTURE OF THE SIMPLE SENTENCE BEFORE YOU START CONSTRUCTING **COMPOUND** AND **COMPLEX** SENTENCES.

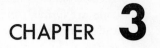

Simple sentence PATTERNS

In Chapter 2 we concentrated on subjects and verbs in the simple sentence. In this chapter, first we will study the interaction of subjects and verbs in various patterns, remembering that the subject-verb core must be present (in some form) in every sentence. Then we will expand the simple sentence by adding words and phrases to the core.

A simple sentence contains only one subject-verb core. Those we worked with in Chapter 2 contained only one subject and only one verb. But a core may contain any number of subjects and verbs, provided that (a) the subjects are *consecutive*, that is, they do *not* alternate with the verbs; and (b) each subject relates to all the verbs, as in the sentence: Al, Joe, and Mae ate, drank, and sang (SSS-VVV pattern).

Once subjects and verbs *alternate* within a sentence (S-V, S-V, S-V), new cores are formed, and the sentence is no longer simple; then new mechanical and grammatical problems arise. Since our goal is to build from simple sentences to compound and complex forms, we must know simple sentence structure thoroughly before moving ahead.

Below is a table showing the simple sentence patterns with examples of each. Study them. All the exercises in this chapter are based on these patterns.

	PATTERN	EXAMPLE
subject understood—verb	—V	Go!
single subject—single verb	S—V	Dictators dictate.
multiple subject—single verb	SSS—V	Men, women, and children died.
single subject—multiple verb	S—VV	The ship foundered and sank.
multiple subject—multiple verb	SS—VVV	Sadie and Tom married, divorced, and remarried.
multiple subject—single verb	SSSSSS—V	The President, his wife and children, members of the Cabinet, the White House staff, 22 reporters, and the President's beagles had a picnic.
single subject—multiple verb	S—VVVVVV	The Olympic athlete ran the 100-yard dash, threw the discus, vaulted 16 feet, swam in the 100-meter backstroke, participated in the cross-country relay, and then slept for 36 hours.

PRACTICE WITH THE SUBJECT-VERB CORE

If one is not sure of his subject and verb, he cannot control his sentence structure. This may well lead him to errors in punctuation, in agreement of subject and verb, and to run-on sentences, comma splices, and fragments. For this reason, let us focus now solely on the subject and verb relationship to reinforce your understanding of its function and its importance.

Single-Word Sentences

Below are examples of single-word sentences. The single word must be a verb in the present tense. The subject *you* is understood in each case. Study the one-word sentences below; then do the quiz.

Run!	Kiss!	Charge!	Give.
Stop!	Eat.	Retreat!	Look.

SELF-QUIZ 1

Put a check mark alongside the words below that can be one-word sentences. They must make sense with "you understood."

Sit_____   Wood_____   Orange_____

March_____   Shoot_____   Disgraceful_____

Beautiful_____   Speak_____   Seeing_____

Teach_____   Jump_____   Ride_____

Scream_____   Hello_____   Leave_____

Movie_____   Bend_____   Raft_____

Stay_____   Horse_____   Drawing_____

SELF-QUIZ 2

Write your answers in the blanks.

1. How many subjects and verbs can a simple sentence contain?

   _____

   _____

2. What changes a simple sentence into a compound or complex sentence?

   _____

   _____

3. One of our aims is to build from _____ sentences

   to _____ and _____ forms.

4. Define *consecutive* as used in the second paragraph of this chapter.

   _____

   _____

5. Define *alternate* as used in the second and third paragraphs.

   _____

   _____

Single-Subject, Single-Verb Sentences

Below are examples of two- and three-word sentences which follow this pattern. Study the examples; then do the quizzes.

Men fight.	It died.	The boy escaped.
A woman sobbed.	Truth hurts.	His picture faded.
He sits.	Crime pays.	A dog barked.
She sings.	Horses snort.	Some cats scratch.

SELF-QUIZ 3

Make single-subject, single-verb sentences by inserting the most appropriate words from the choices given. Punctuate the sentences correctly.

CHOICES: warms, electrocutes, giggled, swim, crowed, dance, development, blowing, gallop, instructor, blow, pours, activity, smelled, lovely

1. Horses _____

2. The girl _____

3. Rain _____

4. A rooster _____

5. Winds _____

6. Dancers _____

7. Fish _____

8. Heat _____

9. Electricity _____

10. Her perfume _____

SELF-QUIZ 4

Make single-subject, single-verb sentences by inserting the most appropriate words.

CHOICES: The pickets, Merry-go-rounds, Lovely, Understand, Lovers, Bigots, Unnecessary, A prisoner, Cowards, Dynamite, Rioters, Advertisers, Students, A child

1. _____ advertise.

2. _____ picketed.

3. _____ riot.

4. _____ explodes.

5. _____ cower.

6. _____ love.

7. _____ escaped.

8. _____ revolve.

9. _____ were studying.

10. _____ was playing.

TEST 1

Write ten of your own one-word sentences. Punctuate them correctly.

TEST 2

Part A: Write verbs to go with the following subjects.

1. Reptiles_____.   6. Birds_____.

2. The penguins_____.   7. The bride_____.

3. Musicians_____.   8. Mathematicians_____.

4. Apricots_____.   9. Miners_____.

5. An American_____.   10. Satellites_____.

Part B: Write subjects to go with the following verbs.

1. _____steal.   6. _____paint.

2. _____buy.   7. _____tasted.

3. _____develop.   8. _____study.

4. _____give.   9. _____curses.

5. _____destroy.   10. _____filed.

Part C: Write ten single-subject, single-verb sentences of your own.

TEST 3

Write five multiple-subject, single-verb sentences.

EXAMPLES:

Joan and Henry were married. Bugs and fleas fly.

TEST 4

Write five single-subject, multiple-verb sentences.

EXAMPLE:

Playing strengthens and relaxes the patients.

TEST 5

Write five multiple-subject, multiple-verb sentences.

EXAMPLE:

Historians, scientists, and novelists research and write.

THE PATTERN IN REVERSE: INVERTED SENTENCES

The subject-verb pattern in the English language is so common that exceptions to the pattern are given a special name. When the verb is placed before the subject, or when the subject is placed between the verb and its auxiliary, the sentence is said to be in reverse or *inverted* order. This occurs in three situations:

1. In most questions
2. When the expletive *there* is used
3. When the sentence starts with an adverbial phrase

Questions that Don't Invert

You can ask a question without inverting the sentence by merely raising your voice at the end of the sentence: He is coming? They are here?

You often don't invert the sentence when you use certain question words like *who, whose, which, what.*

What is going on?
Who went with him?
Which one is guilty?
Whose friend disappeared?

Questions that Do Invert

When forms of the verb *be* are used, the verb changes places with the subject.

You were busy. ——————→ Were you busy?
She is his wife. ——————→ Is she his wife?
They are at home. ——————→ Are they at home?
The girl was my friend. ——————→ Was the girl my friend?

When other types of verbs are used, they combine with auxiliaries to form questions. The subjects are then placed between the auxiliaries and their verbs.

You are coming with us. ——————→ Are you coming with us?
You came with him. ——————→ Did you come with him?
He will help us. ——————→ Will he help us?
They can do the job well. ——————→ Can they do the job well?

SELF-QUIZ 5

In the sentences below, underline the subjects once and the verbs twice.

1. Are the girls coming with us?
2. Can you untie this knot?
3. Will the party be held at your house?
4. Have they won any games this year?
5. John Smetz is coming here?
6. Olga has lumbago?
7. When will the eclipse take place?
8. Why did she marry him?
9. Did the dog have rabies?
10. Who is he?

"There" as an Expletive: Another Type of Inversion

There is a perfectly respectable word that is usually used as an adverb.[1] In the following sentences *there* is an adverb, and you will note that none of these sentences is inverted.

Place the carton over there. He lives there. Leave the money there. Our friends boarded there many years ago. There he is.

Sometimes *there* does not act as an adverb but as an expletive—a filler word on which to hang a sentence. In these cases *there* displaces the subject and shoves it over to the other side of the verb. When writing such sentences (which, by the way, are very common), one must realize that the subject and the verb have been inverted. Here are some examples:

In the room there are twelve people. During the Civil War there were many casualties. There are thirty days in December. There will be many June weddings this year.

SELF-QUIZ 6

Underline subjects once and verbs twice.

1. He placed the jelly beans there.
2. There are 600 red beans.
3. There is a milch cow in his barn.
4. In the auditorium there are many angry people.
5. He is right there.
6. They are sitting there by their parents.
7. After the party there is always a mess to clean up.
8. There by their well there are three pails.
9. There he is.
10. Put it over there.

[1] An adverb is a word that limits or describes a verb, an adjective, or another adverb.

Introductory Adverbial Phrases: A Third Type of Inversion

In order to vary your writing, you may wish to invert your sentences in the following manner:

Out of the cave came the six convicts.
Over the fence jumped the rhinoceros.
Through the hot, festering jungle tramped the exhausted men.

The introductory phrases are called *adverbial* because they modify the verb. Other types of phrases do not work in inversions.

TEST 6

Rewrite the three inverted sentences above in normal order; then in lines 4-10 write seven additional *inverted* sentences of the same type. Underline all subjects once and all verbs twice. Keep the sentences simple. Don't create "phony" or clumsy sentences just to do the exercise.

1. _____

2. _____

3. _____

4. _____

5. _____

6. _____

7. _____

8. _____

9. _____

10. _____

TEST 7: Mid-Chapter Review

General directions: Keep all sentences simple. Underline all subjects once and all verbs twice.

(1–4): Write sentences using the word *dream* as indicated.

1. *to dream* (as subject)_____

2. *dreaming* (as subject)_____

3. *dream* (as verb)_____

4. *dreaming* (as verb)_____

(5–8): Write sentences as in 1–4, using the word *desire*.

5. _____

6. _____

7. _____

8. _____

(9–11): Write three questions in which you invert the subjects and verbs.

9. _____

10. _____

11. _____

(12–13): Write one sentence in which you use *there* as an expletive and one in which you use *there* as an adverb.

12. (expletive)_____

13. (adverb)_____

(14–20): Write sentences as directed.

14. (one word)_____

15. (one subject, one verb) _____

16. (three subjects, one verb)_____

17. (one subject, three verbs)_____

18. (three subjects, three verbs)_____

19. (inverted sentence with adverbial phrase) _____

20. (inverted sentence with adverbial phrase)_____

EXPANDING THE SIMPLE SENTENCE

The simple sentence can be expanded indefinitely and remain simple as long as no new subject-verb cores are added. Once new cores are included the sentence becomes compound or complex.[1]

[1] When a new subject-verb core is added to a simple sentence, each core and the words associated with it are called clauses. This is explained more fully in the chapters on compound and complex sentences.

The exercises in this half of the chapter are designed to help you expand your sentences while at the same time keeping you aware of their basic structures—the subject-verb cores. Although appropriate words can be added anywhere in a sentence, we will work on three specific areas: words added before the subject, words injected between the subject and the verb, and words added after the verb.

The chart below shows the simple sentence patterns[1] with blanks to indicate where words and phrases will be added. Study the chart carefully; then go on to the exercises.

EXPANDED SIMPLE SENTENCE PATTERNS

1. *The "you understood" pattern:*

   Please, go to the store now.
   _____**V**_____.

2. *Words before the subject:*

   Early in the spring, George proposed.
   _____**S-V.**

3. *Words between the subject and verb:*

   George, my darling husband, proposed.
   S_____**V.**

4. *Words after the verb:*

   George proposed to my best friend.
   S   **V**_____.

5. *Words before the subject, between the S-V, and after the verb:*

   Early in the spring, George, my darling husband, proposed a fishing trip.
   _____**S**_____**V**_____.

6. *Pattern 5 with multiple subjects:*

   Before doing their homework each day, Don, Gene, and Leon, eager and ambitious, sold large boxes of candy to melancholy housewives.
   _____**SSS**_____**V**_____.

7. *Pattern 5 with multiple subjects and multiple verbs:*

   Under the old house, a skunk, a raccoon, and an itinerant vagabond snored, fidgeted, and belched throughout the night.
   _____**SSS**_____**VVV**_____.

---

[1] Some of the longer patterns are omitted because they do not present new problems; their only difference lies in the number of subjects and/or verbs.

Check for yourself. You will find no more than one subject-verb core in any of the above patterns. They are all *simple* sentences.

SELF-QUIZ 7

The purpose of these exercises is to make you aware of the presence of more than one subject-verb core. Those sentences with more than one core are not simple sentences.

Under each of the six subject-verb cores below there are ten choices. Place a check-mark alongside the choices that contain S-V cores; leave the others blank.

1. The <u>Senators</u> <u>debated</u> . . .

    a._____and the Representatives adjourned.

    b._____loudly and angrily.

    c._____with the lobbyists.

    d._____until morning.

    e._____without reaching any definite conclusion.

    f._____while the President slept.

    g._____about the tax bill.

    h._____the subject for many long hours.

    i._____long after the bill was passed.

    j._____before the guests arrived.

2. The <u>explorers</u> <u>discovered</u> . . .

    a._____an enemy encampment.

    b._____something that no human had seen before.

    c._____a series of small, isolated, uninhabited islands.

    d._____that men can survive despite intense heat.

    e._____new passages to India.

    f._____ancient villages in the jungle.

    g._____their predecessor's camp.

    h._____dozens of cans of bean soup, cartons of marshmallows, hundreds of cases of stale jelly beans, and thousands of heartburn pills.

    i._____that Jake was gone.

j._____nothing of very great significance.

3. Many <u>people</u> <u>think</u> . . .

    a._____very little of their leaders.

    b._____a great deal about life and death.

    c._____long into the night.

    d._____Sam is smart.

    e._____about God.

    f._____we should help underdeveloped nations.

    g._____that school is boring.

    h._____deeply.

    i._____he should not have gone.

    j._____very little.

4. The <u>pitcher</u> <u>pitched</u> . . .

    a._____a spitball.

    b._____before the catcher was ready.

    c._____a long, looping, deceptive curve.

    d._____two no-hit games.

    e._____and the batter struck out.

    f._____George the ball.

    g._____the fastest ball I ever saw.

    h._____the ball swiftly, carefully, and accurately.

    i._____to the tall, lanky, freckle-faced infielder.

    j._____a greatly improved game.

5. <u>Margaret</u> <u>is</u> . . .

    a._____a beautiful, black-haired, brown-eyed woman with a flat nose and high cheek bones.

    b._____my sister-in-law.

c._____the daughter of a Buddhist priest.

d._____the person for whom they are looking.

e._____the girl who was shot.

f._____ill and very unhappy.

g._____here and Jeff doesn't know it.

h._____a friend of the Queen of England.

i._____stupid, ugly, and bad tempered.

j._____never early or even on time.

6. They will go . . .

a._____very quickly.

b._____before the special luncheon.

c._____before luncheon is served.

d._____to Mexico City sometime next May.

e._____deep into the jungle of Malasia.

f._____after the suspect who disappeared.

g._____unless we contact them immediately.

h._____by sea, by air, and by camelback.

i._____early in the morning.

j._____over the wall and down into the abandoned tunnel.

Adding Words to Expand the S-V Core

The following exercises demonstrate various ways to expand the simple sentence from very brief subject-verb combinations to much longer and more complicated patterns. You are asked to add words before the subjects (Tests 8 and 9), between the subjects and verbs (Tests 10 and 11), and after the verbs (Test 12). You are not given the technical terms for the various words and phrases, but are told that they should *not include new subject-verb patterns*, and that they must add *sensibly*[1] to the existing patterns.

At this stage it is important to concentrate on the basic structure of simple sentences because once you have learned to recognize and handle the subjects and verbs, you tend to make few other errors. Such other errors as you are likely to make will be examined at later points in this book.

[1] In two exercises nonsense is allowed, as long as it is grammatical.

Adding Words Before the Subject

TEST 8:

From the choices listed below, select *three* phrases for each subject-verb core which will make the cores into good *simple* sentences. Do *not* select clauses. (Clauses, remember, contain S-V cores and would make the sentences compound or complex.)

Some of the phrases will fit more than one core. For your first choice in each group select the phrase which makes the most sense. For your other two choices you may select phrases that add humor even if they don't make sense, but be sure that the combination is grammatically correct.

1. _____ priest knelt before the altar.

   _____ // // // // //

   _____ // // // // //

2. _____ books were moved to the attic.

   _____ // // // // // //

   _____ // // // // // //

3. _____ he was attending school.

   _____ // //   //   //

   _____ // //   //   //

4. _____ jewels are extremely expensive.

   _____ // //   //   //

   _____ // //   //   //

CHOICES:

1. Nobody knew that
2. The pink, purple, yellow, and russet
3. The exquisite old, hand-carved
4. They hired a guard because
5. Old, white-haired, and black-frocked, the
6. Quickly, the stolen
7. Unlike his trouble-making friends,
8. After many hours of indecision, the
9. Despite great sacrifices
10. The president realizes that the
11. Although she watered them daily, the
12. Modern in style, beautifully arranged, the
13. Until dawn the
14. His mother was so happy that
15. The girl's
16. One by one the
17. Long after midnight had passed,
18. Before the police arrived, the
19. She objected bitterly when the
20. When the congregation had left, the

TEST 9:

Insert an appropriate phrase of at least three words at the beginning of each subject-verb core. Be sure that the completed sentences are *simple*.

Important: Do not do these exercises mechanically—just to fill in blanks. Select your words carefully and thoughtfully. Try to use a variety of approaches while keeping within the pattern. Note: Write four phrases for *each* number below.

EXAMPLE:

    a. Kind and thoughtful men should love and protect their wives.
    b. Stupid, slovenly, and unkempt men should love and protect their wives.
    c. Against all odds men should love and protect their wives.
    d. In good times and bad men should love and protect their wives.

1. _____ friends now live in France.

    _____ // // // // //

    _____ // // // // //

    _____ // // // // //

2. _____ customs may seem odd to us.

    _____ // // // // // //

    _____ // // // // // //

    _____ // // // // // //

3. _____ student is responsible for the crime.

    _____ // // // // // //

    _____ // // // // // //

    _____ // // // // // //

4. _____ rain and hail damaged the roof.

    _____ // // // // // //

    _____ // // // // // //

    _____ // // // // // //

Inserting Words between the Subject and the Verb

Various words and phrases can be placed between the subject and the verb of a simple sentence without making it compound or complex. There are only three basic restrictions: (1) that no new verb or subject be added, thus changing subject and verb relationships; (2) that no new subject-verb core be injected; (3) that the additional words be pertinent to the idea of the sentence and make sense.

Here are some examples:

The old man walked down the street.
The old man, reeking with whiskey,[1] walked down the street.
The old man, my father's friend, walked down the street.
The old man with the tittering blond on his arm walked down the street.

TEST 10

Select phrases from the list below and insert them in the spaces between the subjects and the verbs. Read all of the sentences and all of the phrases before filling the blanks. Select the most apt phrase for each sentence, unless you prefer to have fun by making some ridiculous combinations. Add commas where necessary.

PHRASES:

half drowned
attending the convention
eyes staring blankly ahead
ever helpful
still shouting for women's rights

typing feverishly
my best friend
on the skinny bicycle
in the middle of the lake
a career soldier

1. The foreign correspondent _____ wrote the story from memory.

2. Boy Scouts _____ came to his assistance.

3. The Suffragettes _____ marched down the street.

4. Drugs salesmen _____ listened to the chemist's speech.

5. After the storm the sailor _____ staggered to his bunk.

6. The blind beggar _____ suddenly collapsed.

7. The lieutenant _____ reenlisted.

8. The rowboat _____ was overturned.

9. Sam _____ loaned me the money.

10. The fat woman _____ rode gaily down the street.

[1] Note that commas are added when the added words are not essential in identifying the subject and when the added words interrupt the flow of the idea.

TEST 11

Part A: In each of the blanks below, write two or more of your own words without adding a subject, a verb, or a S-V core. Your words must make sense as part of the complete sentence.

1. The boy's books _____ were found in the pond.

2. Fireworks _____ illumined the July sky.

3. Horses _____ stampeded wildly from the barn.

4. The little old man and the crazy old woman ___ rocked the creaky old chairs back and forth.

5. The orchestra conductor _____ split the seams of his trousers.

6. Six cheerleaders _____ gaily led the parade.

7. The actor _____ was hooted from the stage.

8. Women _____ baked the cookies.

9. Six kittens _____ were given to the children.

10. The vicious tiger _____ was finally captured.

Part B: Following the above pattern, write ten of your own *simple* sentences. Underline subjects once and verbs twice.

Adding Words to Follow the Verb

TEST 12

Part A: Add at least six words to each of the subject-verb cores below. Be sure that the completed sentence is *simple*. Punctuate correctly.

1. They will decide _____

2. He is coming _____

3. The president, the congressmen, and the judges held _____

4. Don't go _____

5. The conspirators have been planning _____

6. They read and wrote _____

7. Peace <u><u>is</u></u> _____

8. She <u>talked</u> and <u>pleaded</u> _____

9. To <u>work</u> hard <u><u>is</u></u> _____

10. <u>Dancing</u> <u><u>can</u></u> <u><u>be</u></u> _____

Part B : Using the above pattern, write ten of your own *simple* sentences. Underline the subjects once and verbs twice.

FINAL TEST

Part A : *Individual Simple Sentences*

Write ten simple sentences with words preceding the subjects, words between the subjects and verbs, and words following the verbs. In at least three of these sentences use multiple subjects and multiple verbs. Select your words carefully and try to make each sentence distinct and meaningful. Underline your subjects once and your verbs twice.

Part B : *Simple Sentences in Context*

Using one of the topics suggested below, write a ten-sentence paragraph containing *only simple sentences*. BE CAREFUL. Many students who can write good individual sentences lose their sentence sense or "feel" when they write paragraphs. That is one reason for all the drill that you have been subjected to. When you have completed your paragraph, examine each sentence as a separate unit. Underline your subject and verb. If any of your sentences are incomplete, correct them. If they are not simple sentences, make them simple.[1]

TOPICS:

Women (Men) Cannot Be Trusted
TV Commercials Should (Should Not) Be Banned
Grades Should (Should Not) Be Eliminated
Pornographic Words Should (Should Not) Be Used in School Publications

what you have learned in chapter 3

Starting with sentences containing one verb and "you understood" as the subject, this chapter has explored many simple sentence patterns. It has demonstrated that neither the number of subjects and verbs nor the total number of other words in the sentence changes its basic structure. As long as all subjects are together and all subjects relate to all verbs, the sentence is simple. Once the subjects and verbs *alternate,* the sentence usually (there are a few exceptions) becomes compound or complex. Sure knowledge of the simple sentence provides the groundwork for building compound and complex sentences, because both depend on simple sentences as part of their basic structure.

------

[1] You will find it difficult to write a paragraph full of simple sentences. It is more natural to use a variety of sentences. This exercise is aimed at making you *aware* of your sentence structure in context.

KEY 1

Sit, March, Teach, Scream, Stay, Shoot, Speak, Jump, Bend, Ride, Leave

KEY 2

(1) A simple sentence can contain any number of consecutive subjects and consecutive verbs. (2) A simple sentence becomes a compound or complex sentence when subjects and verbs *alternate*, S-V, S-V. (3) simple, compound, complex (4) "Consecutive" means following one after the other without interruption. (5) "Alternate" means to follow each other by turns.

KEY 3

(1) gallop (2) giggled (3) pours (4) crowed (5) blow (6) dance (7) swim (8) warms (9) electrocutes (10) smelled

KEY 4

(1) Advertisers (2) The pickets (3) Rioters (4) Dynamite (5) Cowards (6) Lovers (7) A prisoner (8) Merry-go-rounds (9) Students (10) A child

KEY 5

(1) girls are coming (2) you can untie (3) party will be held (4) they have won (5) Smetz is coming (6) Olga has (7) eclipse will take place (8) she did marry (9) dog did have (10) he is

KEY 6

(1) He placed (2) beans are (3) cow is (4) people are (5) He is (6) They are sitting (7) mess is (8) pails are (9) he is (10) "you understood" put.

KEY 7

Those that contain S-V cores are: (1) a, f, i, j (2) b, d, i (3) d, f, g, i (4) b, e, g (5) d, e, g (6) c, f, g

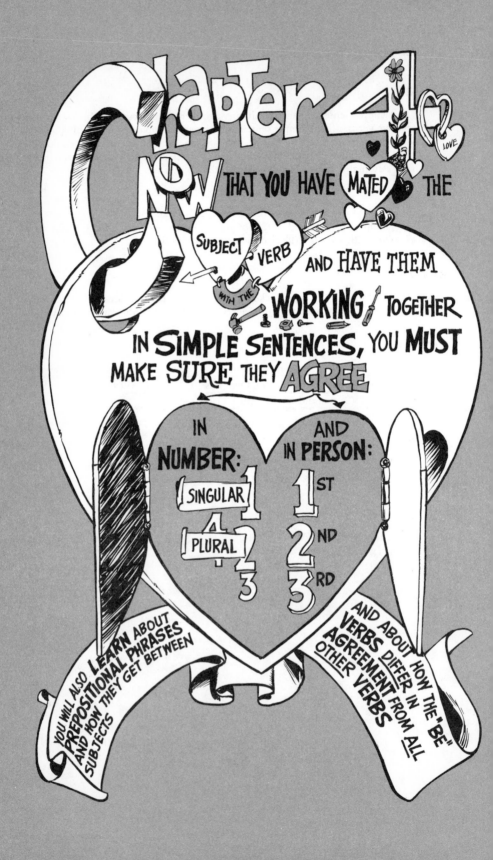

CHAPTER 4

Subject-verb

AGREEMENT

Before moving from the study of simple sentences to the study of compound and complex sentences, we will examine a relationship that exists in every sentence and that creates problems for many students. In every sentence the verb must agree with the subject, and since, by definition, every sentence has some form of subject-verb core, students who have trouble with subject-verb agreement tend to make many errors.

If you do poorly in the following exercises, you have a problem with subject-verb agreement.

SELF-QUIZ 1

Underline the correct verb in the parentheses.

1. The car (run, runs) well.
2. There (were, was) ten people in the room.

3. (Is, are) they coming?
4. I (am, are) ready to work.
5. They (walks, walk) to school every day.
6. The boys and the girl (is, are) here.
7. Our stores (has, have) the option to buy all the grapes.
8. The men in the boat (row, rows) skillfully.
9. Trains of this company always (arrives, arrive) on time.
10. Many men from my former neighborhood (was, were) in the audience.

.n.n.n.n.n.n.n.n.n.n.n.n.n.n.n.n.n.n.n.n.n.n.n.n.n.

Subject-verb agreement is basically very simple: a singular subject requires a singular verb form, and a plural subject requires a plural verb form. The problem, however, is to be able to distinguish clearly whether the subject is singular or plural; whether it is first, second, or third person; and whether you have matched the proper verb form with the subject. Let's examine each of these elements in turn.

THE PROBLEM OF NUMBER: SINGULAR AND PLURAL

When a word (or words) is used as a subject, it is considered a noun or noun form.[1] Most nouns can be made singular or plural. Some are only singular and others only plural.

Listed below are the various methods by which nouns are made plural, with examples of each. You probably know most of them. Study those that are new to you or give you trouble.

1. Most nouns (including proper nouns[2]) add s:

frog	frogs	Smith	Smiths
banana	bananas	toe	toes
trio	trios	pickle	pickles
bicycle	bicycles	night	nights
chief	chiefs	handkerchief	handkerchiefs
attorney	attorneys	turkey	turkeys
Charley	Charleys	Brophy	Brophys
radio	radios	tobacco	tobaccos

2. Some nouns add es:

a. Nouns that end with sh, ch, s, or x add es:

box	boxes	church	churches
brush	brushes	fish	fishes[3]
gas	gases	glass	glasses

[1] Nouns are defined in Chapter 10.
[2] Proper nouns are specific names, for example, George Jeffery, Kleinmetz High School, *The Saturday Review*, Lake Huron.
[3] The usual plural of *fish* is *fish*: *I have other fish to fry.* When referring to different species, the plural is *fishes*: *The lake was stocked with fishes of many varieties.*

b. Some nouns ending with a consonant followed by an *o*, add *es*:

veto	vetoes	potato	potatoes
volcano	volcanoes	embargo	embargoes

3. Some nouns change their final *f* or *fe* to *ves*:

loaf	loaves	half	halves
elf	elves	thief	thieves
knife	knives	leaf	leaves
wife	wives	calf	calves

4. Some nouns change internal vowels:

louse	lice	goose	geese
mouse	mice	man	men
foot	feet	woman	women
		tooth	teeth

5. Nouns that end in *ey* (the vowel *y*[1]) add *s* to form plurals:

valley	valleys	gulley	gulleys
attorney	attorneys	money	moneys

6. Nouns that end in a consonant plus *y*, drop the *y* and add *ies*:

secretary	secretaries	fly	flies
sky	skies	baby	babies
ally	allies	enemy	enemies
variety	varieties	boundary	boundaries

7. Proper nouns ending in *y* add only an *s*. Most other proper nouns add only an *s* or *es*, so that the basic spelling of the names is not changed.

Burke	Burkes	Jones	Joneses	Klatch	Klatches
Wiley	Wileys	Smith	Smiths	Carpenter	Carpenters
Will	Wills	Cohen	Cohens	Onofrio	Onofrios
DiFranco	DiFrancos	Skrscynski	Skrscynskis	Dilly	Dillys

Other categories may be summed up as follows:

1. Some nouns are identical in the singular and in the plural. It is usually necessary to use numerals to tell the reader whether they are singular or plural: *He saw one Japanese. He saw ten Japanese.*

moose	moose	Chinese	Chinese	trousers	trousers
deer	deer	sheep	sheep	scissors	scissors

[1] The vowel-sound *y* is found in words like *money* and *funny*. The consonant-sound *y* is found in words like *you* and *yard*.

2. Some nouns are used only as plurals:

riches	tactics	headquarters
premises	proceeds	athletics
cattle	goods	acoustics

3. Some nouns are used only as singulars:

news	measles	whereabouts	ethics
economics	mumps	molasses	physics

4. Collective nouns may be considered singular or plural depending on their use in the sentence. This will be discussed in Chapter 10.

board	fraternity	audience	troop
club	family	group	class
faculty	crew	crowd	tribe
majority	minority		

5. Pronouns (words used instead of nouns) may also be singular or plural. These must agree in number with the noun they are replacing and also with their verb. This is discussed in Chapter 10.

Handling Your Numbers Problem

Although the foregoing rules may be helpful, learning the correct singular and plural forms is mostly a matter of memorization. The following exercises are intended to give you practice and to make you aware of the numbers problem. The best rule is: when in doubt about a word, look it up. Most standard dictionaries give irregular plurals and indicate whether a word is used as a plural or collective noun.

SELF-QUIZ 2

Write the plural form of the following words.

1. mouse _____

2. fish _____

3. bird _____

4. person _____

5. administrator _____

6. city _____

7. deer _____

8. antelope _____

9. company _____

10. dynamo _____

11. turkey _____

12. box _____

13. bus _____

14. embryo _____

15. enemy _____

16. jelly _____

17. goose _____

18. wheat _____

19. potato _____
20. tooth _____
21. man _____
22. thief _____
23. variety _____
24. boundary _____
25. embargo _____
26. ally _____
27. baby _____
28. moose _____
29. radio _____
30. child _____
31. loaf _____
32. engineer _____
33. Jones _____
34. church _____

35. Japanese _____
36. calf _____
37. foot _____
38. sheep _____
39. key _____
40. lady _____
41. studio _____
42. veto _____
43. attorney _____
44. quantity _____
45. Murphy _____
46. house _____
47. fruit _____
48. Smith _____
49. ox _____
50. study _____

Write the singular form of the following words.

1. eggs _____
2. astronauts _____
3. wheat _____
4. beer _____
5. tomatoes _____
6. chess _____
7. moose _____
8. Chinese _____

9. apples _____
10. Frenchmen _____
11. receivers _____
12. studies _____
13. shelves _____
14. benches _____
15. astronomers _____
16. wreckage _____

17. peasants _____

18. cantelopes _____

19. fraternities _____

20. Abercrombys _____

21. subsidies _____

22. countries _____

23. nations _____

24. alumni _____

25. belles _____

26. stevedores _____

27. trophies _____

28. penguins _____

29. hair _____

30. committees _____

31. Longfellows _____

32. attorneys _____

33. journeys _____

34. ethics _____

35. locomotives _____

36. lettuce _____

37. liabilities _____

38. globes _____

39. elves _____

40. gnus _____

41. G-men _____

42. Fitches _____

43. fruit _____

44. ditties _____

45. phenomena _____

46. estuaries _____

47. plagues _____

48. freemen _____

49. ducks _____

50. localities _____

ı.ıı.

THE PROBLEM OF PERSON

We distinguish person according to who is speaking (*first person*), who is spoken to (*second person*), and who or what is spoken about (*third person*). For each category we also distinguish between singular and plural.

			Singular	Plural
First:	person(s)	speaking	I	we
Second:	"	spoken to	you	you
Third:	"	spoken about	he, she, it	they
			tree, cat, etc.	trees, cats, etc.

Person, Number, and Verb Agreement

All verbs (except *be*) end in *s* or *es* in the third person singular of the present tense.[1] This is the only form of the verb that differs; all the other forms are spelled the same, singular and plural, in the present tense.

>   I run. You run. We run. They run.
>   He (she, it, the dog, the car, etc.) run*s*.
>   I believe. You believe. We believe. They believe.
>   He believe*s*.
>   I have. You have. We have. They have.
>   He ha*s*.
>   I do. You do. We do. They do.
>   He do*es*.

The verb *be* is an exception. It has the following forms in the present:

	Singular	*Plural*
1st person:	I am	We are
2nd person:	You are	You are
3rd person:	He, she, it is	They are

The sentences below contain verbs that students often mismatch with their subjects. Study these examples, bearing in mind that the *s* ending is found only in the *third person singular*.

>   I travel every year. (*first person*)
>   The club travel*s* often.
>
>   We drive to work every day. (*plural*)
>   He rarely drive*s* to work.
>
>   Jerry own*s* a Buick.
>   The company own*s* a fleet of Buicks.
>   You don't even own a bicycle. (*second person*)
>
>   The Smiths and the Kingsleys manage a motel. (*plural*)
>   Ken Smith manage*s* a grocery.
>
>   Marge and Melody select ties for their husbands. (*plural*)
>   Steve select*s* his own ties.
>
>   The cowboys ride into the sunset. (*plural*)
>   The cowboy ride*s* into the sunset.
>
>   We love you all of the time.
>   They love you most of the time.
>   He love*s* you some of the time.
>
>   I win the bet on the baseball game.
>   He win*s* the bet on the horse race.
>   Our team win*s* every twenty years or so.

[1] Verbs ending in *y* (*dry, deny, apply,* etc.) change the *y* to *i* and add *es*: *dries, denies, applies.*

We lose most of the money.

Jerry, Frank and Ed lose a great deal.

The company lose*s* a great deal of money.

SELF-QUIZ 3

Underline the correct verb in the following sentences.

1. The turtle (swim, swims) fairly rapidly.
2. Porpoises (swim, swims) faster.
3. The hens (lays, lay) over 140 eggs per week.
4. Crocodiles and alligators (is, are) reptiles.
5. The lawyers (is, are, am) speaking to the jury.
6. You (runs, run) too slowly.
7. The roosters (crows, crow) every morning.
8. They (fertilizes, fertilize) their grass too often.
9. I (buy, buys) a new car every twenty years.
10. They (is, am, are) coming tomorrow.
11. The freight train (pass, passes) through here every morning.
12. The planes (takes off, take off) on time.
13. Nurses (is, are, am) highly trained.
14. He (adjust, adjusts) the microscope very carefully.
15. She (manipulate, manipulates) the typewriter with great dexterity.
16. The catcher (catch, catches) the ball neatly.
17. Who (claim, claims) to know everything?
18. My neighbors always (win, wins) their bets.
19. They (lose, loses) their money regularly.
20. Cattle (is, are, was) sleeping in the sunshine.

TEST 1

Write simple sentences using the subjects indicated. Use the subject first in its singular form and then in its plural form. Mate each subject with a different verb in the PRESENT tense. Use no *be* forms.

EXAMPLE:

(boat) a. The boat leaks.

        b. The boats sail well.

1. (car)   a. _____

           b. _____

2. (I)   a. _____

           b. _____

3. (man)   a. _____

              b. _____

4. (prune)   a. _____

              b. _____

5. (girl)   a. _____

              b. _____

6. (horse)   a. _____

              b. _____

7. (factory)   a. _____

              b. _____

8. (deer)   a. _____

              b. _____

9. (knife)   a. _____

              b. _____

10. (piccolo)   a. _____

              b. _____

TEST 2

Write ten pairs of simple sentences in the PRESENT tense. Use each word below as a verb twice: (a) in the first person singular, and (b) in the third person singular.

EXAMPLE:

  (eat) a. I eat apples.
          b. She eats worms.

1. (do)   a. _____

              b. _____

2. (desire)   a. _____

              b. _____

3. (stay)   a. _____

              b. _____

4. (go)   a. _____

            b. _____

5. (deny) a. _____

            b. _____

6. (want) a. _____

            b. _____

7. (claim) a. _____

            b. _____

8. (box)   a. _____

            b. _____

9. (receive) a. _____

            b. _____

10. (play) a. _____

            b. _____

Person, Number, and the *Be* Verbs

As you have seen, the present tense of the verb *be* has the forms *am, are, is*. There are only two past tense forms: *was* and *were*. In the table below, these forms are matched up with their subjects in person and number. Memorize this table. It is important to know these forms by heart because they are the most frequently used in the language, not only by themselves but as auxiliaries in combination with other verbs.

	Singular	*Present*	*Past*	*Plural*	*Present*	*Past*
First person:	I	am	was	We	are	were
Second person:	You	are	were	You	are	were
Third person:	He, she, it, etc.	is	was	They	are	were

Study the examples below and identify the *be* forms as to person (first, second, or third), number (singular or plural), and tense (past or present). In some sentences they are used as auxiliaries.

PRESENT TENSES

Singular

First person: I am early. I am going to pay you now.

Second person: You are a good friend. You are working too hard.

Third person: He is a forger. The food is excellent. The weather is terrible. The rabbit is running away. She is screaming.

Plural

First person: We are on time.   We are assuming power.
Second person: You are a fine group.   You are playing a great game.
Third person: They are sick.   They are leaving now.

PAST TENSES

Singular

First person: I was a friend of hers.   I was chasing a rabbit.
Second person: You were her best friend.   You were driving too fast.
Third person: He was sick.   She was unfriendly.   It was red.   The company was bankrupt.   The potato was rotten.   A truce was arranged.

Plural

First person: We were there last year.   We were singing all night. We were delivering the supplies.

Second person: You were slow in getting started.   You were moving erratically.

Third person: They were very happy. They were fishing all night.

SELF-QUIZ 4

Underline the correct word.

1. You three men (are, is) to come with me.
2. The company (were, was) recently incorporated.
3. I (am, are) leaving immediately.
4. Sam and I (am, are) forming a partnership.
5. Australia (are, is) sending a delegation.
6. You (is, are) expected to go to the party.
7. Thelma and Julia (is, are) kissing Edward and Frank now.
8. I (is, am, are) arriving on the noon plane.
9. The men and women (am, is, are) here in the conference room.
10. Lena and Egbert (is, was, were) with us.
11. The soldiers (is, are, were) disembarking now.
12. The bakers (am, are, is) baking day and night.
13. We (were, was) in Afghanistan last week.
14. They (is, are, were) fighting all last week.
15. They (was, were, is) playing.
16. We (are, is) on the island now.
17. I (were, was) going to town.
18. You (was, were) with them at the time.
19. You (was, is, were) riding in the back seat.
20. I (was, am, were) there yesterday.

TEST 3

Part A: Write six simple sentences using the forms of *be* in the first, second, third person singular and plural, PRESENT tense. Underline subjects and verbs in the usual manner.

Part B: Write six sentences as above in the PAST tense. Underline subjects and verbs.

TEST 4

Compose twenty simple sentences by completing the blanks below. Use the correct form of *is, are, am, were, was,* as auxiliaries or as individual verbs. You may use each verb more than once. Underline the subjects and verbs in the usual way.

1. The rhinoceros _____

2. Apples, lemons, and bananas _____

3. The companies _____

4. Lulu and I _____

5. The governors _____

6. After the earthquake, the people _____

7. Despite the warning, the club _____

8. The girl _____

9. We _____

10. The inhabitants of the island _____

11. Members of the club _____

12. His teammates _____

13. The detectives _____

14. Friends _____

15. In the spring I _____

16. Before going to school, the child _____

17. Her friend _____

18. The gift _____

19. The secretary _____

20. I _____

TEST 5

Write twenty sentences of your own using *is, are, am, were, was,* either alone or as auxiliaries. You may skip around but don't leave any out. Mark your subjects and verbs by single and double underlining.

BRINGING IN PREPOSITIONAL PHRASES

In Chapter 3 you learned to insert words and phrases between subjects and verbs without losing track of the subjects and verbs. The type of phrase most frequently used in this in-between position is the *prepositional phrase.* These phrases are groups of words which start with a preposition and end with a noun or noun form called the object of the preposition: *over the hill, under the dam, beyond the horizons.*

When the prepositional phrase is written between the subject and verb, the writer sometimes confuses the object of the preposition with the subject of the sentence and makes errors in agreement of subject and verb. This happens when the subject and object differ in number. For example, if the subject is plural but the object of the preposition is singular, you might make the mistake of using a singular verb:

  incorrect: The ships in old Boston Harbor was small.
  correct: The ships in old Boston Harbor were small.

When checking your sentences for agreement of subject and verb, it is especially valuable to be able to recognize prepositional phrases, because they never contain the subject or verb of the sentence.

SELF-QUIZ 5

1. A prepositional phrase must contain at least two words, a _____

   _____ and its _____.
2. A group of words which starts with a preposition and ends with its object

   is called a _____.
3. The prepositional phrase is often placed between the _____

   and _____ of a sentence.

4. The _____ of a preposition is a noun or a _____
   form.
5. The prepositional phrase is mentioned here in particular because its

   _____ is sometimes confused with the _____ of the
   sentence.
6. Prepositional phrases may contain words other than the _____

   _____ and its _____, but they never contain the _____

   _____ and the _____ of the sentence.

7. If a student confuses the object of his _____ with the

   subject of his _____ he may write the wrong form
   of the verb.
8. This problem in agreement arises because the subject of the sentence may

   be different in _____ from the _____.

Prepositions

The list of words and phrases below are often used as prepositions. Study them and refer to them when you get confused about which word is the subject of your sentence. Few students err in writing prepositional phrases. The greatest value in knowing about them is that they help you to see which words in a sentence are *not* your subject or your verb. If you have no trouble with your subjects and verbs, you have little to worry about in regard to prepositional phrases.

about	besides	into
above	between	of
across	beyond	on
after	but (except)	on account of
against	by	over
along	by way of	since
among	concerning	through
as	down	throughout
as for	during	to
as to	except	toward
at	for	under
before	from	underneath
behind	in	upon
below	in addition to	with
beneath	in place of	within
beside	in spite of	without

Prepositional Phrases

In all of the prepositional phrases below, the first word is the preposition and the last word is its object. Notice, first of all, how common these phrases are, and then remember that there are no subjects or verbs in them.

about time	as for your question
above your head	at night
across the field	before sunrise
after the storm	behind the shed
against the wall	below the deck
along the path	beneath the starry sky
among the people	beside the lovely lady

between the devil and the deep blue sea
but Fred   by way of introduction
concerning your father   to bed
to the house   through the window
without help   from the post office
for you   from him
in place   except Snodgrass
during the night   down the drain

In the sentences below at least one prepositional phrase is inserted in brackets between each subject and verb. Read them carefully and note how a careless writer might confuse the object of the preposition (the last word of the prepositional phrase) with the subject of the sentence.

1. The crate [of apples] was shipped yesterday.
2. His team [of horses] works hard.
3. The men [on top] [of the red roof] are drunk.
4. Butchers [from the eastern part] [of Nova Scotia] are holding a convention.
5. The child [in the blue suit and brown shoes] is crying.
6. One [of those dangerous criminals] is at large.
7. Each [of the contestants] still has a chance to win.
8. The children [in the big red house] [on the other side] [of the dark and muddy river] wave [at us] every day.
9. None [of the men] has signed the contract.
10. The ladies [in the clubhouse] are fighting.

TEST 6

Complete these sentences. Keep them SIMPLE and in the PRESENT tense. Underline your subjects once and your verbs twice. Put brackets around the prepositional phrases.

1. The men on the tree-covered island in the middle of the lake _____

2. Somebody in the upper stands _____

3. Children under the age of six, in the company of an adult _____

4. The old man in the tobacco-stained, baggy suit _____

5. In spite of their troubles the people of Upper Slobbovia _____

6. The girls in the class of 1942 _____

7. Neither of the two terror-stricken teenagers _____

8. The team of carefully-trained firefighters _____

9. Members of the most famous marching band in the country _____

10. The friendly, hungry, chattering birds in our tree house _____

The self-quiz below is designed to show you how other words and phrases as well as prepositions can get between the subjects and the verbs. Keep in mind that we are continuing to work with *simple* sentences. The ground rules are that any number of words which enhance the meaning of the sentence may be added except those which form new subject-verb cores.

SELF-QUIZ 6

Underline the subject of each sentence; then circle the proper verb from the choices in parentheses.

1. The veteran, tired, worn, and discouraged, (is, are, am, were) going home.
2. Professor Limbo, wishing to be friendly, (tell, tells) three jokes to his early morning classes every Monday.
3. The astronauts, daring and resourceful men, (am, is, was, are) planning to land on the moon.
4. The highbrows, filled with dreams of social improvement or self-aggrandizement, (are, is, am, was) leaving the universities.
5. In early autumn the leaves, saturated with the colors of the sun, slowly (drop, drops) from the trees.
6. The miser, hated by many, finally (give, gives) his money to the poor.
7. His childhood, full of sweet and sour memories, (comes, come) back to him on days like this.
8. India, with its countless starving and its royal rich, its myriad views, its starkness and its pageantry, (beckon, beckons) the adventurous traveler.
9. The contents of the test tube, bubbling furiously, (spill, spills) on the floor.
10. The actress, gay and charming, (have, has) a deep baritone voice.
11. The rabbi, deep in meditation, (do, does) not hear the thunder.
12. The soldier, obeying his orders, (shoot, shoots) the stranger.
13. The children, dressed in Nature's own apparel, (dive, dives) into the pool.
14. Computers, precise, efficient, accurate-appearing (is, am, are, was) far from perfect.
15. The house on the corner of Bog and Jay Streets (lean, leans) to one side.
16. Elephants, gray, lumbering, quizzical beasts, (lie, lies) in the shade of the tree.
17. There by the pond (are, is, am, was) ten nuts.
18. There, but for the grace of God, (go, goes) I.

19. Where (do, does) he, the man in the yellow tent (lives, live)?

20. The Ancient Mariner, starved and tortured, (cry, cries) for help.

TEST 7

Part A: Underline the subjects in the phrases below and complete the sentences. Underline your verbs. Keep all of your writing in the PRESENT tense. Do not use any form of *be*.

1. The maniac, screaming and shouting,_____

2. In the late afternoon, the dog in the apartment next door_____

3. The baritone, bowing from the waist,_____

4. Fishermen in small, unseaworthy boats_____

5. Jane, ill for many months,_____

6. The rescue squad, sirens shrilling,_____

7. Winston Churchill, speaking before Parliament,_____

8. The boa constrictor, its body curled tightly around the antelope,_____

9. Love and peace, together_____

10. His car, rusty and dilapidated,_____

Part B: Write ten simple sentences of your own in which your subjects are separated from your verbs by words or prepositional phrases (no new subject-verb cores). Use different subjects and verbs in each sentence. Keep them all in the PRESENT tense. Underline your subjects once and your verbs twice.

what you have learned in chapter 4

Making subjects and verbs agree involves an understanding of *number* (singularity and plurality) and of first, second, and third *person*. Most verbs change only in the *third person singular* of the *present tense*, but "be" verbs require special study because they change into various forms, and they change in the *past* as well as the *present tense*. It is also important to recognize prepositional phrases because they often come between subject and verb and cause agreement problems.

(If you are still uncertain about subjects and verbs, the subject-verb core, the simple sentence, or agreement of subject and verb, review the necessary sections of chapters 2, 3, and 4 before proceeding to chapter 5.)

KEY 1

(1) runs (2) were (3) are (4) am (5) walk (6) are (7) have (8) row (9) arrive (10) were

KEY 2

Plural

1. mice
2. fish, fishes
3. birds
4. people
5. administrators
6. cities
7. deer
8. antelopes
9. companies
10. dynamos
11. turkeys
12. boxes
13. buses, busses
14. embryos
15. enemies
16. jellies
17. geese
18. wheat
19. potatoes
20. teeth
21. men
22. thieves
23. varieties
24. boundaries
25. embargoes
26. allies
27. babies
28. moose
29. radios
30. children
31. loaves
32. engineers
33. Joneses
34. churches
35. Japanese
36. calves
37. feet
38. sheep
39. keys
40. ladies
41. studios
42. vetoes
43. attorneys
44. quantities
45. Murphys
46. houses
47. fruit
48. Smiths
49. oxen
50. studies

Singular

1. egg
2. astronaut
3. wheat
4. beer
5. tomato
6. chess
7. moose
8. Chinese
9. apple
10. Frenchman
11. receiver
12. study
13. shelf
14. bench
15. astronomer
16. wreckage
17. peasant
18. cantelope
19. fraternity
20. Abercromby
21. subsidy
22. country
23. nation
24. alumnus
25. belle
26. stevedore
27. trophy
28. penguin
29. hair
30. committee
31. Longfellow
32. attorney
33. journey
34. ethics
35. locomotive
36. lettuce
37. liability
38. globe
39. elf
40. gnu
41. G-man
42. Fitch
43. fruit
44. ditty
45. phenomenon
46. estuary
47. plague
48. freeman
49. duck
50. locality

KEY 3

(1) swims   (2) swim   (3) lay   (4) are   (5) are   (6) run   (7) crow   (8) fertilize   (9) buy   (10) are   (11) passes   (12) take off   (13) are   (14) adjusts   (15) manipulates   (16) catches   (17) claims   (18) win   (19) lose   (20) are

KEY 4

(1) are   (2) was   (3) am   (4) are   (5) is   (6) are   (7) are   (8) am   (9) are   (10) were   (11) are   (12) are   (13) were   (14) were   (15) were   (16) are   (17) was   (18) were   (19) were   (20) was

KEY 5

(1) preposition, object   (2) prepositional phrase   (3) subject, verb   (4) object, noun   (5) object, subject   (6) preposition, object, subject, verb   (7) preposition, sentence   (8) number, object of the preposition.

KEY 6

(1) <u>veteran</u> <u>is</u>   (2) <u>Professor Limbo</u> <u>tells</u>   (3) <u>astronauts</u> <u>are</u>   (4) <u>highbrows</u> <u>are</u>
(5) <u>leaves</u> <u>drop</u>   (6) <u>miser</u> <u>gives</u>   (7) <u>childhood</u> <u>comes</u>   (8) <u>India</u> <u>beckons</u>
(9) <u>contents</u> <u>spill</u>   (10) <u>actress</u> <u>has</u>   (11) <u>rabbi</u> <u>does</u>   (12) <u>soldier</u> <u>shoots</u>
(13) <u>children</u> <u>dive</u>   (14) <u>computers</u> <u>are</u>   (15) <u>house</u> <u>leans</u>   (16) <u>elephants</u> <u>lie</u>
(17) <u>nuts</u> <u>are</u>   (18) <u>I</u> <u>go</u>   (19) <u>he</u> <u>does</u> <u>live</u>   (20) <u>Ancient Mariner</u> <u>cries</u>

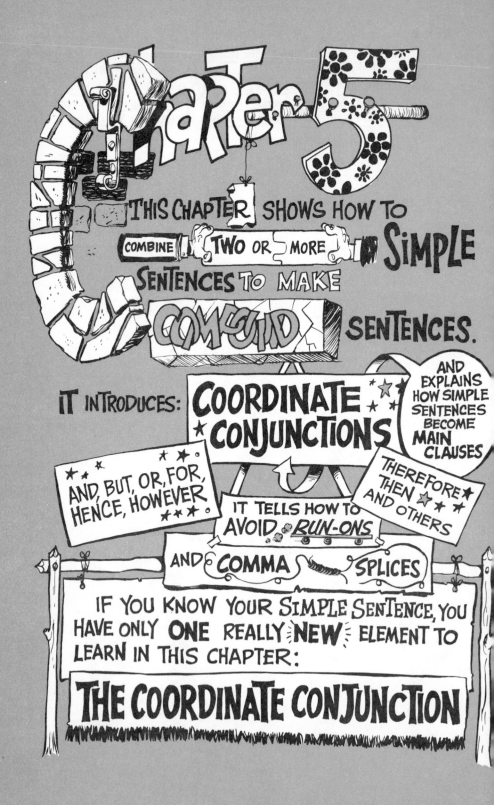

CHAPTER 5

Writing

COMPOUND SENTENCES

Adding new S-V cores is easy. It comes naturally because writing that is limited to simple sentences tends to be choppy and often sounds childish. Maturer minds tend to think in compound and complex sentences. The student's problem is to write his thoughts with a conscious effort at obeying the rules of standard English. This means that he must continue to keep control of his sentences as he changes from simple to more complex patterns.

The purpose of this section is to give you practice with expanding simple sentences into compound sentences. The many exercises in this section will help you recognize and eliminate sentence faults such as run-ons and comma splices by making you more aware of how compound sentences are structured.

WHAT IS A COMPOUND SENTENCE?

A compound sentence consists of two or more simple sentences joined together by one or more coordinate conjunctions or by a semicolon. Various patterns are possible, as shown in the diagrams below.

Main (Independent) Clauses. The parts of compound sentences that separately would be considered simple sentences are called main clauses. In other words, once two or more simple sentences have been combined to make a compound sentence, the simple sentences become main clauses.

Coordinate Conjunctions. Coordinate conjunctions are key elements in the structure of the compound sentence. They are used to tie two or more main clauses together. Coordinate conjunctions may also connect words and phrases,[1] but in this and the next two chapters you will study them primarily as connectors of main clauses.

Types of Coordinate Conjuctions

Listed below are the four categories of coordinate conjunctions. It is important to memorize this list, because coordinate conjunctions are the keys to the compound sentence.

1. *The most common conjunctions, used with a comma:*
   , and   , but   , or   , for   , yet

2. *Conjunctions that are used with a semicolon* (only the most frequently used are listed):

; accordingly	; however	; then
; consequently	; moreover	; therefore
; furthermore	; nevertheless	; thus
; hence	; otherwise	

3. Sometimes semicolons by themselves act as conjunctions.

4. *Conjunctions that come in pairs:*
   either . . . or   not only . . . but (also)
   neither . . . nor

COMPOUND SENTENCE PATTERNS

1. *The "and-but" pattern.* This pattern is the most common and is used with the first group of coordinate conjunctions: *and, but, or, for,* and *yet.*

S-V	, coordinate conjunction	S-V
main clause	(CC)	main clause

The President arrived early, **yet** he missed the Prime Minister.

---

[1] Examples of coordinate conjunctions which connect words or phrases: cat *or* dog; into the house *and* over the new rug; kind *but* firm; *neither* naughty *nor* nice.

There can, of course, be more than two subject-verb cores. In this case the conjunction is added before the last clause in the series.

| _____S-V_____ | , | _____S-V_____ | , | _____S-V_____ | , CC | _____S-V_____ . |

Some bury their dead in tombs, some burn their dead, some throw the bodies into the river, **and** some give their dead to the vultures.

2. *The coordinate conjunction-semicolon pattern.* This pattern is very similar to the *and* pattern. In both, the conjunctions are always placed between main clauses.

| _____SS-V_____ | ; CC | _____S-VV_____ . |

The governor and mayor agree privately; **however,** they will not release a statement or make a speech.

3. *The semicolon alone.* The semicolon alone acts as a weak period or a strong *and* in compound sentences. Writers use it between two main clauses whose ideas are closely related when they feel that the period would interrupt the idea too much and the *and* is unnecessary or inappropriate. Avoid using it too often. A period is usually better.

Hans went to Denmark; Elsa followed shortly.
The trainmen went on strike; all rail shipment was delayed.
We do not seek power; we do not seek glory.

4. *The "either . . . or" pattern.* In this pattern one of the paired conjunctions is placed at or near the beginning of the sentence, and the other is placed between the clauses.

| C | _____S-V_____ | C | _____S-V_____ . |

Either John will go to Mary **or** Mary will come to John.
Neither did the enemy appear **nor** did the fog lift.
Not only did the delegation reach Iran quickly, **but** they **also** brought good news with them.

Avoid pattern 4 when the simple sentence form would be more effective:
correct:　Either Ben or Louise will go.
incorrect: Either Ben will go, or Louise will go.

Most patterns used in the simple sentence can be used in the main clauses of compound sentences.[1]

| _____SSS-V_____ | , CC | _____S-VV_____ . |

The basketball team, the band, and the chorus went to Chicago, **but** the cheerleaders stayed home and sulked.

---

[1] Exceptions are sentences using expletives and "you understood."

S-VVV	CC	S-V

Simon left early, climbed the hill, and chased goats, **but** Lillian only sl

V-S	, CC	V-S-V

Who are you, **and** where are you going?

V-S	;	V-S

Into the hills went the bandits; into the swamps went the posse.

SELF-QUIZ 1

Fill in the blanks.

1. Once you have mastered the _____, you sho

   find the _____ relatively easy to write.
2. It is imperative to remember what you have learned about the _____

   _____ and to apply it to the writing of

   _____ .

3. A _____ consists of two or more sim

   sentences joined together by one or more _____

   or by a _____ .
4. The parts of compound sentences that separately would be conside

   simple sentences are called _____ .
5. List the five most common coordinate conjunctions.

   _____
6. List the eleven coordinate conjunctions that are used with semicolons.

   _____

   _____

   _____
7. What punctuation mark can act like a coordinate conjunction?

   _____
8. List three coordinate conjunctions which come in pairs. _____

   _____
9. End punctuation, conjunctions, or semicolons are needed when the wr

   adds new _____ cores.

MEANINGS AND USES OF SOME COORDINATE CONJUNCTIONS[1]

The conjunctions listed below are grouped in two general categories:

A. Conjunctions which indicate that the ideas they introduce follow *as a result of* or *in agreement with* the preceding idea.

accordingly
I received my orders at midnight; **accordingly** I was on my way at one a.m.

consequently
The strike took place in the middle of the harvest; **consequently** much food was spoiled.

hence
He did not report to work; **hence** he did not receive his pay.

thus
The peace negotiations were begun, and the major issues were settled; **thus** the war was finally ended.

therefore
We received no information; **therefore** we did not vote.

moreover
We had wanted to travel for many years; **moreover,** we finally had the money.

furthermore
They will sue you for damages if you don't pay them; **furthermore,** they may press criminal charges against you.

then
The jury listened to the testimony; **then** they passed judgment.

B. Conjunctions which indicate that the ideas they introduce are *in opposition to* or *in spite of* what preceded.

nevertheless
They were invited by the President himself; **nevertheless** they decided not to go.

however
She wanted to marry John desperately; **however,** Peter had more money.

otherwise
I will pay you the money today if you need it; **otherwise** I will mail it to you next month.

---

[1] The coordinate conjunctions listed here are called *conjunctive adverbs.* Commas are placed after some of them when they immediately follow the semicolon. It is up to the writer to decide. Note that some of the conjunctive adverbs can be used in different positions. In these cases, commas are always used: They were invited by the president himself; they decided, *nevertheless,* not to go. They were invited by the President himself; they decided not to go, *nevertheless.* The strike took place during the harvest; much food, *consequently,* was spoiled. She wanted to marry John desperately; Peter had more money, *however.*

Write fifteen compound sentences, using the conjunctions indicated. Try to write varied, thoughtful sentences. Place the proper commas or semicolons before the conjunctions. Underline subjects once and verbs twice.

1. (either . . . or)_____
2. (consequently)_____
3. (and)_____
4. (then)_____
5. (but)_____
6. (thus)_____
7. (otherwise)_____
8. (furthermore)_____
9. (yet)_____
10. (nevertheless)_____
11. (accordingly)_____
12. (or)_____
13. (moreover)_____
14. (therefore)_____
15. (however)_____

THE RUN-ON AND THE COMMA SPLICE

The run-on sentence and the so-called comma splice are considered substandard writing and should be avoided. As the term suggests, a run-on occurs when you start a new sentence without placing a period at the end of the previous one. A comma splice occurs when you place only a comma between sentences instead of a period, a comma and conjunction, or a semicolon.

Avoid the run-on:	Friendly governments contributed funds relief workers fed and nursed the hungry.
Avoid the comma splice:	Friendly governments contributed funds, relief workers fed and nursed the hungry.
Corrected with a period:	Friendly governments contributed funds. Relief workers fed and nursed the hungry.
Corrected with a comma and a conjunction:	Friendly governments contributed funds, and relief workers fed and nursed the hungry.
Corrected with a semicolon:	Friendly governments contributed funds; relief workers fed and nursed the hungry.

If one is constantly aware of his subject-verb cores, he can avoid run-ons and comma splices by inserting a conjunction or the proper punctuation before developing a sentence around a new core.

SELF-QUIZ 2

All of the following are run-on sentences or comma splices. Correct them by adding periods (and the necessary capital letters). Do not add commas or semicolons. Underline subjects once and verbs twice.

1. George, Sally, and Millie found Sam in the pond he was eating goldfish.
2. The hounds ran over the bridge, around the lake, and deep into the woods, the skunk had no chance at all.
3. Up to the square marched the protestors, singing and shouting there they ended the parade.
4. After the battle the men rested on the ground some drank French wine.
5. The psychologist listened carefully for many hours the patient talked.
6. Later in the day they had a picnic the sun set quickly.
7. Everyone ate heartily after the program they fell asleep.
8. Long after dawn the fog held tight to the ground, it kissed the grass, almost smothering it with love.
9. Come home with me, give me your hand you are my best friend.
10. The antelope darted daringly in front of the car there was a screech of brakes, Sarah screamed.

.ıı.ı

SELF-QUIZ 3

Some of these are correct. If they are, place a C to the left of the number. If they are incorrect, correct them by adding periods and capital letters. Do not add conjunctions, commas, or semicolons. Underline subjects once and verbs twice.

_____ 1. Dagwood went home, Selma stayed with Lucy, and Babbs left town.

_____ 2. The organization voted Millie the money after the meeting was over she resigned.

_____ 3. The little boy deflated the tires of his father's car all by himself his sick father reinflated them.

_____ 4. The angry settlers chased the Indians far across the plains before dawn the Indians regrouped and attacked again.

_____ 5. Write carefully and clearly, indent for paragraphs, punctuate as necessary.

_____ 6. Industry needs you; you need industry.

_____ 7. He saddled the horse and rode quickly after his brother the horse took him rapidly out of sight into the sun it sank suddenly hiding the disappearing silhouette.

_____ 8. She was black as the night she was sweet she was kind.

_____ 9. He destroyed all before him and left the women and children sobbing in the dust.

_____ 10. The child ran home the house burned down, and the ashes glowed all night.

I.II.II.II.II.II.II.II.II.II.II.II.II.II.II.II.II.II.II.II.II.II.II.II.II.I

SELF-QUIZ 4

In the paragraphs below, correct the run-ons and comma splices by inserting periods and capital letters only. Do not change sentences that are correct.

(2 run-ons, 1 comma splice)
1. There is no need for study halls in high school they are a waste of time and effort. Some students want to study, rooms should be provided for them. Others should be allowed to take extra classes, participate in recreational activities, or go home it should be up to each student to decide for himself.

(2 run-ons, 1 comma splice)
2. My friend, Liza, works at St. John's Hospital in the morning she takes me to work every day, and I pay her $4.00 a week. I would like to get a job there myself, I am qualified for the work it is highly specialized.

(2 run-ons, 1 comma splice)
3. The draft has been a major problem in America since the 1950's. Demonstrations have taken place in many cities New York had one of the worst over one hundred students were arrested during one demonstration. This has shocked many people, it is a very serious situation.

(2 comma splices, 2 run-ons)
4. Many drivers are very careless, a careful driver must be doubly on the alert. He must constantly scan the road as far ahead as possible he must check his side and rear view mirrors. He must expect someone to overlook a stop sign or "jump" a red light too quickly in this way he can be ready to compensate for the errors of others and help avoid an accident, this is called defensive driving.

I.II.II.II.II.II.II.II.II.II.II.II.II.II.II.II.II.II.II.II.II.II.II.II.II.II.

what you have learned in chapter 5

Compound sentences are formed by adding two or more *simple sentences* together with *coordinate conjunctions*. Each simple sentence is then called a *main clause*.

To avoid writing *run-ons* or *comma splices*, you must place the proper conjunctions and/or punctuation between the main clauses. In most cases a comma *and* a coordinate conjunction are required. Sometimes a semicolon is used. When a sentence is comprised of a series of main clauses, commas are placed between each clause, and a comma and coordinate conjunction is placed before the final clause.

Writing compound sentences is simple if you have learned to write simple sentences well and have learned the coordinate conjunctions.

KEY 1

(1) simple sentence, compound sentence   (2) simple sentence, compound sentence
(3) compound sentence, coordinate conjunctions, semicolon   (4) main clauses
(5) and, but, or, for, yet   (6) accordingly, consequently, furthermore, hence,
however, moreover, nevertheless, otherwise, then, therefore, thus   (7) semicolon
(8) either-or, neither-nor, not only-but (also)   (9) subject-verb

KEY 2

Check not only whether you put the periods in the right places, but also whether you underlined the S-V cores properly.

1. George, Sally, and Millie found . . . pond. He was eating goldfish.
2. The hounds ran . . . woods. The skunk had . . . all.
3. . . . marched the protestors . . . shouting. There they ended the parade.
4. . . . men rested . . . ground. Some drank . . .
5. The psychologist listened . . . hours. The patient talked. (*Or*) The psychologist . . . carefully. For . . . patient talked .
6. . . . they had . . . picnic. The sun set quickly.
7. Everyone ate . . . program. They fell asleep. (*Or*) Everyone ate heartily. After . . . they fell asleep.
8. . . . fog held . . . ground. It kissed . . . love.
9. Come home with me. Give me your hand. You are my best friend.
10. The antelope darted . . . car. There was a screech of brakes. Sarah screamed.

KEY 3

1. C
2. The organization voted . . . money. After . . . she resigned.
3. boy deflated . . . himself. His father reinflated them. (*Or*) boy . . . car. All by himself . . . father reinflated them.
4. The angry settlers chased . . . plains. Before dawn the Indians regrouped and attacked again. (*Or*) The angry . . . before dawn. The Indians . . . again.
5. Write . . . clearly. Indent for paragraphs. Punctuate as necessary.
6. C
7. He saddled . . . rode . . . brother. The horse took . . . sun. It sank . . .
8. She was . . . night. She was sweet. She was kind.
9. C
10. The child ran home. The house burned down, and the ashes glowed all night.

KEY 4

1. There . . . school. They . . . effort. Some . . . study. Rooms . . . them. Others . . . home. It . . . himself.
2. My . . . morning. She . . . week. I . . . myself. I . . . work. It . . . specialized.
3. Demonstrations . . . cities. New York . . . worst. Over . . . demonstration. This . . . people. It . . . situation.
4. Many drivers are very careless. A . . . alert. He . . . possible. He . . . mirrors. He . . . quickly. In . . . accident. This . . . driving.

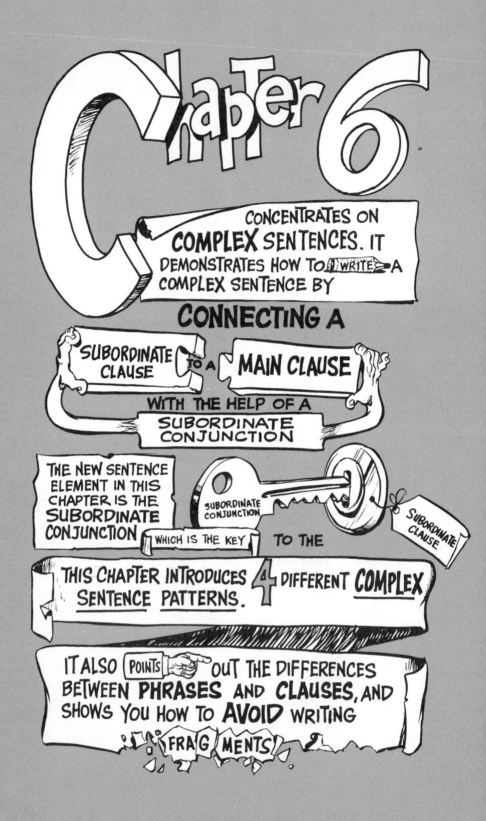

CHAPTER 6

Writing

COMPLEX SENTENCES

The final step in sentence development is the building of the complex sentence.[1] The basic structure is relatively simple. Just as in the writing of compound sentences, it is based on a knowledge of the subject-verb core and the use of conjunctions. The subordinate conjunctions used in connecting the clauses of complex sentences, however, are somewhat more difficult to work with. The reason is that the words used as conjunctions can also be used as various other parts of speech. Also, the complex sentence patterns are more varied than compound sentence patterns.

[1] All sentences are simple, compound, complex, or combinations of these three types.

WHAT IS A COMPLEX SENTENCE?

A complex sentence consists of a main clause and at least one subordinate (dependent) clause. The subordinate clause can be placed before or after the main clause or can be inserted between the subject and the verb of the main clause.

Subordinate Clause. A subordinate clause is a group of words which is usually introduced by a subordinate conjunction and which contains one subject-verb core. A *subordinate conjunction* is any word on the list below which introduces a subordinate clause and which connects that clause to a main clause.

SUBORDINATE CONJUNCTIONS

It is important to memorize the conjunctions listed below because they are the keys to the complex sentence. It is also important to note that these words can act as parts of speech other than conjunctions. They are conjunctions only if they introduce subordinate clauses and connect them to main clauses. You will also occasionally find other words or other combinations of the words below which act as subordinate conjunctions.

after	how	till	whether
although	if	unless	which
as	in order that	until	while
as if	provided that	what	who
as far as	since	whatever	whoever
as long as	so	when	whom
as soon as	so that	whenever	whomever
because	that	where	why
before	though	wherever	

THE SUBORDINATE CONJUNCTION—A HANDY TOOL

While the coordinate conjunctions *add* clauses together, the subordinate conjunctions literally *weave* them together. The examples below illustrate some of the results that are possible when you combine two simple sentences into one complex sentence. Notice how important the conjunction (shown in italics) can be to the meaning of the new complex sentence.

Simple: John is a fool.
John does not like girls.

Complex: *Because* John is a fool, he does not like girls.
John is a fool *because* he does not like girls.
John, *who* does not like girls, is a fool.

Simple: Mary had been ill for weeks.
Mary went away.

Complex: *After* Mary had been ill for weeks, she went away.
Mary, *who* had been ill for weeks, went away.
Since she had been ill for weeks, Mary went away.

Although we will concentrate on two-clause sentences in this chapter, note how easy it is to get complicated by weaving in more subordinate clauses.

Simple: Ned is in trouble again.
Ned is my neighbor.
Ned has been in jail before.
Ned is worried.

Complex: *Because* he has been in jail before, Ned, *who* is my neighbor, is worried, *as* he is in trouble again.

SELF-QUIZ 1

1. Sentences are of three types:_____, _____, and_____, or a_____of these three.

2. In writing compound sentences we combine two or more_____ clauses by using _____.

3. In this section we will use_____conjunctions to form _____sentences.

4. A complex sentence consists of a_____clause and at least one _____clause.

5. A subordinate clause is a group of words which contains one_____ core and is usually introduced by a_____conjunction.

6. When a main clause is combined with a subordinate clause, the result is a_____sentence.

7. A_____sentence is made up of two or more main clauses connected by one or more_____.

8. A_____sentence is made up of a main_____and a _____clause. The two clauses are usually connected by a _____conjunction.

9. A_____conjunction is any word on the_____ conjunction list which introduces a subordinate_____and connects that clause to a_____clause.

10. _____ are the keys to complex sentences.

11. It is important to note that the words used as _____ conjunctions can act as _____ other than _____ conjunctions.

12. They are _____ conjunctions only if they introduce _____ clauses and connect them to _____ clauses.

13. _____ are the keys to compound sentences.

.ıı

DISTINGUISHING BETWEEN A PHRASE AND A CLAUSE

By definition a subordinate conjunction must introduce a subordinate clause, and by definition a clause must contain a subject and a verb. Therefore if a word on the subordinate conjunction list is not followed by a subject and verb, it is introducing a phrase, not a clause.

SELF-TEST 2

In the exercises below, place a C next to the clauses and a P next to the phrases. In the subordinate clauses, underline the subjects once and the verbs twice.

1. _____ after the fight in the old, red barn

2. _____ until they arrive

3. _____ because of the earthquake in Lower Slobbovia

4. _____ although the people of the province want peace

5. _____ while she watches the baby

6. _____ when the clock strikes

7. _____ before the early hours of misty dawn

8. _____ since the beginning of recorded time

9. _____ as deep as the deepest ocean

10. _____ whether he wishes

.ıı.ı

In this list there are other words and phrases along with subordinate clauses. Find the subordinate clauses and underline the subjects once and the verbs twice.

1. slowly, carefully, inch-by-inch
2. as soon as they left
3. into the stream, over the hill, under the bridge, across the valley
4. learning about the arrival of their friends
5. running as swiftly as he could
6. jeering, chanting, shouting, screaming
7. since you were sleeping
8. though we love you dearly
9. provided that you do not fight back
10. in order that we can be sure of your loyalty

RECOGNIZING COMPLEX SENTENCES

A complex sentence must have a main clause and at least *one* subordinate clause. The simple sentences below do not, of course, contain subordinate clauses. They have only one subject-verb pattern. Study the examples; then do the exercises.

Simple: The delegates did not know when to speak.
Complex: The delegates did not know *when* they should speak.
Simple: His sister will be here before the Tuesday deadline.
Complex: His sister will be here *before* the Tuesday deadline passes.

SELF-QUIZ 4

Place an S by the sentences which are simple and a Cx by the sentences which are complex. Underline subjects once and verbs twice. Circle the subordinate conjunctions.

1. _____ The people in the city have short tempers.

2. _____ In the winter, after the heavy snows had fallen, Jeff visited his old farm.[1]

3. _____ She wrote to him before he left.

4. _____ She loved him when others did not.

5. _____ After lunch they left.

[1] If there were no comma between *winter* and *after,* would the meaning of the sentence be changed?

6. _____ Before they left, they voted.

7. _____ They spent money which was not theirs.

8. _____ Which of them will go?

9. _____ He did not know why they came.

10. _____ My friend, who lives near here, is ill.

SELF-QUIZ 5

List from memory the 35 subordinate conjunctions on page 88. Continue to retest yourself until you know all of them by heart.

1. _____   19. _____

2. _____   20. _____

3. _____   21. _____

4. _____   22. _____

5. _____   23. _____

6. _____   24. _____

7. _____   25. _____

8. _____   26. _____

9. _____   27. _____

10. _____   28. _____

11. _____   29. _____

12. _____   30. _____

13. _____   31. _____

14. _____   32. _____

15. _____   33. _____

16. _____   34. _____

17. _____   35. _____

18. _____

Try to list from memory the 19 coordinate conjunctions you learned in Chapter 5.
See page 78 to check yourself.

1. _____	11. _____
2. _____	12. _____
3. _____	13. _____
4. _____	14. _____
5. _____	15. _____
6. _____	16. _____
7. _____	17. _____
8. _____	18. _____
9. _____	19. _____
10. _____	

COMPLEX SENTENCE PATTERNS

Complex sentences fall into four general patterns. We will look at each in turn; then we will work with them one at a time.

Pattern One: *The main clause comes first.* It is connected to the subordinate clause by a subordinate conjunction.

Pattern Two: *The subordinate clause comes first.* It is followed by the main clause. The conjunction is often, but not necessarily, the first word in the sentence. A comma separates the clauses when the subordinate clause is placed first.

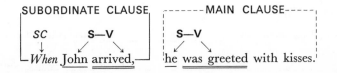

Pattern Three: *The subordinate clause is placed between the subject and the verb of the main clause.* There are two variations of this pattern.

3A. *The subordinate conjunction acts only as a connector.*

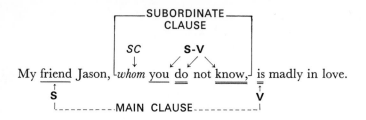

3B. *The subordinate conjunction acts both as connector and as subject of the subordinate clause.*

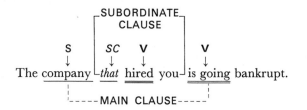

Pattern Four: *An entire clause acts as subject of a sentence.* When the "subordinate" clause functions in this manner, it is called a *noun clause*.

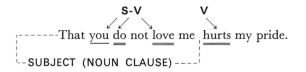

SELF-QUIZ 7

1. Complex sentences fall into＿＿＿＿＿＿general patterns.

2. In the first pattern, the＿＿＿＿＿＿clause comes first, and it is connected

   to the＿＿＿＿＿＿＿＿clause by a＿＿＿＿＿＿＿＿＿＿＿

   ＿＿＿＿＿＿.

3. In the second pattern, the＿＿＿＿＿＿＿＿clause comes first,

   and it is followed by the＿＿＿＿＿＿clause.

4. In the second pattern, the＿＿＿＿＿＿＿＿is often the first
   word of the sentence.

5. In the third pattern, the＿＿＿＿＿＿＿＿clause is injected between

   the＿＿＿＿＿＿and the＿＿＿＿＿＿of the＿＿＿＿＿＿clause.

6. In some cases (in the third pattern) the subordinate conjunction also acts as the_____of the_____clause.

7. In Pattern Four complex sentences, an entire subordinate clause can act as the_____of a sentence.

8. A complex sentence is made up of a_____ and a_____clause. The two clauses are usually joined by a _____.

9. A subordinate conjunction is any word on the_____ _____list which introduces a_____ _____and connects that clause to a_____clause.

10. A clause is a group of words which contains a_____ _____core.

Practice with Pattern One

The main clause comes first. It is connected to the subordinate clause by a subordinate conjunction.

EXAMPLES:

1. She was angry *because* George was late.
2. The thief hid *until* the policeman left.
3. The boy was examined *while* his parents waited.
4. The conference will adjourn *until* the new delegate arrives.
5. European diplomats met in secret conference *before* the American ambassador arrived.

TEST 1

Write ten Pattern One sentences, using the conjunctions indicated. Underline your subjects once and your verbs twice.

1. _____ *after*_____

2. _____ *since*_____

3. _____ *that*_____

4. _____ *if*_____

5. _____ *where*_____

6. _____ *although*_____

7. _____ *when*_____

8. _____ *which*_____

9. _____ *whatever*_____

10. _____ *as long as*_____

Following Pattern One, write five complex sentences of your own. Underline your subjects once, your verbs twice, and circle your subordinate conjunctions.

Practice with Pattern Two

The subordinate clause is placed *before* the main clause.

EXAMPLES:

1. *Before* they left, it rained.
2. *As soon as* the message arrives from the Vatican, we will call a meeting of the Bishops.
3. In spite of all the complaints *that* he made, he really loved the camp.

Don't let introductory words or phrases fool you. The next three sentences are also examples of Pattern Two complex sentences.

4. Early in the spring *when* everything begins to grow, he arrives.
5. Wondering *if* help would ever come, she waited, shivering, on the narrow ledge.
6. In our part of the country, *when* strangers arrive, we welcome them warmly.

SELF-QUIZ 8

Rewrite the Pattern One sentences below to change them to Pattern Two, and rewrite the Pattern Two sentences to change them to Pattern One.[1] Change only the order of the clauses and the necessary punctuation and capitalization.

1. We will stay here until we hear from you._____

_____

2. If the emergency is really great, the people will respond._____

_____

[1] The clauses in Pattern One and Two sentences cannot always be interchanged: When the boy heard your scream, he ran home. Although the company polluted the water, it denied its guilt. If Betty cannot come, she should go somewhere else.

3. As long as everyone agrees, we will continue the meeting._____

_____

4. Solutions cannot be found to many of our problems while the war continues to rage._____

_____

TEST 2

Using the conjunctions listed, write ten Pattern Two complex sentences. Underline your subjects once and your verbs twice. Be sure that your sentences have two subject-verb cores.

1. In order that _____

2. Unless _____

3. Until _____

4. Whoever _____

5. Since _____

6. So that _____

7. Wherever _____

8. After _____

9. Before _____

10. Whether _____

Following Pattern Two, write five complex sentences of your own. Underline your subjects once, your verbs twice, and circle your subordinate conjunctions. Use different conjunctions in each sentence.

Practice with Pattern 3A

EXAMPLES:

1. The man *whose* horse was stolen is here now.
2. The woman *on whom* we relied has disappeared.[1]
3. The employment agency *to which* I applied did not answer.

[1] Note how prepositions sometimes work together with conjunctions in this position.

TEST 3

Using the conjunctions listed below, write five Pattern Three A sentences. Underline your subjects once and your verbs twice.

1. _____ whom _____

2. _____ where _____

3. _____ which _____

4. _____ that _____

5. _____ whatever _____

Practice with Pattern 3B

EXAMPLES:

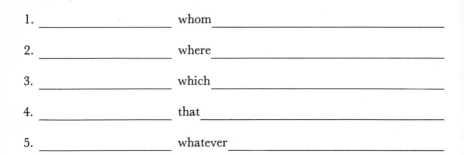

1. The engine *that* was wrecked cannot be repaired.

2. The statement *which* was proven to be a lie has been published.

3. The lady *who* left us the estate has disappeared.

TEST 4

Using the following conjunctions, write three Pattern Three B complex sentences: *who, which, that*. Underline subjects and verbs.

Don't Confuse Pattern Three with Simple Sentences

In Chapter 3 you were told that as long as your subjects and verbs are consecutive, as long as they don't alternate, your sentence is simple. If, however, you look at the Pattern Three complex sentences, you find SS-VV which appears to be the same as the simple sentence pattern. The difference is that, although the subjects and verbs are consecutive in Pattern Three complex sentences, each subject relates to a *different* verb. In simple sentences with multiple subjects and verbs, all of the verbs and subjects relate to each other. Note the examples below:

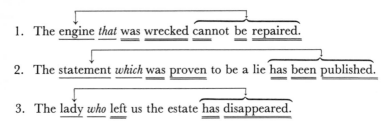

Simple Sentence: The males and females dined and debated.

Pattern Three
Complex Sentence: The friends *whom* Hester invited were silent.

The same test applies to those complex sentences in which the conjunction is omitted.

Practice with Pattern Four

EXAMPLES (The noun clause is in brackets):

[What he said] was not clear.

[Who sent the gift] is still a mystery.

[When it will happen] is not yet revealed.

[Which message was delivered] may never be known.

TEST 5

Write five Pattern Four sentences of your own. Underline your subjects and verbs. Put brackets around your noun clauses.

Omitting the Subordinate Conjunction

In complex sentences based on Patterns One and Three, there is a tendency to omit the conjunction, especially *whom, which,* and *that.* Omitting the subordinate conjunction does not change the nature of the sentence. It is still complex. Here are some examples of complex sentences without conjunctions.

Pattern One
He likes the car [*that*] I bought.
She thinks [*that*] apricots are delightful.
We met a couple [*whom*] we have known for many years.
Pattern Three
The man [*whom*] he shot still haunts him.
The mushrooms [*that*] they ate were poisonous.
The opinions [*which*] I hold are shared by many other people.

SELF-QUIZ 9

Insert the appropriate conjunction wherever it is missing.

1. The lawyer pointed to the man he hated.
2. She feels immoral movies should be banned.
3. He returned all the land he had stolen.
4. They thought dirty words should be deleted.
5. Florence believed nothing was sacred.
6. The dog he feared was dead.[1]
7. Early last year the girl we loved so much eloped.
8. The cattle he purchased were slaughtered.
9. Jim, the man she wanted to marry, refused to see her.
10. The animals they saw in the park were graceful.

---

[1] Note how the meaning of this sentence changes when commas are added: The dog, he feared, was dead.

THE SENTENCE FRAGMENT

When working with compound sentences you learned that a lack of knowledge about simple and compound sentences may cause you to write run-ons. Similarly, a lack of understanding about subordinate clauses leads to the writing of fragments. Both run-on and fragment writing are considered serious errors because they indicate a lack of understanding of what a sentence is. There are, however, certain circumstances when sentence fragments may be written intentionally. This will be discussed at the end of the chapter.

To review, a subordinate clause is a group of words which contains one subject-verb core and which is usually introduced by a subordinate conjunction *that ties it to a main clause.* Together, the two clauses are a complex sentence. The subordinate clause alone is not a sentence.

A *fragment* is a subordinate clause which is not connected to a main clause but is punctuated as if it were a complete sentence. A fragment can also be any group of words which is punctuated as a sentence but which does not fulfill the basic S-V requirements.

Why Students Write Fragments

Students who write fragments seem to be unaware that subordinate clauses begin with subordinate conjunctions and that it is the conjunction which makes it necessary to add main clauses. One reason for the confusion is that much of our spoken language is carried on by means of sentence fragments. For example:

1. "When did you leave?"
   "After the show was over."
2. "Why did she fall out?"
   "Because the car turned the corner too sharply."
3. "Does your mother wear that outfit often?"
   "Whenever she goes out."
4. "When will they know?"
   "As soon as the mail arrives."
5. "What made him plead guilty?"
   "So that he might get a lighter sentence."

The five questions are all complete sentences; the replies are fragments. Fragments are correct when used as direct quotations in dialogue, as shown above, but they are incorrect when included as part of expository paragraphs. They are incorrect because they begin with a subordinate conjunction (*after, because, whenever,* etc.) but they are not connected to a main clause. If you cover up the question in each example and read only the reply, you become aware that it is an incomplete fragment as it stands. Something is missing if you don't add a main clause.

Let's see what happens when we attach a main clause to the fragments. Compare each of the following complex sentences with the dialogue from which it was created.

1. I left *after* the show was over.
2. She fell out *because* the car turned the corner too sharply.
3. My mother wears that outfit *whenever* she goes out.
4. They will know *as soon as* the mail arrives.
5. He pleaded guilty *so that* he might get a lighter sentence.

SELF-QUIZ 10

Convert each question-answer dialogue into a complex sentence. Underline your subjects once and your verbs twice; circle your subordinate conjunction. Don't write questions.

EXAMPLE: "Did he tell the truth?"
"As far as I know."

As far as I know, he told the truth. (or) He told the truth *as far as* I know.

1. "Would you vote for him for president?"
"If he were the best man."

_____

2. "Why did you give him the money?"
"So that he could leave town."

_____

3. "Will you join the fraternity?"
"Provided that you lower the dues."

_____

4. "Why did he commit suicide?"
"Because no one seemed to care about his welfare."

_____

More Examples of Fragments

We went to the theater. After the performance was over. We decided to get a bite to eat, but it was very late.

"After the performance was over," is, of course, a fragment. The writer obviously *thought* in terms of the complete idea, "After the performance was over, we decided to get a bite to eat, but it was very late." He punctuated the subordinate clause, however, as if it were a complete sentence. Or, perhaps, he knew that he had written a subject-verb core, "performance was," but he forgot that "after" is a subordinate conjunction.

SELF-QUIZ 11

Correct the fragments below by using these proofreading marks:

Use a slash (/) to reduce a capital letter to lower case.
Use a delete sign ($\mathscr{g}$) to remove a period.
If you change a period to a comma, underline it (,).

EXAMPLE: Because he had been late all week, He knew that she would be angry. He loved her in a selfish way, Although he tried not to show it. She recognized it in time, however, and refused to see him again.

1. They went for months at a time without sufficient food. Because they were stubborn. No one knew that they needed help. Until it was too late.
2. After the long, muggy, rainy season. Jeffrey tried to get through to the aid station. They died in agony. In spite of all his efforts.
3. They headed for cover as quickly as they could. Skidding and sliding over the icy snow they went. Until darkness covered everything.
4. When you decide. We will join you. Since you are now undecided. We will have to wait.
5. The child opened the heavy oak door. Not knowing what to expect. He trembled inwardly.

.II.II.II.II.II.II.II.II.II.II.II.II.II.II.II.II.II.II.II.II.II.II.II.I

SELF-QUIZ 12

1. A lack of knowledge about_____and_____

   sentences may lead to the writing of run-ons and comma splices.

2. A lack of knowledge of phrases and_____clauses may lead to the writing of fragments.

3. Fragments and run-ons are considered basic writing errors because they

   demonstrate ignorance of what a_____is.

4. One tends to write run-ons when he is not sure where one_____

   ends and the next_____begins.

5. One writes fragments when he punctuates a_____clause or

   a phrase as if it were a complete_____.

6. It is the_____conjunctions which make it necessary to

   add_____clauses.

7. The _____ conjunction makes a clause _____,

therefore requiring the addition of a _____ clause.

8. A simple sentence contains one _____ core.

9. A compound sentence consists of two or more _____

connected by one or more _____.

10. A complex sentence consists of a _____

joined to a _____ by a _____.

.ıı.

SELF-QUIZ 13

Identify the items below as sentences (S), run-ons (R.O.), comma splices (C.S.), or fragments (Frag.).

1. _____ He went to the movies, his wife went too.

2. _____ After the long and tiresome lecture which no one understood.

3. _____ Read this carefully.

4. _____ Gregory delivered the mail that Lena wanted.

5. _____ Give the mayor your carefully considered advice.

6. _____ Despite the fact that he ignored the advice of all his friends of long standing.

7. _____ Before he went.

8. _____ Until you hear from me, don't answer the phone.

9. _____ Who never believed a word.

10. _____ He ran through the alley and into the street without thinking he was struck by a car and badly injured.

11. _____ Kiss me.

12. _____ Which some very lovely and scintillating person requested.

13. _____ The delegate requested the majority to vote.

14. _____ The armies of the Republic moved swiftly into position on the plains the enemy waited in tense expectation.

15._____Men fight, women wait and sob, and children hide in fear.

16._____Men fight, women wait.

17._____After which everyone—man, woman, and child—on the slowly sinking ship was satisfied.

18._____Whatever you, the cause of all my trouble and worries, may think.

19._____So that no one, not even our enemies, will have to be hurt.

20._____In the spring he entered the far end of the tunnel and worked his way toward the middle of the bats and poisonous snakes he knew little until he was attacked by them.

TEST 6

After correcting Self-Quiz 13, punctuate the three run-ons to make them into simple sentences and add main clauses to the eight fragments to change them into complex sentences.

A FINAL WORD ABOUT CONJUNCTIONS

Now that you have learned how conjunctions function in sentences, you need not worry so much about whether specific words are coordinate or subordinate conjunctions. The *meanings* of the words, after all, are *connective*, and you are not likely to substitute an "and" for a "who" or "although" or vice versa. But you must be aware that they are connectives, and you must be aware of *what* they connect.

When to Start Sentences with "Ands" or "Buts"

When you use coordinate conjunctions (*and, but, or, consequently, however,* etc.), you are doing so to connect a following statement with a previous one. In general, this is done *within* sentences. Sometimes, however, it is permissible to start sentences with these conjunctions. Usually this is done to emphasize the part of the sentence introduced by the conjunction:

We will fight if we must. But we desperately want peace.
You have been my friend for years. And I want it to stay that way.
We have decided to send the money. However, you must guarantee its return.

It is considered substandard writing to overuse coordinate conjunctions at sentence beginnings. When you do this, you lose the effect that is gained by occasional use, your writing becomes rambling and indefinite, and you give the impression that you are not sure of your own sentence structure.

When to Use Fragments

Sentence fragments are acceptable in the same sense that sentences may occasionally be begun with a coordinate conjunction. Now and then in order to emphasize certain ideas introduced by a subordinate conjunction, it is acceptable to write a fragment. For example:

> We should allow more students into the college only under the conditions stipulated. When we have the facilities. When there is enough money. When they are eager to come.

You will see this technique used fairly often in advertising and in editorial writing. To overuse it makes your writing choppy, ineffective, and poorly structured. *As a general rule, it is wise to avoid writing fragments or starting sentences with coordinate conjunctions until you are a very skillful sentence writer.*

what you have learned in chapter 6

Complex sentences are formed by connecting *subordinate clauses* to *main clauses* with *subordinate conjunctions*.

A subordinate clause must not be treated as a simple sentence. If it is not attached to a main clause, it is considered a *fragment*. The subordinate conjunction prevents the clause from acting as an independent sentence.

Some students get confused about the difference between clauses and phrases because words used as subordinate conjunctions are also used to introduce many phrases. Simply remember that a clause contains a subject-verb core; a phrase does not.

The flexibility of the complex sentence is made possible by the various positions in which the subordinate clause can be placed: before the main clause, after it, or between the subject and verb of the main clause. Sometimes the entire subordinate clause acts as the subject of a sentence.

(You now know the three basic sentence types: simple, compound, and complex. All other sentences are combinations of these three. The many exercises that you have worked with were intended to give you a *feeling* for sentence structure as well as a theoretical knowledge of it. Chapter 7 puts it all together.)

KEY 1

(1) simple, compound, complex, combination   (2) main, coordinate conjunctions   (3) subordinate, complex   (4) main, subordinate   (5) subject-verb, subordinate   (6) complex   (7) compound, coordinate conjunctions   (8) complex, clause, subordinate, subordinate   (9) subordinate, subordinate, clause, main   (10) subordinate conjunctions   (11) subordinate, parts of speech, subordinate   (12) subordinate, subordinate, main   (13) coordinate conjunctions

KEY 2

Clauses: (2) *until* they arrive   (4) *although* the people ... want   (5) *while* she watches   (6) *when* the clock strikes   (10) *whether* he wishes

KEY 3

Clauses: (2) *as soon as* they left   (5) ... *as swiftly as* he could   (7) *since* you were sleeping   (8) *though* we love ...   (9) *provided that* you do not fight back   (10) *in order that* we can be sure ...

Complex sentences: (2) ... *after* <u>snows</u> <u>had fallen</u>, <u>Jeff</u> <u>visited</u> ... (3) <u>She</u> <u>wrote</u> ... *before* <u>he</u> <u>left</u> (4) <u>She</u> <u>loved</u> him *when* <u>others</u> <u>did</u> not. (6) *Before* <u>they</u> <u>left,</u> <u>they</u> <u>voted.</u> (7) <u>They</u> <u>spent</u> ... *which* <u>was</u> (9) <u>He</u> <u>did</u> not <u>know</u> *why* <u>they</u> <u>came</u> (10) My <u>friend</u> *who* <u>lives</u> ... <u>is ill.</u>

KEY 7

(1) four   (2) main, subordinate, subordinate conjunction   (3) subordinate, main   (4) subordinate conjunction   (5) subordinate, subject, verb, main   (6) subject, subordinate   (7) subject   (8) subordinate clause, main, subordinate conjunction   (9) subordinate conjunction, subordinate clause, main   (10) subject-verb

KEY 8

(1) Until we hear from you, we will stay here.   (2) The people will respond if the emergency is really great.   (3) We will continue the meeting as long as everyone agrees.   (4) While the war continues to rage, solutions cannot be found to many of our problems.

KEY 9

(1) The lawyer pointed to the man *whom* he hated.   (2) She feels *that* immoral movies should be banned.   (3) He returned all the land *that* (which) he had stolen.   (4) They thought *that* dirty words should be deleted.   (5) Florence believed *that* nothing was sacred.   (6) The dog *that* he feared was dead.   (7) Early last year the girl *whom* we loved so much eloped.   (8) The cattle *that* (which) he purchased were slaughtered.   (9) Jim, the man *whom* she wanted to marry, refused to see her.   (10) The animals *that* (which) they saw in the park were graceful.

KEY 10

(1) *If* <u>he</u> <u>were</u> the best man, <u>I</u> <u>would</u> <u>vote</u> for him for president. (or) <u>I</u> <u>would</u> <u>vote</u> for him for president *if* <u>he</u> <u>were</u> the best man. (Each sentence in this exercise may be turned around, that is, it may begin with either the main or the subordinate clause.)   (2) <u>I</u> <u>gave</u> him the money *so that* <u>he</u> <u>could</u> <u>leave</u> town.   (3) <u>I</u> <u>will</u> <u>join</u> the fraternity *provided that* <u>you</u> <u>lower</u> the dues.   (4) *Because* no <u>one</u> <u>seemed</u> to care about his welfare, <u>he</u> <u>committed</u> suicide.

KEY 11

1. They went for months at a time without sufficient food. Because they were stubborn. No one knew that they needed help. Until it was too late. (or) They went for months at a time without sufficient food. Because they were stubborn, No one knew that they needed help. Until it was too late.
2. After the long, muggy rainy season, Jeffrey tried to get through to the aid station. They died in agony. In spite of all his efforts.
3. They headed for cover as quickly as they could. Skidding and sliding over the icy snow they went, Until darkness covered everything.
4. When you decide, We will join you. Since you are now undecided, We will have to wait.

5. The child opened the heavy oak door, ~~N~~ot knowing what to expect. He trembled inwardly. (*or*) The child opened the heavy oak door. Not knowing what to expect, ~~H~~e trembled inwardly.

KEY 12

(1) simple, compound   (2) subordinate   (3) sentence   (4) sentence, sentence   (5) subordinate, sentence   (6) subordinate, main   (7) subordinate, subordinate, main   (8) subject-verb   (9) main clauses, coordinate conjunctions   (10) subordinate clause, main clause, subordinate conjunction

KEY 13

(1) C.S.   (2) Frag.   (3) S   (4) S   (5) S   (6) Frag.   (7) Frag.   (8) S   (9) Frag. (10) R.O.   (11) S   (12) Frag.   (13) S   (14) R.O.   (15) S   (16) C.S.   (17) Frag.   (18) Frag.   (19) Frag.   (20) R.O.

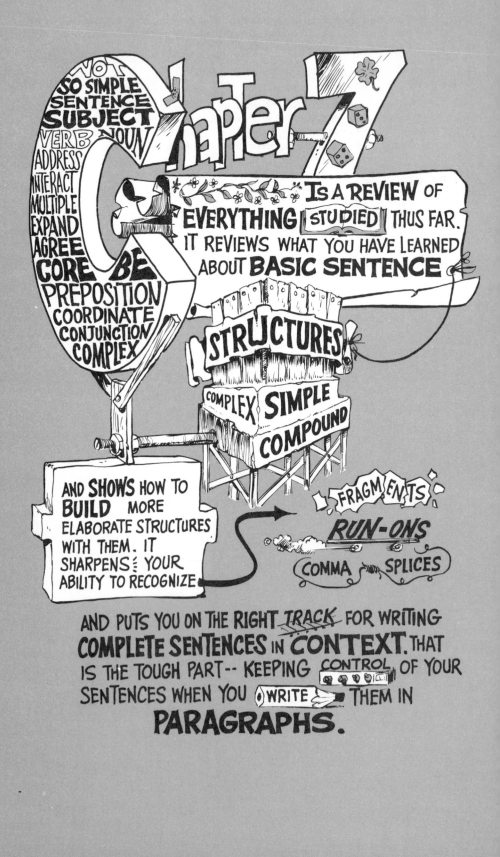

CHAPTER 7

Review of

SENTENCE STRUCTURE

You have been building sentences from the simplest one-word to the compound and the complex. Those are the basic structures. They can be combined in all sorts of ways to build compound-complex and complex-complex sentences (see page 112). Before we turn to more elaborate sentences, it will be helpful to review all the basic forms studied thus far.

The structures illustrated below are, of course, oversimplified. They do not include the many words and phrases that usually flesh out sentences. They do illustrate, however, the basic simplicity and flexibility of the English sentence. They reaffirm the point that if you know your subjects, verbs, and conjunctions, you can build any kind of sentence. They also show the dominance of the simple sentence in all the patterns.

Below are diagrams of the three basic structures. In the following pages we will review the variations of these patterns to sum up the sentence work that you have done so far.

Simple: SUBJECT—VERB.

Compound: SUBJECT—VERB, | coordinate conjunction | SUBJECT—VERB.

Complex: SUBJECT—VERB | subordinate conjunction | SUBJECT—VERB.

THE SIMPLE SENTENCE

The simple sentence contains a subject and a verb that agree in number and person. It may contain a series of subjects and a series of verbs, but these subjects and verbs may not alternate, and all subjects must relate to all verbs. The simple sentence contains no clauses. All the possible patterns are reviewed below.

The simple sentence can be comprised of one word, a verb. It must be in the present tense. "You," the subject, is understood.	V.
In all other simple sentences there must be at least one subject and one verb.	S-V.
There may be an unlimited number of subjects and one verb.	SSS-V.
There may be one subject and an unlimited number of verbs.	S-VVV.
There may be an unlimited number of subjects and an unlimited number of verbs.	SSS-VVV.
Words may precede the subject.	____S-V.
Words may be placed between the subject and the verb.	S ____ V.
Words may be placed after the verb.	S-V ____.
All of these situations are often present.	____S ____V ____.

But the sentence remains simple as long as the subject and verb do not alternate and all subjects relate to all verbs.

THE COMPOUND SENTENCE

The compound sentence contains two or more simple sentences (called main clauses), connected by one or more coordinate conjunctions (see Chapter 5). It may *not* contain any subordinate conjunctions.

A coordinate conjunction is one which connects main clauses together to form compound sentences.

Each main clause in a compound sentence can include all the pattern variations noted in the above description of the simple sentence.

This is the basic compound sentence pattern. Note the addition of the comma.

SUBJECT-VERB, [CC] SUBJECT-VERB.

With some coordinate conjunctions, it is customary to add a semicolon. (See page 78).

SUBJECT-VERB; [CC] SUBJECT-VERB.

In some instances the semicolon is used without a conjunction.

SUBJECT-VERB; SUBJECT-VERB.

When there are more than two main clauses in a compound sentence, the coordinate conjunction is used only between the last two clauses. Commas are used between the other clauses. (See page 79.)

S-V, S-V, S-V, [CC] S-V.

Paired conjunctions like "either-or" and "not only-but also" form the only basically different compound sentence pattern. To be considered coordinate conjunctions each half of the pair must be followed by a subject-verb core.

[C] SUBJECT-VERB [C] SUBJECT-VERB.

THE COMPLEX SENTENCE

The complex sentence contains a main clause connected to a subordinate clause by a subordinate conjunction. (See Chapter 6 for list of subordinate conjunctions.)

Since the subordinate clause must, like the main clause, contain a subject and a verb, its basic difference lies in the presence of the subordinate conjunction. This connector sometimes acts as both conjunction and subject of the clause. The subordinate clause can contain all the patterns of the simple sentence except the "You" understood one.

Pattern One

The main clause comes first and the subordinate clause follows.

SUBJECT-VERB [SC] SUBJECT-VERB.
main clause | subordinate conjunction | subordinate clause

Pattern Two

Here the subordinate clause comes first and the main clause follows. The comma indicates that the usual order of the clause has been reversed.

[SC] SUBJECT-VERB, SUBJECT-VERB.
subordinate clause | main clause

Pattern Three-A

The subordinate clause is placed between the subject and the verb of the main clause. Sometimes the subordinate clause is separated from the main clause by commas. The subordinate conjunction acts only as a connector.

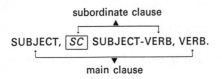

Pattern Three-B

In this case the subordinate conjunction is also the subject of the subordinate clause. Words like *who*, *which*, and *that* serve this function in many of the complex sentence patterns. Although there are two consecutive subjects and two consecutive verbs, this pattern is unlike the simple sentence because one subject is a subordinate conjunction and because each subject relates to a different verb.

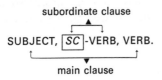

Pattern Four

The subject of the sentence is an entire clause (known as a noun clause).

```
Subject-Verb
SUBJECT  -  VERB.
(Noun Clause)
```

BUILDING ELABORATE SENTENCE STRUCTURES

By using various combinations of the basic structures, you can build longer and more elaborate sentences. New clauses can be added to modify or develop your ideas, the way you might build new wings or stories on a house. The only requirement is that your architectural plan must never lose sight of the correct subject-verb relationships, no matter how elaborate your sentence gets to be.

By way of illustration, examine the following blueprint for constructing compound-complex sentences.

Take one simple sentence:

Simple   Jim, Sam, and Sally meditated and debated about life and death.

Add main clause:

Compound   Jim, Sam, and Sally meditated and debated about life and death, *but* they could not agree about anything.

Build in a subordinate clause:

Compound-
complex

Jim, Sam, and Sally, *who* had met at a church party,
meditated and debated about life and death, *but* they
could not agree about anything.

Attach a second subordinate clause:

Complex-
complex

Jim, Sam, and Sally, *who* had met at a church party,
meditated and debated about life and death *while* they
were waiting for the minister, *but* they could not agree
about anything.

TEST 1

Write a paragraph containing five compound-complex sentences about any subject
that comes to mind. Underline subjects and verbs and circle your conjunctions as
usual.

THE SENTENCE IN CONTEXT

While many students have no trouble with single sentences, they lose track of
the beginnings or endings of them when they write paragraphs. If you have
done your sentence work conscientiously, however, you should be able to
handle the sentences in context whether the ideas are complicated or simple,
deep or shallow. This ability to recognize the sentence in context is, in fact,
one of the key tests of your understanding of the sentence. The final and most
important test will come when you write your own paragraphs.

CORRECTING THE RUN-ON AND COMMA SPLICE IN CONTEXT

Let's review what you need to remember about these writing faults, so that
you may be able to recognize and correct them in paragraphs (and, of course,
to avoid them when you write your own).

1. A run-on exists when two sentences are punctuated as if they were one.

2. A comma alone is not considered sufficient punctuation between two
main clauses. This error is called a *comma splice.*

3. Each sentence must contain at least one subject-verb core.

4. If more than one subject-verb core are contained in one sentence, the
proper punctuation mark and conjunction must be present.

5. In a complex sentence the conjunction (subordinate) may correctly be
at or near the beginning of the sentence.

SELF-QUIZ 1

In the paragraphs that follow, you will find a given number of run-ons and/or comma
splices. Correct the run-ons by inserting periods and capital letters in the proper
places. Correct the comma splices by adding periods or proper conjunctions. Do not
change any sentences which are punctuated correctly. Don't go about this mechanically. Use your good common sense as well as your knowledge of structure. Each
sentence must make *sense.* NOTE: *Do one exercise at a time and correct it before doing
the next one.*

(1) The Failure of Lighter-Than-Air Craft

(3 run-ons, 2 comma splices)

Lighter-than-air craft, those stately dirigibles that once sailed so smoothly through the skies, have never quite recovered from the world's two worst airship disasters, the first disaster occurred when the British R101 went down in 1930 the second happened when the German Zeppelin "Hindenburg" crashed in New Jersey in 1936. Eighty-three persons died in those crashes that number is not overwhelming in this age of jets that seat many hundreds of people, but the disasters finished the airship as a means of travel.

Plentiful supplies of nonflammable gas helium are now available for airship use, few people seem interested in building the ships. In Germany, however, an Austrian engineer recently approached the Bonn government with a proposal to build a helium-filled, nuclear-propelled airship capable of carrying 500 passengers and 100 tons of freight their aim is to attract some of the holiday tours that have been so popular in recent years.

(2) College Reform

(3 run-ons, 2 comma splices)

Universities have been too slow in making changes, and campus unrest has served a purpose in helping to bring about some needed reforms this is the opinion of one prominent educator from a well-known Eastern college the educator also said that reform would probably have come to the colleges anyway, it would have come more slowly. At his university more young administrators have been hired, the administration has also included more students in decision-making committees. Students now control all of their own social activities the situation is quite different from what it was a few years ago.

(3) The Courts Get Tougher on Youths

(4 run-ons, 1 comma splice)

The rebellious conduct of minors seems to be producing changes in the attitudes of the courts toward young people hitherto, the law has been gentle to minors, expecting from them only the degree of care and considerateness that is normal for persons of their age and experience in one recent case a young teenager who was playing golf was careless about the safety of other golfers he drove a ball without giving warning and severely injured another golfer. When sued for damages, the youth claimed that he could not be expected to be as careful as an adult it might be compared to a case where a young man murdered his parents and then asked for mercy because he was an orphan. The court ruled against the youth, the judge said, in effect, that a youth who participates in adult activities must take adult responsibilities.

(4) The "Cheated" Woman

(4 run-ons, 2 comma splices)

Almost half of all working-age American women are working today, women comprise one-third of our labor force they are performing in almost every area of business, industry, government, the professions, and the arts despite the fact that many of them are working quite capably in these areas, their promotions and pay are not equal to those of men at identical jobs. As of 1968 about 75% of the women were working in jobs paying less than $5000 a year, most of these jobs were clerical, sales, factory, or service jobs according to recent surveys only about 2% of all the executives in this country are women, and no women are in top management positions in any major corporation. In many cases women who do the same job as men are doing get paid much less to succeed in business a woman has to be twice as good as a man—and sometimes better!

(5) All Whites Are *Them*

(*6 run-ons, 2 comma splices*)

A Black teenager, born in Alabama, spent a summer at the Yale University Summer High School several years ago he spent seven weeks on campus, sometimes he wondered whether he could ever feel comfortable in a crowd of "them." At home he had heard "Nigger!" shouted at him from passing cars here, at Yale, he was accepted and treated well, but he kept on thinking of all Whites as "them" some of that wore off after the first few weeks, however, and he could begin to think of his white acquaintances as Larry and Tom and Jack. He had begun to differentiate he could see that some Whites were different from other Whites some of them were aloof some of them were funny. In a way he knew that he was experiencing the same kinds of feelings that Whites experience who get to know individual Negroes as people, he wondered whether back in Alabama he would start to hate *them* all again.

CORRECTING THE FRAGMENT IN CONTEXT

Review the following points before you do the quiz exercises.

1. A fragment is usually a subordinate clause which is treated as if it were a complete sentence. It can be any group of words without an S-V core that is punctuated as if it were a sentence.

2. A careful reading will usually indicate that the fragment should have been included with the previous sentence, or should be added to what follows.

SELF-QUIZ 2

Correct the paragraphs below by incorporating the fragments properly. Use the following markings to show your corrections:

To change a capital letter to a small letter, write a slash through it: W̶
Where you change a period to a comma, underline the comma: ,
To take out unwanted punctuation, use the deletion sign: ȡ

EXAMPLE: After dinner, he lay down, W̶hich was a blessing.

(1) The WASP Flies High

(7 fragments)

From time to time various minority groups, religious, racial, or political, have been accused of controlling the policies of U.S. institutions. The WASP (White Anglo-Saxon Protestants), however, are still very much in control. According to an article published in *Look* magazine in 1968. The 1968 figures showed that there are about 50 million Roman Catholics in the U.S., 22 million Negroes, 6 million Jews, 4 million Eastern Orthodox, and a little more than 2 million members of other denominations. Which include Orientals, Polynesians, Eskimos, Muslims, and Bhutanese. Roughly 58 percent or about 116 millions, however, are WASP. Whose influence far outweighs their numbers. About 88 percent of the boards of directors of the 10 largest corporations, 83 percent of the 10 largest commercial banks, and about 80 percent of the five largest insurances companies are controlled by WASP. While all of our Presidents but one have been WASP. As well as most cabinet members and most members of Congressional committees and other influential political bodies. Catholics, Jews, and Negroes hold only a very small portion of such positions. Of 775 leading public and private nondenominational private universities, less than 1% had Catholic or Jewish presidents. One recent survey showed that 67 percent of the private "business-social" clubs. Where many of the official transactions of large corporations are initiated do not admit members of minority groups. While membership limits to Catholics have been relaxed greatly in recent years. Few of the clubs admit Jews, and almost all exclude Negroes, Puerto Ricans, Mexican Americans, and members of other minority groups. All in all, the WASP still flies high.

(2) Gandhi and the King

(6 fragments)

No leader relied more on symbolic gestures or achieved more with them than did Mahatma Gandhi. He asked Indians to wear homespun cloth. Because he felt that small home industry would help the Indian economy. When they did not follow his urgings. He often "punished" them by undergoing long fasts. Of course, he used his fasts more often as a political weapon against the British. Who feared that his death would cause a nationwide uprising. Another of his symbols was his loin cloth. A symbol of simplicity and poverty. When he was invited to an audience with the King of England. Ghandi entered Buckingham Palace wearing only his loin cloth. In answer to a question about the propriety of this. He replied, "The king had on enough for both of us."

(3) Fair Taxes?

(6 fragments)

Many citizens are under the impression that people who have higher incomes pay proportionately higher taxes. This isn't necessarily true. In 1968 there were some 381 Americans with incomes of $100,000 or more. Who did not pay any income tax at all. There were even some millionaires who paid no income tax. There were also more than a thousand taxpayers with incomes over \$200,000. Who paid only the same proportion of their total income as did the typical person in the \$15,000 to \$20,000 group. The reason for this is that there are many loopholes in the tax laws. Which help some of the very rich to avoid paying their fair share of the taxes. Some of the loopholes were brought to light at a Congressional hearing in 1969 by former Treasury secretary Joseph W. Barr. At that time he warned. That there could be a "taxpayers revolt." If the loopholes weren't closed.

(4) When People Died Young

(*5 fragments*)

Not many people who are currently concerned about the generation gap, seem to realize. That the world leaders just a few centuries ago were the same age as today's college students. During the Neolithic Age the average age of the population was 25. Which means that many of the greatest inventions—the wheel, the sail, the plow—were the work of a very young population. Francis I became King of France at the age of 21. While Henry the VIII became King of England at 18. Although youth today tend to blame the older generation for all the ills of the world. One can point to the past and say that young people created great inventions, beautiful poetry, *and* devastating wars. Which may indicate that it is wisdom, patience, and perhaps love that are the decisive factors, not age.

(5) Letitia and the Cats

(*4 fragments*)

Letitia, my brother's sister-in-law, hated cats. Whenever she saw a cat, in someone else's house, at the movies, or at a formal dance. She would let out a gasp. Which sounded as if she were having a heart attack; then she would start to hiccup violently. It got so bad that my brother's brother-in-law, Letitia's husband, would call ahead to find out whether there were any cats at their point of destination. Either the host would have to vow to lock up the cat, or my brother's brother-in-law would refuse to go. This was particularly hard on people. Who loved cats. Some of them became lifelong enemies. To avoid this sort of thing, my brother's brother-in-law would often tell them that Letitia was allergic to cats. That she turned deep purple and stayed that way for several weeks at the sight of a cat. Most cat lovers accepted this. They could always understand allergies. You might say that every time Letitia came into contact with one of those friendly, furry little house pets, it was a real *cat*astrophe.

SELF-QUIZ 3

In the following group of exercises, you will find examples of run-ons and fragments but *not* of comma splices. There is only internal punctuation, no end punctuation. You are to supply only the end punctuation. When you add a period or question mark, underline it. When you change a letter from lower case to upper case, write the capital letter over the small letter. Check yourself with the key for each paragraph before you go on to the next one.

(1) One Way to Stop War?

Do the descriptions of the horrors of war that one finds in various books and movies help people to hate the idea of war, or do they make people more callous toward the suffering of others in his book, "Nagasaki: The Forgotten Bomb," Frank W. Chinnock describes the terrible suffering of the people of Nagasaki after the atomic bomb blast an old man, for example, had bent down next to a wall to pick some weeds just when the bomb exploded before he straightened up the heat waves from the explosion killed his wife who had been standing next to him a boy who had dived into a river to find something for his sister came up to hear people all about him screaming in a burned streetcar one could see dead passengers sitting like charred mummies there are many such graphic descriptions in this book do they help to make people seek ways toward peace?

(2) Teetotalling Mama

My maternal grandmother had a tendency to drink a bit too much as a result my mother refused to sip even a carbonated beverage she believed that the resultant "burp" was as sinful as a drunken stagger my brothers and I were brought up on milk, hot chocolate, lemonade, and an occasional iced punch after we grew a bit older, we once indulged in an ice cream soda at a nearby ice cream parlor, but we had to worry through a whole evening in fear that our "burps" might upset Mama and cause a major family crisis even after we were married, Mama would smell everything we drank to be sure that we weren't straying from her teachings if there was any doubt at all we would get a stern lecture this might have gone on until we were grandparents except for the fact that Mama found her Waterloo in a bowl of Hawaiian punch at the wedding reception of a family friend something attracted her to that punch for refill after refill it may have been the heat of the evening or the unusually good taste of the punch before the evening was over Mama was thoroughly "stewed" my friend swore that he had "doctored" that punch very little, but little was too much for a complete abstainer like Mama in the garden she sang several fairly risque songs in a fairly loud voice in the house she tried to unscrew several light bulbs and mix the potato chips, which were in a large cake bowl, with an electric cake mixer we took her home and put icebags on her head nobody ever said anything to Mama about how drunk she had been in turn Mama never smelled our drinks again.

(3) Those Shocking Frogs

Frogs are more "shocking" creatures than most people think in 1793 Alessandro Volta saw a fellow Italian scientist take a dissected frog's leg and place it between two different metals the experiment was so arranged that when one metal touched a nerve and the other touched a muscle, the leg twitched and contracted after many experiments Volta realized that the power came not from the frog's leg but from the metal the saline solution in the leg had acted as a conductor this experiment eventually led to Volta's invention of the storage battery in a much more recent experiment, Dr. Wolfgang Karger of the University of Ruhr in Germany demonstrated that frogs and toads carry electric energy in their skin a small amount of electric energy is generated when water is drawn into the frog's skin, enough energy to run a tiny direct current motor scientists have since found that certain human parts act in the same way this electricity may someday be used to run pacemakers these are little instruments that are used to stimulate the hearts of people with heart trouble next time you eat frogs' legs, you might meditate a little about the little fellows' contribution to human welfare it might even bring a "frog" to your throat.

.ıı

(4) Dyslexia

Don't make fun of the child who spells words backwards or sees numbers in reverse order these children are sometimes suffering from a special learning deficiency called "dyslexia," or specific language disability they may see the number 29 as 92 or the word "cat" as "tac" their d's are written as b's and their b's are written as d's because that is how they see them of course you should be careful not to get upset every time you notice someone occasionally making such errors some specialists claim that many children go through a brief period in early life when they "mirror" read it is only when this type of thing continues for a period of time and the child does not seem to be able to read correctly after patient prompting that one should seek professional help it is estimated that as many as six million children may suffer from this difficulty when their problem is recognized, they can be helped with special teaching techniques and a great deal of patience when it is not recognized, they often suffer terribly in school because of constant frustration and failure.

'.ıı.

(5) Aunt Snell's Diet

Aunt Snell was rather careful about the food she ate in the spring time she would eat only the eggs of the youngest hens, and brown eggs they must be in the fall she would take maple syrup right from the maple tree, chestnuts from the chestnut tree, and as much rhubarb as she could buy these she would bake into a horrible concoction which she would dare to call pie, and she would feed it to her family and guests several times a week in the winter she bought exotic food like sharkstail soup and fried grasshoppers her children were all brought up on goat's milk and raw cabbage she would use radishes only from Western Pennsylvania and meat from kosher butcher shops, although she was Presbyterian, not Jewish from Florida came her oranges and from California her iceburg lettuce when she decided on a particular food, there would be no change for years sometimes she claimed that she studied the rate of atomic fallout to decide what areas to avoid in her choice of farm products at other times it was based on the fertilizer content of the soil in a particular state her children seem to be reasonably healthy but she died rather suddenly several years ago by choking on a "chaw" of tobacco somehow she had kept this habit hidden from her family all those years up to the time of her death they had always thought that she had just liked to spit a lot.

ı.ıı

FINAL TEST ON SENTENCES

Part A: Write a short paragraph of about 200 to 300 words on one of the topics suggested below. Underline your subjects once, your verbs twice, and circle your conjunctions. In the process of doing this, correct any errors you may have made in sentence structure. You may modify these topics if you wish. Take either side of those that are controversial.

1. The U.S. should police the world for the good of all.

2. Beer drinking should be allowed on campus.

3. Schools and colleges should emphasize intramural sports rather than intercollegiate sports.

4. Funds for political campaigns should be greatly limited to allow men of more modest means to run.

5. Religion should be taught in the schools.

6. The present drug laws should be changed to. . . .

7. We should preserve more land for parks and wildlife.

Part B: Write a short theme (about 200 to 300 words) on one of the topics below. Proofread your paper carefully, keeping in mind what you have learned about sentence structure.

1. Sex education should be taught in the elementary and secondary schools.

2. The U.S. should spend less money on space and more on slums.

3. Pollution control should be made mandatory for all municipalities and all industry.

4. Habitually alcoholic drivers should be relieved of their drivers' licenses permanently.

5. Obscenity laws should be made tougher.

6. Less stress should be placed on private cars, and public transportation should be greatly improved.

7. Police should use tranquilizer pellets instead of bullets.

what you have learned in chapter 7

Chapter 7 has given you an overview of the three sentence types so that you can more clearly see their similarities and differences. It has shown the relationship of compound and complex sentences to the simple sentence. It has again demonstrated how the basic structure of the simple sentence depends on only two sentence parts, the subject and the verb, and how the structure of compound and complex sentences relies on three sentence parts: subjects, verbs, and conjunctions. This knowledge should help you write better sentences, punctuate them correctly, and avoid the common errors made in paragraph writing: run-ons, comma splices, and fragments.

KEY 1

(1) Lighter . . . disasters. The first . . . 1930. The second . . . 1936. Eighty-three . . . crashes. That number . . . travel. Plentiful . . . use, *but* . . . ships. In Germany . . . freight. Their aim . . . years.

(2) Universities . . . reforms. This is . . . college. The educator . . . anyway, *but* it . . . slowly. At his . . . hired, *and*[1] . . . committees. Students . . . activities. The situation . . . ago.

(3) The rebellious . . . people. Hitherto, . . . experience. In one . . . golfers. He drove . . . golfer. When sued . . . adult. It might . . . orphan. The court . . . youth, *and*[1] the judge . . . responsibilities.

(4) Almost half . . . today, *and*[1] women . . . force. They are . . . arts. Despite . . . jobs. As of 1968 . . . year, *and*[1] . . . service jobs. According . . . corporation. In many cases . . . less. To succeed . . . better!

(5) A Black . . . ago. He spent . . . on campus, *and*[1] sometimes . . . "them." At home . . . cars. Here, at Yale, . . . as "them." Some of that . . . Jack. He had . . . differentiate. He could see . . . Whites. Some . . . aloof. Some . . . funny. In a way . . . people, *and* . . . again.

KEY 2

(1) The WASP Flies High

From time to time various minority groups, religious, racial, or political, have been accused of controlling the policies of U.S. institutions. The WASPs (White Anglo-Saxon Protestants), however, are still very much in control, According to an article published in *Look* magazine in 1968. The 1968 figures showed that there are about 50 million Roman Catholics in the U.S., 22 million Negroes, 6 million Jews, 4 million Eastern Orthodox, and a little more than 2 million members of other denominations, Which include Orientals, Polynesians, Eskimos, Muslims, and Bhutanese. Roughly 58 percent or about 116 millions, however, are WASP, Whose influence far outweighs their numbers. About 88 percent of the boards of directors of the 10 largest corporations, 83 percent of the 10 largest commercial banks, and about 80 percent of the five largest insurances companies are controlled by WASP, While all of our Presidents but one have been WASP, As well as most cabinet members and most members of Congressional committees and other influential political bodies. Catholics, Jews, and Negroes hold only a very small portion of such positions. Of 775 leading public and private non-denominational private universities, less than 1% had Catholic or Jewish presidents. One recent survey showed that 67 percent of the private "business-social" clubs, Where many of the official transactions of large corporations are initiated, do not admit members of minority groups. While membership limits to Catholics have been relaxed greatly in recent years, Few of the clubs admit Jews, and almost all exclude Negroes, Puerto Ricans, Mexican-Americans, and members of other minority groups. All in all, the WASP still flies high.

(2) Gandhi and the King

No leader relied more on symbolic gestures or achieved more with them than did Mahatma Gandhi. He asked Indians to wear homespun cloth, Because he felt that small home industry would help the Indian economy. When they did not follow his urgings, He often "punished" them by undergoing long fasts. Of course, he used his fasts more often as a political weapon against the British, Who feared that his death would cause a nationwide uprising. Another of his

---

[1] A period instead of *and* would also be correct here.

symbols was his loin cloth, A symbol of simplicity and poverty. When he was invited to an audience with the King of England, Gandhi entered Buckingham Palace wearing only his loin cloth. In answer to a question about the propriety of this, He replied, "The king had on enough for both of us."

(3) Fair Taxes?
Many citizens are under the impression that people who have higher incomes pay proportionately higher taxes. This isn't necessarily true. In 1968 there were some 381 Americans with incomes of $100,000 or more, Who did not pay any income tax at all. There were even some millionaires who paid no income tax. There were also more than a thousand taxpayers with incomes over $200,000, Who paid only the same proportion of their total income as did the typical person in the $15,000 to $20,000 group. The reason for this is that there are many loopholes in the tax laws, Which help some of the very rich to avoid paying their fair share of the taxes. Some of the loopholes were brought to light at a Congressional hearing in 1969 by former Treasury secretary Joseph W. Barr. At that time he warned, That there could be a "taxpayers revolt," If the loopholes weren't closed.

(4) When People Died Young
Not many people who are currently concerned about the generation gap seem to realize, That the world leaders just a few centuries ago were the same age as today's college students. During the Neolithic Age the average age of the population was 25, Which means that many of the greatest inventions—the wheel, the sail, the plow—were the work of a very young population. Francis I became King of France at the age of 21, While Henry the VIII became King of England at 18. Although youth today tend to blame the older generation for all the ills of the world, One can point to the past and say that young people created great inventions, beautiful poetry, *and* devastating wars, Which may indicate that it is wisdom, patience, and perhaps love that are the decisive factors, not age.

(5) Letitia and the Cats
Letitia, my brother's sister-in-law, hated cats. Whenever she saw a cat in someone else's house, at the movies, or at a formal dance, She would let out a gasp, Which sounded as if she were having a heart attack; then she would start to hiccup violently. It got so bad that my brother's brother-in-law, Letitia's husband, would call ahead to find out whether there were any cats at their point of destination. Either the host would have to vow to lock up the cat, or my brother's brother-in-law would refuse to go. This was particularly hard on people, Who loved cats. Some of them became lifelong enemies. To avoid this sort of thing, my brother's brother-in-law would often tell them that Letitia was allergic to cats, That she turned deep purple and stayed that way for several weeks at the sight of a cat. Most cat lovers accepted this. They could always understand allergies. You might say that every time Letitia came into contact with one of those friendly, furry little house pets, it was a real *cat*astrophe.

KEY 3

Punctuation marks that have been added to the original paragraphs are underlined in the Key to aid you in checking yourself. The subjects, verbs, and conjunctions have also been indicated so that you can once again see how the subject-verb cores rule the sentence patterns. If you have punctuated certain paragraphs differently and disagree with the Key, check with your instructor. You may be right. Different interpretations are sometimes possible.

(1) One Way to Stop War?
Do the descriptions of the horrors of war *that* one finds in various books and movies help people to hate the idea of war, *or* do they make people more callous

toward the suffering of others? In his book, "Nagasaki: The Forgotten Bomb," Frank W. Chinnock describes the terrible suffering of the people of Nagasaki after the atomic bomb blast. An old man, for example, had bent down next to a wall to pick some weeds just *when* the bomb exploded. *Before* he straightened up, the heat waves from the explosion killed his wife who had been standing next to him. A boy *who* had dived into a river to find something for his sister came up to hear people all about him screaming. In a burned streetcar one could see dead passengers sitting like charred mummies. There are many such graphic descriptions in this book. Do they help to make people seek ways toward peace?

(2) Teetotalling Mama

My maternal grandmother had a tendency to drink a bit too much. As a result my mother refused to sip even a carbonated beverage. She believed *that* the resultant "burp" was as sinful as a drunken stagger. My brothers and I were brought up on milk, hot chocolate, lemonade, and an occasional iced punch. *After* we grew a bit older, we once indulged in an ice cream soda at a nearby ice cream parlor, *but* we had to worry through a whole evening in fear *that* our "burps" might upset Mama and cause a major family crisis. Even *after* we were married, Mama would smell everything we drank to be sure that we weren't straying from her teachings. *If* there was any doubt at all, we would get a stern lecture. This might have gone on until we were grandparents except for the fact that Mama found her Waterloo in a bowl of Hawaiian punch at the wedding reception of a family friend. Something attracted her to that punch for refill after refill. It may have been the heat of the evening or the unusually good taste of the punch. Before the evening was over Mama was thoroughly "stewed." My friend swore *that* he had "doctored" that punch very little, *but* little was too much for a complete abstainer like Mama. In the garden she sang several fairly risque songs in a fairly loud voice. In the house she tried to unscrew several light bulbs and mix the potato chips, *which* were in a large cake bowl, with an electric cake mixer. We took her home and put icebags on her head. Nobody ever said anything to Mama about how drunk she had been. In turn Mama never smelled our drinks again.

(3) Those Shocking Frogs

Frogs are more "shocking" creatures *than* most people think. In 1793 Alessandro Volta saw a fellow Italian scientist take a dissected frog's leg and place it between two different metals. The experiment was so arranged *that when* one metal touched a nerve and the other touched a muscle, the leg twitched and contracted. After many experiments Volta realized *that* the power came not from the frog's leg but from the metal. The saline solution in the leg had acted as a conductor. This experiment eventually led to Volta's invention of the storage battery. In a much more recent experiment, Dr. Wolfgang Karger of the University of Ruhr in Germany demonstrated *that* frogs and toads carry electric energy in their skin. A small amount of electric energy is generated *when* water is drawn into the frog's skin, enough energy to run a tiny direct current motor. Scientists have since found *that* certain human parts act in the same way. This electricity may someday be used to run pacemakers. These are little instruments *that* are used to stimulate the hearts of people with heart trouble. Next time [*when*] you eat frog's legs, you might meditate a little about the little fellows' contribution to human welfare. It might even bring a "frog" to your throat.

(4) Dyslexia

Don't make fun of the child *who* spells words backwards or sees numbers in reverse order. These children are sometimes suffering from a special learning deficiency called "dyslexia," or specific language disability. They may see the number 29 as 92 or the word "cat" as "tac." Their *d*'s are written as *b*'s and their *b*'s are written as *d*'s *because* that is *how* they see them. Of course you should be careful not to get upset every time you notice someone occasionally making such errors. Some specialists claim *that* many children go through a brief period in early life *when* they "mirror" read. It is only *when* this type of thing continues for a period of time and the child does not seem to be able to read correctly after patient prompting *that* one should seek professional help. It is estimated *that* as many as six million children may suffer from this difficulty. *When* their problem is recognized, they can be helped with special teaching techniques and a great deal of patience. *When* it is not recognized, they often suffer terribly in school because of constant frustration and failure.

(5) Aunt Snell's Diet

Aunt Snell was rather careful about the food [*that*] she ate. In the springtime she would eat only the eggs of the youngest hens, *and* brown eggs they must be. In the fall she would take maple syrup right from the maple tree, chestnuts from the chestnut tree, *and* as much rhubarb as she could buy. These she would bake into a horrible concoction *which* she would dare to call pie, *and* she would feed it to her family and guests several times a week. In the winter she bought exotic food like sharkstail soup and fried grasshoppers. Her children were all brought up on goat's milk and raw cabbage. She would use radishes only from Western Pennsylvania and meat only from kosher butcher shops, although she was Presbyterian, not Jewish. From Florida came her oranges and from California her iceburg lettuce. When she decided on a particular food, there would be no change for years. Sometimes she claimed *that* she studied the rate of atomic fallout to decide what areas to avoid in her choice of farm products. At other times it was based on the fertilizer content of the soil in a particular state. Her children seem to be reasonably healthy, *but* she died rather suddenly several years ago by choking on a "chaw" of tobacco. Somehow she had kept this habit hidden from her family all those years. Up to the time of her death they had always thought *that* she had just liked to spit a lot.

NOW that you have a good understanding about the basic structure of the sentence, you are ready to work on other aspects to polish and improve your sentences. In the next three chapters you will study punctuation, time and tense, parts of speech, and word usage. As we move along, refresh your memory: Refer back to the earlier chapters when you have forgotten or are unsure about something. Reviewing what you have learned thus far will be most helpful when you work on

PART III

polishing

sentences . . .

CHAPTER 8

Handling

PUNCTUATION

In working your way through this book, you have already learned much about punctuation. Your understanding of the structure of simple, compound, and complex sentences is a key factor in handling many punctuation problems.

Punctuation is an integral part of language. It helps the writer to group ideas in a meaningful manner, to emphasize important points, and to differentiate between questions and statements. It represents in written form what intonation, pauses, and volume do in speech. While a speaker, for example, indicates a question by a rising tone at the end of a sentence, a writer represents it with a question mark. A speaker may signal subordinate ideas by pauses, while a writer signals them by commas.

The tendency in modern publishing is to establish maximum clarity in sentence structure and to use as little punctuation as possible. It is just as incorrect to overpunctuate as to underpunctuate. *Punctuation marks should never be inserted without a good reason.*

SELF-QUIZ 1

1. Three of the functions of punctuation are _____

   _____

2. Punctuation represents in written form what _____,

   _____, and _____ do in speech.

3. What is a key factor in your handling of many punctuation problems?

   _____

4. The tendency in modern publishing is to establish maximum clarity in

   _____ and to use as _____ punctuation as possible.

5. It is just as incorrect to _____ as to _____

   _____ .

6. _____ should never be inserted without a good reason.

ı.ıı

END PUNCTUATION

In learning basic sentence structure, your understanding of where to place end punctuation (periods, question marks, and exclamation points) should have been reinforced. This, of course, means that you also learned how to avoid fragments, run-ons, and comma splices.

In this section you will review the various uses of end punctuation.

The Period

1. Periods mark the ends of sentences that are statements. These are called *declarative* sentences. They do not include questions or exclamations.

> New York is one of the most densely populated cities in the world.
> Frank is insane.
> "Come home immediately," said Clarence.
> Leave the room.

2. Periods are used in dialogue for statements which may or may not be complete sentences.

> "Hello, Jennie."

"Hi, Slink."
"Nice day."
"Yeah."

3. Periods are used in abbreviations.

Dr. Paul D. Daniels
S.O.S.
two a.m.
U.S. Post Office

Sometimes the periods are left out of abbreviations that have become well known: UN, GOP, USSR. Consult your dictionary for the correct usage and be consistent in how you handle such abbreviations.

4. Periods are used to indicate ellipses, that is, intended omissions of words from quoted material. Ellipses are usually indicated by three periods if the deleted material is within a sentence and four periods if it comes at the end of a sentence.

"I pledge allegiance to the flag . . . and to the Republic for which it stands."

". . . where the grapes of wrath are stored. . . . His truth is marching on."

The Question Mark

A question mark is used at the end of a direct question. These are called *interrogative* sentences.

Who are you?
Where is the can opener?
What did George Washington whisper to Martha?
How can the project succeed?
The president asked his advisors, "What will be history's judgment of our actions?"

Note the use of both question mark and period below.

"What will be history's judgment of our actions?" the president asked his advisors.

Sometimes a question is worded like a statement, that is, the subject comes before the verb.

You will be here on time tomorrow?

EXCEPTION: When a so-called question is really an order or a statement, it is called a *rhetorical* question and it ends in a period.

Will you please deliver the goods promptly.
How can news like this be broken gently.
Who knows when the end will come.

The Exclamation Point

Exclamation points are used after utterances that express strong feelings or that bear a sense of urgency. Sentences that end with exclamation points are called *exclamatory* sentences.

> Ughh! How she repels me!
> Ouch! You hurt me!
> Oh, what a beautiful day it is!
> You are a rotten scoundrel!
> Don't move!
> "Apologize immediately!" screamed Mr. Horly.

Ughh, ouch, and *oh* are called *interjections.* They are not considered as grammatical parts of any sentence.

TEST 1

1. Periods mark the ends of sentences that are _____ .

   They are not _____ or _____ .
2. Write three unrelated declarative sentences.
3. Write four lines of informal dialogue.
4. Correct the punctuation where necessary:

   USO   nine pm.
   G B Shaw   Baltimore and Ohio R R
   Rev Carl B Struthers   St. Vincent's Hospital
   He got his BA and went to work for the BBC.
   Howard U is located in Washington DC.
   She attended Mt Vernon Junior College.
5. Copy a short paragraph from this book in which you use ellipses correctly. Indicate the page number of your source.
6. Write a question that is worded like a statement.
7. Write a statement that is worded like a question (rhetorical question).
8. Write a sentence which includes a question in direct quotations.
9. Write three interjections.
10. Write an exclamatory quotation within a sentence.

INTERNAL PUNCTUATION

The principal tools of internal punctuation are the colon, the semicolon, and the comma. Of the three the comma is, by far, the most common and the most confusing. In studying this section, concentrate first on the colon and semicolon, which you should be able to master quickly and easily. With these under your belt, the more complicated comma will be easier to handle.

The Colon

The colon is often called the mark of anticipation because it announces to the reader that he should look for something. That something may be a series of directions, a list, or a quotation.

1. Colons are usually used after the term "as follows" or when "as follows" is implied.

> Pay careful attention to these directions:
> Handle the dynamite gingerly.
> Light the fuses carefully.
> Run rapidly!
> Here are a few subjects for you to write about: "The Dreams of High School Students," "On Annoying Professors," and "Cheating Can Be Stopped."

2. Colons are used to introduce quotations that are more than a sentence or two long. Quotes of paragraph-length and poems are placed in separate paragraphs.

> In the *Dhammapada,* a book of Buddhist sayings, one will find this quotation: "A man should first direct himself in the way he should go. Only then should he instruct others; a wise man will do so and not grow weary."

3. Colons are used after the salutations of business letters.

> Dear Sirs:
> Gentlemen:
> Dear Miss Wallingford:

The Semicolon

The semicolon is considered to represent a greater pause than that of a comma and a lesser pause than that of a period. The semicolon is used in three ways:

1. As indicated in Chapter 5, it is used in compound sentences before certain coordinate conjunctions (called conjunctive adverbs).[1]

; accordingly	; however	; otherwise
; consequently	; therefore	; moreover
; nevertheless	; then	; furthermore
; hence	; thus	

Remember that the semicolons and the coordinate conjunctions are used together in this way only when they bridge two main clauses.

2. A semicolon may be used between two main clauses instead of a period (see page 79). When you are in doubt, it is safer to use the period.

3. Semicolons are used in series of words, phrases, or clauses that become too complicated for commas alone to handle with clarity. This will be discussed again later in the chapter.

> Members of the band included Harold Epstein, clarinetist; Tony Zaluppo, tuba player; Angelo Smetano, drummer; and Luella Turnop, trumpeter.

---

[1] Modern usage often allows for a period preceding these words and their use as transitional or introductory words of new sentences. For example: *Thus, the deed was successfully accomplished. However, they did arrive on time.* It is not acceptable to use only a comma or no punctuation in this situation, as the result would be a comma splice or a run-on.

SELF-QUIZ 2

1. The three principal tools of internal punctuation are _____

   _____

2. The colon is called the mark of _____.

3. List the three conditions under which the colon is used.

   _____

   _____

   _____

4. List the three situations in which semicolons are used.

   _____

   _____

   _____

5. List the eleven compound conjunctions that are used with semicolons.

   _____

   _____

Insert the proper internal punctuation in paragraphs 6 and 7 below. Only colons, semicolons, and commas are needed.

6. A partial list of baseball players and their respective positions is as follows Melvin Pew, first base Harlow Ellison, second base John Holly, third base Clement Ordl, short stop and Simon Klein, catcher.

7. We were invited to the Inaugural Ball last year accordingly, we had to buy new clothes for both my wife and me. This affected our clothing bill quite a bit because she ordered these items from the stores indicated a mink stole, $2,000, Gunter's Fur Shoppe a satin formal, $250, Hunter's Department Store a calfskin purse, $72.00, Lee's Leather Goods.

The Comma

Commas represent in writing what short pauses represent in speech. They are used more often than any other punctuation mark because speech is so full of short pauses. The pauses help the speaker to group his words into meaningful units, to emphasize certain ideas, and to separate some words, phrases, and clauses from the rest of the sentence.

As indicated earlier, the trend today is toward the use of fewer punctuation marks, and the use of commas is affected most. For this reason we will discuss those comma rules first whose use appears to be remaining most stable, and then present those that appear to be undergoing change.

1. *Commas in series.* To separate words, phrases, and clauses in series is one of the simplest and most common functions of the comma.

   a. *Words in series:*
      I bought peanuts, popcorn, ice cream, and jelly beans.

   b. *Phrases in series:*
      We ran into the house, up the stairs, through the bedroom, and onto the back porch.

   c. *Clauses in series:*
      They are men who have fought for their country, who would die for their country, but who would prefer to love and live in peace.

2. *Commas with semicolons in series.* When a series becomes too complicated for commas alone to clarify the meaning, semicolons can be of great help.

   Jerry lives at 1225 East 105 Street, Detroit, Michigan; Ken lives at 12206 Kenworthy Road, Akron, Ohio; and Bert lives at 1406 Budd Street, Los Angeles, California.

3. *Commas with adjectives in a series.* Since all adjectives do not carry out quite the same function in a sentence, they are not always separated by commas in the same way. Those that are considered *coordinate* are separated by commas. Adjectives that are considered *non-coordinate* are not separated by commas.
   Coordinate adjectives in a series can be interchanged without changing the meaning of the sentence, and they can be separated by *and.*

   The dog's coat was wet, muddy, and bloody.
   The look on his face was serene, thoughtful, and bemused.

Non-coordinate adjectives do not take *and* between them, and changing their order changes the meaning of the sentence.

   The pilot followed the huge low-flying oblong object.
   He bought a battered Ford pickup truck.

SELF-QUIZ 3

Part A: Correct these sentences by adding commas. Two sentences are correct.

1. At the meeting were Buddhists Hindus and Moslems.
2. He gave her the money to buy some eggs at the corner store.
3. She kissed him on the nose on both eyes and on the left ear.
4. They fed the chubby chortling and dimpled Black baby.
5. She bought a second hand Chrysler convertible.
6. They came to the party they bothered everyone and they refused to leave.
7. He bought nuts beans pickles apples and fish.

The team consisted of Tony Batista 12201 Blank Road Steve Mentor 1802 Snell Street Pete Totle 2291 Kemp Avenue and Bill Smick 707 Cleet Street.

The girls listed their addresses as follows: Mary Glass 1616 Bell Street Madison Wisconsin Jean Tease 1813 Todd Road Akron Ohio and Minnie Weed 601 Memp Avenue Friendship New York.

ıı.

4. *Commas used to influence the flow of ideas.* In the most general sense, this is the primary use of all commas—to prevent misreading of a sentence. A comma should be used at any point in a sentence where words running together might be ambiguous or convey the wrong meaning.

Read the following pairs of sentences and notice the effect of adding a comma.

> As far as I know Jim will join us.
> As far as I know, Jim will join us.
> When the plane flies over the children will cheer.
> When the plane flies over, the children will cheer.
> Scurrying below the people looked like ants.
> Scurrying below, the people looked like ants.
> To Lulu Belle told her innermost secrets.
> To Lulu, Belle told her innermost secrets.
> Above the stars were shining brightly.
> Above, the stars were shining brightly.

SELF-QUIZ 4

Add commas where needed.

1. After I shot it was Leonard's turn.
2. Below the lights were twinkling brightly.
3. When he wasn't looking down came the pile of boxes.
4. If they gave up the tree would be removed.
5. Before they drowned the sharks attacked.

ıı.

5. *Commas that separate "intruders."* Words that add afterthoughts, emphasis, or shades of meaning are set off from the rest of the sentence by commas.

> a. *Nouns of address.* These are used when the writer is reproducing direct conversation. The name of the person, animal, or thing spoken to is separated from the rest of the sentence by a comma or commas. Remember, the noun of address is *not* the subject of the sentence. "You understood" is the subject.
>
> > Fido, come here.
> > Shine on, harvest moon.
> > You, Frank, are an opinionated ass.

b. *Mild interjections.* These are interjections that are not strong enough to warrant the use of exclamation points.

> My, what a lovely place you have.
> Dear me, I didn't expect you so early.
> Well, what did you expect?

c. *Parenthetical expressions.* These are words added to or inserted in the basic sentence pattern.

> Yes, I agree with you.   No, it isn't too late.
> You are, in effect, breaking the law.
> Women are more gentle than men, in general.
> As a matter of fact, they did not come anywhere near here.

6. *Commas that separate words used out of their usual order.*

usual:	The clever and resourceful detective quickly discovered the clues.
not usual:	The detective, clever and resourceful, quickly discovered the clues.
usual:	The once swift and clear brook was completely dry.
not usual:	The brook, once swift and clear, was completely dry.

SELF-QUIZ 5

Place commas where needed.

1. Why don't you talk to me more civilly George?
2. You are as a matter of fact breaking the law.
3. In general dogs are more faithful than cats.
4. The lakes ill-smelling and filthy turned his stomach.
5. Well I told you so.
6. You will do it Steve whether you want to or not.
7. Oh I didn't know that.
8. Fred keen-eyed and alert caught the thief.
9. They will needless to say be glad to see you.
10. Some campers careless and inconsiderate had left their garbage in full view.

7. *Commas that separate non-restrictive appositives.* The easiest way to understand what is meant by appositives is to look at examples.

restrictive:	His friend Steve lives in Boston.
non-restrictive:	Steve, his friend, lives in Boston.

In these sentences the words *Steve* and *his friend* are said to be in apposition, which means standing side by side. Appositives are restrictive if they must remain together in order to make a definite identification. If you dropped *Steve* from the first sentence, there would be no way of identifying the appositive, *his friend*. Appositives are called non-restrictive if they merely provide additional information which is not essential for positive identification. In the second sentence you could drop *his friend* and still know who was meant. Non-restrictive appositives are set off by commas. No commas are used with restrictive appositives.

restrictive:	He was discussing Lionel Smith the banker, not Lionel Smith the actor.
non-restrictive:	Lionel Smith, the actor, met Ken Dodd, the painter.

8. *Commas that separate non-restrictive clauses.* Like appositives, subordinate clauses can be restrictive or non-restrictive depending on whether they are vital to the meaning of the main clause or add new information. Restrictive clauses do not require commas; non-restrictive clauses do.

restrictive:	People who like sports are our best customers.
	Do not go until you have read all the directions.
	It was a report which he desperately needed.
non-restrictive:	Boston, which is the site of the famous Tea Party, is a very old city.
	He gave the money to Leonard Sedder, who is my father-in-law.
	You are all invited to come, although the weather might be fairly cool.

SELF-QUIZ 6

Add commas where necessary.

1. Jean Dawson president of the sewing club was badly injured.
2. The girl who lived here was married last week.
3. People who lie should be punished.
4. The Essex company which is located in a beautiful wooded area is known for its fine products.
5. The Essex Company which produces steel is not connected with the Essex Company which produces chemicals.
6. The team that practices hardest is not always the winner.
7. Steve Brody my best friend is in Florida.
8. His brother Melvin left town.
9. Mrs. Eliajal Walleer the first woman to drive an Army tank was cited for bravery.
10. St. Louis my hometown is an interesting city.

9. *Other common uses of the comma.*

> *In dates.* Commas are used to separate the day of the month from the year.

March 2, 1918
July 26, 1923

In addresses. Commas are used to separate the parts of an address: house number and street name, city or town, state, country.

12201 Burcheye Road, Fayette, Nebraska, U.S.A.
16 Neff Road, St. Louis, Missouri

In correspondence. Commas are used in the salutations of friendly letters and in the complimentary closings of both business and social correspondence.

Dear Mary,   Sincerely yours,
Dear Uncle Talbot,   Very truly yours,

In direct quotations. Commas are used to separate words of direct quotations from the rest of the sentence.

Clarence said, "Give my love to Luella," and his blush spread like catsup.
"I don't like her," replied Esmeralda, "but it's your life."

When end punctuation is used within the quotation marks, the commas are unnecessary.

"I hate her!" screamed Ella.
"Why should you of all people hate her?" shouted Rock.

REMINDER: Don't forget the use of commas between the main clauses of compound sentences and after subordinate clauses that begin complex sentences.

The angry crew refused to follow the captain's orders, and he finally had to change them.
After they had ridden fiercely for many days, the men reached home safely.

The Dash

The principal uses of the dash are to set off a series using commas, to emphasize a point, and to set off a disconnected expression.

1. *To set off a series using commas:*

Some of the city's service departments—water, heat, sanitation, and safety—are vitally in need of funds.
The men in question—Harold Keene, Jim Peterson, and Gerald Greene—deserve awards.

2. *To emphasize a point:*

Thousands of young men were killed and many more were permanently injured in the Vietnamese War—the longest war in our history.

Many people in this country suffer from malnutrition—in this, the richest country in the world.

3. *To set off a disconnected or parenthetical remark:*

His idea—one which just suddenly popped into his head—seems like a very sound approach.
The automobile—he had always dreamed of owning a fleet of them—lay in ruins at the bottom of the cliff.

Parentheses

The principal uses of parentheses are to inject a disconnected idea into a sentence (similar to the third use of the dash listed above), to enclose letters or numbers in a series, and to list sources of statements.

1. *To set off a disconnected idea:*

The second lieutenant and the major (Robert could never understand why they had been commissioned) never saw action at the front.
Before arriving at the station, the old train (someone said that it was a relic of frontier days) caught fire.

2. *To enclose letters or numbers in a series:*[1]

The fact that the school imposed such severe discipline taught him (1) to avoid taking any chances, (2) to be almost compulsively neat and clean, and (3) to be suspicious of any kind of informality or lack of order.

3. *To list sources of statements:*

Several historians have demonstrated conclusively that the war could have been averted. (Cass and Cass, *History of War*, p. 202.)

what you have learned in chapter 8

In addition to reviewing the use of punctuation as related to sentence structure, this chapter has demonstrated how to treat series of words, phrases, and clauses, how to group words together or separate certain ideas from others, how to emphasize or question, and how to handle restrictive and non-restrictive phrases and clauses. It has also shown how to punctuate abbreviations, addresses, dates, salutations, and other special situations.

Punctuation should help the reader to read your words as you intend them to be read. Use it carefully and sparingly.

KEY 1

(1) group ideas meaningfully, emphasize important points, differentiate between questions and statements (2) intonation, pauses, volume (3) understanding of sentence structure (4) sentence structure, little (5) overpunctuate, underpunctuate (6) punctuation marks

[1] This technique is used when the writer wishes to emphasize the number or order of his items.

KEY 2

(1) colon, semicolon, comma   (2) anticipation   (3) after the term "as follows" or when it is implied, to introduce long quotations, after the salutation of business letters   (4) before conjunctive adverbs, between two main clauses, to separate series that are too complicated for commas alone   (5) accordingly, consequently, nevertheless, hence, however, therefore, then, thus, otherwise, moreover, furthermore

(6) A partial list of baseball players and their respective positions is as follows: Melvin Pew, first base; Harlow Ellison, second base; John Holly, third base; Clement Ordl, short stop; and Simon Klein, catcher.

(7) We were invited to the Inaugural Ball last year; accordingly, we had to buy . . . stores indicated: a mink stole, $2,000, Gunter's Fur Shoppe; a satin formal, $250, Hunter's Department Store; a calfskin purse, $72.00, Lee's Leather Goods.

KEY 3

Part A: (1) Buddhists, Hindus,   (2) correct   (3) nose, eyes,   (4) chubby, chortling,   (5) correct   (6) party, everyone,   (7) nuts, beans, pickles, apples,

Part B: The team consisted of Tony Batista, 12201 Blank Road; Steve Mentor, 1802 Snell Street; Pete Totl, 2291 Kemp Avenue; and Bill Smick, 707 Cleet Street.

The girls listed their addresses as follows: Mary Glass, 1616 Bell Street, Madison, Wisconsin; Jean Tease, 1813 Todd Road, Akron, Ohio; and Minnie Weed, 601 Memp Avenue, Friendship, New York.

KEY 4

(1) shot,   (2) Below,   (3) looking,   (4) up,   (5) drowned,

KEY 5

(1) civilly,   (2) are, fact,   (3) general,   (4) lakes, filthy,   (5) Well,   (6) it, Steve,   (7) Oh,   (8) Fred, alert,   (9) will, say,   (10) campers, inconsiderate,

KEY 6

(1) Dawson, club,   (2) correct   (3) correct   (4) company, area,   (5) correct
(6) correct   (7) Brody, friend,   (8) correct   (9) Walleer, tank,   (10) Louis, hometown,

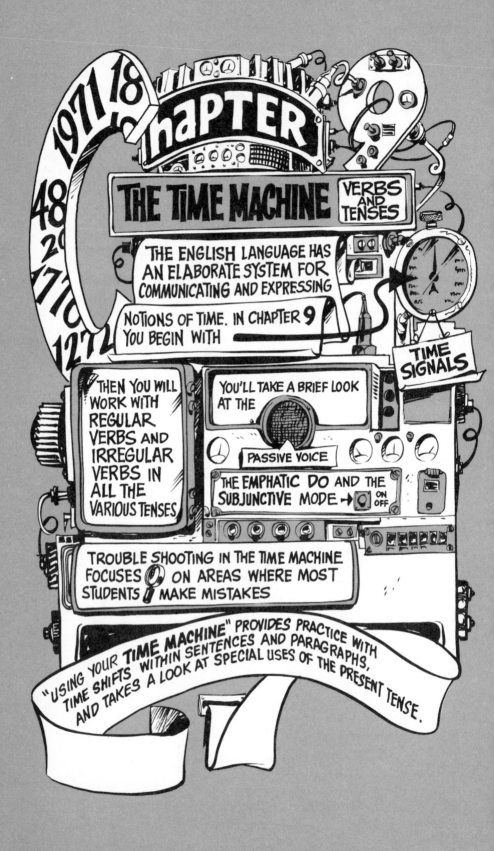

The time machine—
VERBS AND TENSES

TIME SIGNALS

The English language provides a finely calibrated set of signals by means of which a writer can describe the time of events in a very precise manner. It does this through specific "time" words and phrases and through a complex set of signals based on the tenses of the verb. The most evident kinds of time signals are words, such as the following, which state the time in specific terms:

now	July 26, 1923
immediately	at noon today
tomorrow at 6:00 p.m.	22 B.C.

The author sets the exact time with specific time designations such as the above words; then he keeps the time consistent throughout the paragraph by his control over the verb. The verb not only plays an important part in setting the time, but it must also agree with the subject in both number and person. (See Chapter 4.)

The basic tenses are *past*, *present*, and *future*, but there is a wide range of intermediate tenses which help the writer to specify the time in various ways. He can specify whether an action is in progress at the moment, whether it has been continuing over a period of time or has just occurred occasionally, and whether one action in the past happened before another action in the past.

The table below (Tracking "Kiss" Through Time) will give you an idea of the many shades of meaning that are made possible by the various tenses.

Tracking "Kiss" Through Time

Study the sequence of tenses below. Note how one can describe the exact time of an event with the proper combination of verb and auxiliaries (forms of *have* or *be*). *Have* and *be* are the most commonly used auxiliaries.

PRESENT TENSES

present	I kiss her whenever I leave.
present perfect	I have kissed her every day.
present progressive	I am kissing her right now.
present perfect progressive	I have been kissing her ever since I arrived.

FUTURE TENSES

future	He will kiss her (tonight or never!).
future perfect	He will have kissed her by 3:00 p.m. tomorrow.
future progressive	He will be kissing her tomorrow morning.
future perfect progressive	He will have been kissing her for three hours by noon.

PAST TENSES

past	We kissed.
past perfect	We had kissed just once before her mother arrived.
past progressive	We were kissing when they walked in.
past perfect progressive	We had been kissing for several minutes before the bell rang.

Tracing Time Through Two Paragraphs

To make you aware of how important the time system is in English, note the numerous time words and tense words (verbs) in the paragraphs below:

The explorers' supplies *did* not *reach* them *until long after* they *had arrived* at the base camp. Mud, rock slides, and swollen rivers *had impeded* the progress of supply trucks *when* they *had attempted* to reach the stranded men. *When* the supplies *reached* the camp, there *was* great rejoicing and the explorers and the truck drivers *shared* a sumptuous meal.

The teenagers of Clifton Beach *will hold* their *Annual* Beach Ball on *Tuesday, February 2* at *nine p.m.* Since the weather *will be* extremely cold *at that time*, the ball *will be held* in the beach house on Canal Street. The Beach Ball *was* originally *scheduled* for *August 26*, but there *was* an oil leak from an offshore pumping station *at that time*, and it *contaminated* the beach for the balance of the season. This *will be* the *first time* in the history of Clifton Beach that a beach party *will be held* in *mid-winter*.

SELF-QUIZ 1

1. Write three words or phrases (not verbs) which indicate time: _____

_____

2. _____ work with time words and phrases to maintain a consistent time pattern throughout a paragraph.

3. The _____ must help set the _____ and must also agree with the subject in both _____ and _____.

4. The three basic tenses are _____, _____ and

_____.

5. The two verbs most commonly used as auxiliaries are _____ and

_____.

6. The auxiliary _____ signals future action.

7. Progressive tenses can be identified by the _____ ending.

Which tense would you use in the following situations? Refer to the table of tenses.

8. An action that takes place repeatedly, on a regular basis. _____
9. An action that took place regularly in the past and is continuing in the

present. _____
10. An intended future action that will continue over a period of time.

_____

11. An action that took place at a particular time in the past before something

else happened. _____
12. An action that had been taking place for a period of time before something

else happened. _____

13. An action that is taking place at this very moment. _____

14. An action that will have been completed by a certain time in the future.

_____

15. An action that will be taken at some time in the future. _____

16. An action that has been completed. _____

ılıl.ıl.ıl.ıl.ıl.ıl.ıl.ıl.ıl.ıl.ıl.ıl.ıl.ıl.ıl.ıl.ıl.ıl.ıl.ıl.ıl.ıl.ıl.ıl.

Your Tour Through Time

As indicated at the beginning of this chapter, writers set the initial time of their sentences by using time words; then they adjust their verbs to fit that time by changing the form of the verbs and by using auxiliaries.

There are two types of verbs, *regular* and *irregular*. The regular verbs are much simpler to use because they all change in the same way, while the irregular verbs change in many ways. For this reason we will study the regular and irregular verbs separately.

In this section you will work your way through all twelve tenses, seeing how each is formed and how each is used. You don't have to memorize the names of the tenses or any set of rules about tense. You may refer to the descriptions and examples whenever necessary. Doing the exercises carefully will reinforce all that you have learned about verbs as well as help you to handle tenses correctly. It should give you a *feeling* for tense as well as a better understanding of it.

REGULAR VERBS

Regular verbs are verbs which add *d* or *ed* to their present tense to form the past and perfect tenses. Most verbs are regular. Here are some examples:

talk	talk*ed*
twitter	twitter*ed*
glance	glance*d*
deny	deni*ed*[1]
submit	submitt*ed*[2]

The Present Tenses of Regular Verbs

Present

The present tense is used (among other functions) in commands, suggestions, and to indicate habitual action or continuing ability.

command:	*Deliver* this message immediately, Private Gross.
suggestion:	*Discourage* them from coming if you can.
habitual action:	She *sews* well. He *paints* beautifully.

[1] Note that *y* changes to *i*.
[2] Final *t* is doubled.

Present Perfect [*have | has* ﹏﹏﹏*ed*]

The present perfect tense is used to indicate a past action with a continuing present effect. This tense is formed by a combination of *have* or *has* plus the past tense.[2]

> We *have loved* each other for a long time.
> They *have declined* our offer, but we will try again.
> She *has devoured* her steak raw and is still hungry.

Present Progressive [*am | are | is* ﹏﹏﹏*ing*]

This tense indicates that something is taking place now and will continue to occur for a while. It requires a *be* auxiliary plus the *ing* form of the verb. Remember that the *ing* alone doesn't do the job. *Ing* freezes the verb (see p. 30).

> I *am* driv*ing* carefully.
> In her petition she *is* demand*ing* equal pay for equal work.
> The defendents *are* deny*ing* the allegations.

Present Perfect Progressive [*have | has been* ﹏﹏﹏*ing*]

This tense indicates an action that has been occurring in the past and is continuing to occur. It is formed by a combination of *have been* or *has been* and the *ing* form of the verb.

> In my opinion, they *have been* support*ing* the wrong candidate all along.
> It *has been* rain*ing* steadily for weeks.
> People *have been* visit*ing* here for years.

TEST 1: The Present Tenses, Regular Verbs

Write sentences using each of the verbs in parentheses as in the example below. Underline your subjects once, your verbs twice.

EXAMPLE: (dice)

Present: His mother dices the carrots.
Present perfect: She has diced the carrots many times.
Present progressive: She is dicing the carrots now.
Present perfect progressive: She has been dicing carrots all day.

1. (fish) _____

2. (chop) _____

3. (chew) _____

4. (glue) _____

5. (argue) _____

---

[2] When used with *have, has,* or *had* to form the perfect tenses, the verbs in the past tense are called perfect (or past) participles.

The Future Tenses of Regular Verbs

Future   [*will* ⁓⁓⁓]

This tense signals action that is to take place in the future at a time which may or may not be specified. It is formed by *will* plus a verb in the present tense.

> I *will walk* alone today.
> The people *will laugh* at us.
> The teachers *will demand* smaller classes.

After the tense of a sentence has been established by *will*, or when a time word is used, *will* is sometimes omitted.

> I will cheer when we (will) arrive.
> We (will) leave tomorrow.

Future Perfect   [*will have* ⁓⁓⁓*ed*]

The future perfect tense indicates an action which is carried from the present to a specific time in the future. It is formed by a combination of *will have* plus the past tense of the verb.

> He has suffered for many years. He *will have suffered* long enough by the time his pardon is granted.
> The turtles have begun to cover their eggs in the sand. They *will have covered* all of them before the tide rises.
> They started studying yesterday. They *will have studied* for twenty hours by tomorrow afternoon.

Future Progressive   [*will be* ⁓⁓⁓*ing*]

This tense indicates a future action in progress. It is formed by *will be* plus the *ing* form of the verb.

> I *will be* rowing there tomorrow while you are driving.
> The Senate *will be* discussing one bill while the House *will be* debating a different one.

Future Perfect Progressive   [*will have been* ⁓⁓⁓*ing*]

This tense indicates an on-going action which will be continued into the future. It is formed by combining *will have been* plus the *ing* form of the verb.

> They *will have been* climbing for 24 hours by tomorrow afternoon.
> The council *will have been* debating for two whole weeks by 5:00 p.m.
> By nightfall the girls *will have been* talking for six hours.

TEST 2: The Future Tenses, Regular Verbs

Write sentences using each of the verbs in parentheses as in the example below. Underline your subjects once and your verbs twice.

> *EXAMPLE*: (pick)
>
> Future: We will pick apples today.
> Future perfect: They will have picked all of the apples by noon.
> Future progressive: The men will be picking cotton tomorrow.
> Future perfect progressive: By midnight she will have been picking nuts
> for 18 hours.

1. (trim)_____

2. (pluck)_____

3. (shovel)_____

4. (sneeze)_____

5. (pitch)_____

The Past Tenses of Regular Verbs

Past [_____d/ed]

The past tense is formed by adding *d* or *ed* to the present tense of the verb.

> He stumbled into the house.
> They presented him with the medal.

Past Perfect [*had* _____d/ed]

The past perfect tense goes one step further back into time than the past tense. To form it you use *had* plus a verb in the past tense. It is often used in combination with a past tense to show which action occurred before the other.

> I *had* jumped before his parachute opened.
> You arrived long after they *had* departed.
> They *had* already ordered dinner before we joined them.

Past Progressive [*was/were* _____ing]

This tense describes an on-going event in the past. It is formed with *was* or *were* plus the *ing* form of the verb.

> He *was* drilling the well.
> They *were* slicing the bread.
> The Earth *was* turning on its axis.

Past Perfect Progressive [*had been* _____ing]

The past perfect progressive tense describes an action that was an on-going occurrence over a period of time in the past before something else occurred. To form it you use *had been* and the *ing* form of the verb.

They *had been* rac*ing* all day when we found them.
The birds *had been* chatter*ing* in the treetops when the storm engulfed them.
We *had been* travel*ing* all day but had arrived late.

TEST 3: The Past Tenses, Regular Verbs

Write sentences using each of the verbs in parentheses as in the example below. Underline subjects once and verbs twice.

EXAMPLE: (start)

Past: He started the car every morning.
Past perfect: He had started the motor.
Past progressive: She was starting her singing lessons.
Past perfect progressive: They had been starting out early for many years
until his heart attack occurred.

1. (greet)_____

2. (place)_____

3. (state)_____

4. (scream)_____

5. (blame)_____

Summary: Formation of Tenses, Regular Verbs

The regular verb goes back and forth in time rather consistently, as charted below.

PRESENT TENSE
The present tense is formed
by dropping *to* from the
infinitive.

to vary	vary
to rate	rate
to pit	pit

PAST TENSE
The past tense is formed by
adding *d* or *ed* to the present
tense of the verb.[1]

vary	vari*ed*
rate	rate*d*
pit	pit*ted*

FUTURE TENSE
The future tense is formed by using
will before the present
tense of the verb.

will vary
will rate
will pit

PERFECT TENSES
The perfect tenses are formed
by using *have, has, had,* or *will
have* with the past tense of the
verb.

pres. perf.	have (has) varied
past perf.	had rated
fut. perf.	will have pitted

[1] Note: *y* changes to *i*; final consonant is sometimes doubled.

PROGRESSIVE TENSES

The progressive tenses are formed by using a *be* auxiliary (*am, are, is, was, were, will be*) with the *ing* form of the verb.

pres. prog.	am (are, is) varying
past prog.	was (were) rating
fut. prog.	will be pitting

PERFECT PROGRESSIVE TENSES

Not employed often, these tenses use *have, has,* or *had* with *been* plus the *ing* verb form.

pres. perf. prog.	have (has) been varying
past perf. prog.	had been rating
fut. perf. prog.	will have been pitting

IRREGULAR VERBS

Irregular verbs differ in several ways from regular verbs. The principal parts of the irregular verbs must be memorized in order to master them. Most students already know how to handle many of the irregulars and are wise enough to refer to a list, such as the one below, when they are not sure.[1]

Irregular verbs have three principal parts:

1. **Present:** This part is formed from the infinitive by dropping the word *to.* For progressive tenses, add *ing* to this part and make necessary spelling changes (see column two below).

2. **Past:** Unlike regular verbs which add *d* or *ed* in the past tense, irregular verbs change in various ways.[2]

3. **Perfect Participle:**[3] This part is used with *have, has,* or *had* in the present, past, and future perfect tenses. The perfect participle creates no problem when you write regular verbs, because the past tenses of the verbs and the participles are identical. In irregular verbs, however, most of the perfect participles are different from the past tenses. In the present perfect tense, *have* or *has* is used with the perfect participle: He *has chosen.* They *have flown.* In the future perfect, *will* and *have* are used: He *will have chosen.* They *will have flown.* In the past perfect, *had* is used with the perfect participle: He *had chosen.* They *had flown.*

Principal Parts of the Irregular Verbs

PRESENT		PAST	PERFECT PARTICIPLE
arise	*arising*	arose	arisen
awake	*awaking*	awoke	awaked
(be) am	*being*	was	been
beat		beat	beaten
become	*becoming*	became	become
begin	*beginning*	began	begun
bend		bent	bent

[1] Lists of the parts of irregular verbs are found in most grammar books. Individual words can be checked in a dictionary.

[2] Some verbs are identical in all three parts. See, for example, *bid* and *burst.*

[3] A perfect participle differs from a participle in that the perfect participle combines with *have, has,* or *had* to form the perfect tenses. The participle alone can be used as an adjective but *not* as a verb: *stolen* goods, *driven* snow.

PRESENT		PAST	PERFECT PARTICIPLE
bet	*betting*	bet	bet
bid (offer)	*bidding*	bid	bid
bite	*biting*	bit	bitten
blow		blew	blown
break		broke	broken
bring		brought	brought
breed		bred	bred
build		built	built
burst		burst	burst
buy		bought	bought
catch		caught	caught
choose	*choosing*	chose	chosen
cling		clung	clung
come	*coming*	came	come
cost		cost	cost
creep		crept	crept
deal		dealt	dealt
dig	*digging*	dug	dug
dive	*diving*	dove, dived	dived
do		did	done
draw		drew	drawn
drink		drank	drunk
drive	*driving*	drove	driven
eat		ate	eaten
fall		fell	fallen
feed		fed	fed
feel		felt	felt
fight		fought	fought
find		found	found
flee		fled	fled
fling		flung	flung
fly		flew	flown
forbid	*forbidding*	forbad(e)	forbidden
forget	*forgetting*	forgot	forgotten
freeze	*freezing*	froze	frozen
give	*giving*	gave	given
go		went	gone
grind		ground	ground
grow		grew	grown
hang (a person)		hanged, hung	hanged, hung
hang (a thing)		hung	hung
hide	*hiding*	hid	hidden
hold		held	held
keep		kept	kept
know		knew	known
lay (put or place)		laid	laid

PRESENT		PAST	PERFECT PARTICIPLE
lead		led	led
leave	*leaving*	left	left
lend		lent	lent
lie (recline)	*lying*	lay	lain
light		lighted, lit	lighted, lit
lose	*losing*	lost	lost
make	*making*	made	made
mean		meant	meant
pay		paid	paid
put	*putting*	put	put
quit	*quitting*	quit	quit
read		read	read
rid	*ridding*	rid	rid
ride	*riding*	rode	ridden
ring		rang	rung
rise	*rising*	rose	risen
run	*running*	ran	run
say		said	said
see		saw	seen
sell		sold	sold
send		sent	sent
set	*setting*	set	set
shake	*shaking*	shook	shaken
shine (glow)	*shining*	shone, shined	shone, shined
shoot		shot	shot
show		showed	shown, showed
shrink		shrank	shrunk
sing		sang	sung
sink		sank	sunk
sit	*sitting*	sat	sat
slay		slew	slain
speak		spoke	spoken
spend		spent	spent
spin	*spinning*	spun	spun
spring		sprang	sprung
stand		stood	stood
steal		stole	stolen
sting		stung	stung
stink		stank	stunk
stride	*striding*	strode	stridden
strike	*striking*	struck	struck
strive	*striving*	strove	striven
swear		swore	sworn
swim	*swimming*	swam	swum
swing		swung	swung
take	*taking*	took	taken

PRESENT		PAST	PERFECT PARTICIPLE
teach		taught	taught
tear		tore	torn
tell		told	told
think		thought	thought
throw		threw	thrown
wake	*waking*	woke	waked
wear		wore	worn
wring		wrung	wrung
write	*writing*	wrote	written

Tracking "Sing" and "Drive" Through Time

The sentences below should help you more clearly visualize how the irregular verbs are used in the twelve tenses.

present tense:	**sing**	**drive**
future tense:	**will sing**	**will drive**
past tense:	**sang**	**drove**
perfect participle:	**sung**	**driven**

PRESENT — They *sing* while they *drive*.

pres. perf. — We *have sung* for years.
He *has driven* for years.

pres. prog. — I *am singing* because I'm happy.
She *is driving* recklessly today.

pres. perf. prog. — You *have been singing* since this morning.
It *has been driving* me insane.

FUTURE — They *will sing* while they (will) *drive*.

future perf. — John *will have sung* many songs by noon tomorrow.
They *will have driven* many miles by noon tomorrow.

future prog. — Lulu *will be singing* many times next week.
Mike *will be driving* all day tomorrow.

fut. perf. prog. — They *will have been singing* for weeks by Easter.
She *will have been driving* for ten years by next August.

PAST — They *sang* to us last night.
I *drove* her home yesterday.

past perf. — They *had sung* for hours before we got there.
My brother *had driven* for hours before he was located.

past prog. — The chorus *was singing* when the neighbors complained.
He *was driving* slowly when he was apprehended.

past perf. prog. — The group *had been singing* loudly before the ceiling fell.
His uncle *had been driving* there every day before the road was closed.

TEST 4: The Present Tense, Irregular Verbs

Write sentences using each of the verbs in the parentheses as in the example below. Underline your subjects once and your verbs twice.[1]

EXAMPLE: (take)

Present: I take aspirins every four hours.
Present perfect: The dog has taken the cat's ball.
Present progressive: We are taking the bus home.
Present perfect progressive: We have been taking soil from here for years.

1. (shake)_____

2. (break)_____

3. (hang)_____

4. (grind)_____

5. (blow)_____

TEST 5: The Future Tense, Irregular Verbs

Write sentences using each of the verbs in the parentheses as in the examples below. Underline your subjects once and your verbs twice.

EXAMPLE: (teach)

Future: I will teach every week day.
Future perfect: She will have taught for 10 years by next June.
Future progressive: Her mother-in-law will also be teaching.
Future perfect progressive: Henry will have been teaching for ten years by 1976.

1. (steal)_____

2. (catch)_____

3. (think)_____

4. (bend)_____

5. (bite)_____

TEST 6: Past Tense, Irregular Verbs

Write sentences using each of the verbs in the parentheses as in the examples below. Underline your subjects once and your verbs twice.

[1] In doing these irregular verb exercises, do not hesitate to check the irregular verb list for the proper forms of the past tense and the perfect participle of various verbs.

EXAMPLE: (write)

Past: I <u>wrote</u> six letters yesterday.

Past perfect: He <u>had written</u> six letters.

Past progressive: The <u>student was writing</u> letters all day.

Past perfect progressive: <u>People had been writing</u> to him for many years before his execution.

1. (tear)_____

2. (swim)_____

3. (stand)_____

4. (slide)_____

5. (run)_____

PASSIVE VOICE, THE EMPHATIC "DO," AND THE SUBJUNCTIVE

With a knowledge of regular and irregular verbs behind you, you may profit from a brief look at the verb from several other points of view: the passive voice, the emphatic "do," and the subjunctive mode.

The Active and the Passive

In the active voice the subject-verb relationship is such that the subject *does* the acting, the possessing, the feeling. In the passive voice the subject, in a sense, *receives* the action of the verb.

It is usually considered preferable to write in the active voice, but situations do arise fairly often in which the passive voice is more appropriate. Compare the uses of the two voices in the sentences below. Note how the passive voice changes tenses as readily as the active voice. Note that in most of the sentences the active voice is more direct and succinct than the passive voice.

PASSIVE	ACTIVE
You are requested by Mr. Jones to deliver this box.	Mr. Jones requests you to deliver this box.
He is denied his rights by the new law.	The new law denies him his rights.
I was seen by several witnesses.	Several witnesses saw me.
You were detained by the police.	The police detained you.
I will be followed by many people.	Many people will follow me.
You will be greeted by the Queen.	The Queen will greet you.

SELF-QUIZ 2

Rewrite the following sentences to change them from passive voice to active voice. Do not change the tense or the meaning. (You may have to add a subject in some cases.)

1. We are cautioned not to go.

_____

2. You are expected to attend the party.

_____

3. They were invited to the Anniversary Ball by the President.

_____

4. We were carried to the ambulance by the medics.

_____

5. She was informed of the accident.

_____

6. The actor was given a standing ovation.

_____

7. The diplomat will be kept under observation by a battery of spies.

_____

8. My uncle was kept prisoner by a tribe of pygmies.

_____

9. Many of them were sent "greetings" from the government.

_____

10. His girlfriend was seen by a psychiatrist.

_____

The Emphatic "Do"

The irregular verb *do* is used in many situations, and its usual use needs no special consideration. Some of its usual uses are shown in the following statements: I did the work. You have done a good job. He will do very well. They have been doing this job for many years. He had done that work long before his son was born.

The verb *do* is also used as an auxiliary with verbs in the present and past tense to emphasize the ideas contained in these verbs.

PRESENT	PAST
I do believe you.	I did believe you.
You do make her laugh.	You did make her laugh.
The mule does show promise.	The mule did show promise.
We do follow the rules.	We did follow the rules.
You do avoid the issues.	You did avoid the issues.
They do disobey the law.	They did disobey the law.

Change the following sentences to make them emphatic. Don't change the tense.

1. We appreciate your work.

   _____

2. They needed the money.

   _____

3. He helps.

   _____

4. The Senate appropriated the money.

   _____

5. His team won the game.

   _____

ı.ıl.ıl.ıl.ıl.ıl.ıl.ıl.ıl.ıl.ıl.ıl.ıl.ıl.ıl.ıl.ıl.ıl.ıl.ıl.ıl.ıl.ıl.-

The Subjunctive

The verbs *were* and *be* are sometimes used in the subjunctive mode. You should be acquainted with these forms.

The subjunctive "were"

Were is used as a subjunctive primarily to express wishes or hopes and to make statements contrary to fact when the writer knows that they are contrary to fact.

WISHES

> I wish you were here now.
> I wish there were some other way of doing the job.

STATEMENTS CONTRARY TO FACT

These statements are usually expressed in a subordinate clause introduced by *if*.

> If I were king, you would be my queen.
> If the general were here, he would signal a retreat.
> If she were you, she would have committed suicide.

The subjunctive "be"

Be is sometimes used as a subjunctive when one wishes to express a command or a desire. It is usually found in subordinate clauses introduced by *that*.

> He stipulated that all firearms be registered.
> They asked that the buildings be torn down.

It is the President's wish that Sergeant Tawny be given the Medal of Honor.

TROUBLE-SHOOTING IN THE TIME MACHINE

In this section we will examine some of the problems that students often have with tenses when they write.

Problem 1: You may forget to write the *ed* endings which signal the past tense because they are scarcely heard in spoken language. (Try saying *walked, talked, searched*.) This is a serious error in writing because you are not making a clear distinction between your past and present tenses.

Solution: Become aware of what tenses you are using when you write. Remember that the past tense of all regular verbs (and the majority of verbs are regular) ends in *d* or *ed*.

Problem 2: You do not know the principal parts of the irregular verbs.

Solution: Quiz yourself on the list of irregular verbs. Cover all but the first column and write the past and participle forms on a sheet of paper. Don't stop working at it until you achieve between 90 and 100 percent correct. Since you will forget some of them, get in the habit of checking this list or a dictionary when you are unsure.

Problem 3: You may misspell the verb forms.

Solution: Pay attention to the spelling rules that apply when adding *ed* or *ing*, such as doubling of consonant (*tag—tagged, swat—swatted, begin—beginning*) or changing *y* to *i* (*hurry—hurried, carry—carried*). If you are unsure, check the dictionary.

Problem 4: You may fail to use auxiliaries when writing the perfect or progressive tenses.

Solution: This can be corrected by adding an auxiliary to the participle to make it a verb, or by leaving the participle alone and adding a new verb.

incorrect: The fat, old chicken dressed and plucked for market.
  (*There is no verb in this sentence. The chicken didn't dress and pluck itself.*)
correct: The fat old chicken was dressed and plucked for market.

incorrect: The boy's jalopy stolen from the used car lot.
correct: The boy's jalopy has been stolen from the used car lot.

Problem 5: You use the participle without an auxiliary: *I sung, We done, She begun, He drunk* instead of *I have (had) sung, We have (had) done, She has (had) begun,* and *He has (had) drunk*.

Solution: This nonstandard pattern may have become a habit. If you wish to change, you have to drill yourself on the perfect participle forms of the irregular verbs until you stop using them without the *have* auxiliaries.

SELF-QUIZ 4

1. _____ verbs are far more numerous than _____

   _____.

2. Once you memorize the list of _____ verbs, you know

   that the rest are _____.

3. The past tense and the past participle of _____ verbs
   end in *ed* or *d*.

4. Some students omit the *ed* endings when they write because they do not

   _____ them.

5. The best cure for misspelling verb forms when you add *ed* or *ing* is to pay

   attention to spelling rules regarding _____ consonants

   and changing _____.

6. Write the *ing* form and the past tense alongside each of the following verbs:

   tag_____

   beg_____

   disturb_____

   call_____

   spot_____

   love_____

   approach_____

   deny_____

   hurry_____

   carry_____

   ferry_____

   vary_____

Correct the following sentences by adding an auxiliary.

7. The large cumbersome package delivered very late.

8. In the morning the pretty girls soaked by the pouring rain.

9. After arriving on the plane from Ethiopia, the envoy tired and disappointed.

10. Some of the brown and white pigeons frightened by the shot.

SELF-QUIZ 5

Correct each of the following incorrect constructions and complete the sentences. (Do not change the form of the verb. Add a suitable auxiliary.)

EXAMPLE: (I eaten) I have eaten there many times.

1. (I sung)_____

2. (He thrown)_____

3. (I swum)_____

4. (They eaten)_____

5. (She begun)_____

6. (I drunk)_____

7. (Sam and Tom taken)_____

Clarifying Some Confusing Verbs

Three pairs of common verbs often cause a great deal of confusion because they are so similar: *rise—raise, sit—set,* and *lie—lay.* Let's try to clarify them. (We will not go into all possible meanings; only the troublesome ones will be dealt with.)[1]

Rise versus Raise

Present	Past	Perfect Participle
rise	rose	risen
raise	raised	raised

Rise is an irregular verb. It usually refers to a steady or customary upward movement. For example: The sun *rises.* The people *rise* to applaud the President. Dust *rises* from the pavement. Fog *rises* from the meadow. Your fever *rose* yesterday. You have *risen* from bed against the doctor's orders. The farmer *rose* at 4 a.m.

Raise is a regular verb. It usually means "to cause to rise, move to a higher level, lift, elevate." For example: The boy *raised* and lowered the flag. The

[1] These verbs are used in so many different ways that it would be worth your while to compare them in a collegiate dictionary.

crocodile *raised* its huge head. (But it *rose* from the mud in one rapid motion.) The crane *raised* the car from the bottom of the river. The girl *raised* her hand. Senator Crabbe *raised* many objections.

Sit *versus* Set

Present	Past	Perfect Participle
sit	sat	sat
set	set	set

Sit is an irregular verb usually meaning to be seated or come to a resting position: Our cat *sits* on the fence. The judge *has been sitting* in his chambers for a long time. Let's *sit* down and talk.

Set usually means to put or place: I *set* the table. I *set* the hot pot on the cot. He *sets* the tomato plants in long, even rows.

Lie *versus* Lay

Present	Past	Perfect Participle	
lie, lying	I lied	I have lied	(to tell a falsehood)
lie, lying	I lay	He has lain	(to recline)
lay, laying	I laid	We have laid	(to put, place, arrange, etc.)[1]

EXAMPLES

After laying down his weapon, the soldier lay down to sleep.
He was lying there when the moose lay down beside him.
We lied to each other.
Will you lie down and rest?
They have lain in bed all day.
Who laid out my clothing?

If you continue to have difficulty with the proper use of these verbs, always check yourself, using this book or a dictionary. When you cannot do so (during an exam, for example) it might be advisable to substitute a synonym that you are sure of.

TEST 7

Write a sentence using each of the following words correctly. You may use any tense.

1. rise _____

2. sit _____

3. set _____

[1] For other meanings (including slang) see Webster's *New World Dictionary,* second college edition.

4. lie (recline) _____

5. lay (put)_____

6. lie (tell a falsehood)_____

7. raise_____

*Ing*ed Verbs Revisited

In Chapter 2 you learned that *ing*ed verbs are "frozen" unless auxiliaries are added to them. Unless an *ing*ed verb is activated by adding an auxiliary or unless another verb is added to make a sentence, you have written a fragment.

incorrect:	The rugged sailor sailing far out to sea.
corrected by adding auxiliary:	The rugged sailor is sailing far out to sea.
corrected by adding new verb:	The rugged sailor, sailing far out to sea, is slightly intoxicated.
incorrect:	The two lovers roaming through the wooded back acres of the farm.
corrected by adding auxiliary:	The two lovers were roaming through the wooded back acres of the farm.
corrected by adding new verb:	The two lovers, roaming through the wooded back acres of the farm, were secretly married yesterday.

Switched Verbs Revisited

Like *ing*ed verbs, perfect participles are "frozen" when they are used without auxiliaries. Unless the participle is activated by adding *have, has,* or *had,* or another verb is added to make a sentence, you are writing a fragment.

incorrect:	The sensitive young doctor disturbed by the rumors.
corrected by adding auxiliary:	The sensitive young doctor was disturbed by the rumors.
corrected by adding new verb:	The sensitive young doctor, disturbed by the rumors, left town.
incorrect:	During the game the children frozen by the icy blasts.
corrected by adding auxiliary:	During the game the children were frozen by the icy blasts.

corrected by add-
ing new verb: During the game the <u>children,</u> frozen by the icy
blasts, <u>huddled</u> together.

TEST 8

Complete the sentences below and punctuate correctly.

EXAMPLE: The twelve angry senators on the agricultural committee,
worrying and fretting, *decided to investigate the danger of crop dusting.*

1. In spite of the rain, large beetle-like insects covered with mud _____

   _____

2. Nearly every varsity member of the girls' swimming team tired but vic-

   torious _____

3. The sinking freighter in the Gulf of Mexico almost completely destroyed

   by fire _____

4. The new sociology professor frightened by the noisy class _____

5. Before the night baseball game, the wind sweeping across the field _____

   _____

6. The mysterious and legendary creature known as the Loch Ness monster

   _____

7. In planning to descend into the angry volcano, the men, fully realizing the

   danger _____

8. The fraternity men and women excited about the possibility of having an

   open door policy in the women's dormitories _____

9. The kindly benefactor of the county orphanage seen only occasionally by

   the children _____

10. The little girl unable to swim _____

TEST 9

Part A: Write sentences using the verbs below in the tenses indicated.

1. run (*past*)

   _____

2. go (*present*)

   _____

3. sail (*past perfect*)

_____

4. begin (*past*)

_____

5. think (*present progressive*)

_____

6. do (*future*)

_____

7. deny (*past progressive*)

_____

8. deliver (*present perfect*)

_____

9. bring (*future*)

_____

10. learn (*past progressive*)

_____

11. give (*future*)

_____

12. fish (*present progressive*)

_____

13. admit (*past perfect*)

_____

14. burst (*past*)

_____

15. kidnap (*future perfect*)

_____

16. speak (*present*)

_____

17. saw (*past perfect*)

_____

18. take (*present*)

_____

19. work (*future perfect*)

_____

20. cry (*past perfect*)

Part B: Using whichever tense you prefer, write a ten-sentence paragraph in which you maintain that tense throughout. Underline your verbs.

USING THE TIME MACHINE

In the first section of this chapter we were largely concerned with the mechanism of the time machine. You learned the parts and how to use them. That took you a long way toward mastering the machine. In this section we will, of course, continue to be concerned about the mechanics, but we will focus primarily on using the time signals logically and consistently.

Whenever you write a sentence, you are dealing with at least one time period. In many sentences you work with more than one period, and in paragraphs and themes you may find it necessary to switch back and forth between time periods.

Tense Shifts in Sentences

The Past and Perfect Tenses. When dealing with time changes from past to present, one does not often run into difficulty. For example, one readily says, "I went to the dentist yesterday, and I am going there again today," or "I played chess last week, and I am playing again tonight." But when students are dealing with the past tense, and the logic of their statements goes back one time period further, they often forget to use the past perfect tense.

incorrect: After I visited India, I went to Japan.
correct: After I had visited India, I went to Japan.
(The visit to India was in an earlier time period than the trip to Japan.)

A Series of Tenses. Consistency, as stated above, is an important part of tense writing. One should establish a particular tense and maintain it unless there is a good reason for changing it. When writing about a series of actions which happen at the same time, there is no reason to change the tense.

incorrect: She starts to scream at me, she throws pots and pans and dishes at me, and then she changed her mind and kissed me.
correct: She started to scream at me, she threw pots and pans and dishes at me, and then she changed her mind and kissed me.
(*or*)
She starts to scream at me, she throws pots and pans and dishes at me, and then she changes her mind and kisses me.

Uses of the Present Tense

There are four special variations in the use of the present tense.

1. Universal Present Tense. If a statement was true at a particular time in the past and continues to be true today, we often write that statement in the present tense (called the universal present) even though a past tense may introduce it.

incorrect: The learned astronomer proved that the earth revolved around the sun.

correct: The learned astronomer proved that the earth *revolves* around the sun.

2. Habitual Present.

The habitual present indicates a continuing ability.

The car *runs* well.
He *learns* rapidly.
They *play* regularly.

3. Historic Present.

In order to describe a past action more vividly, a writer sometimes uses the present tense. When he does this he makes clear to the reader what he is doing by paragraphing the section separately.

The queen *descends*, trembling, from the throne. Her usually impenetrable eyes *show* the faintest signs of inward terror. "I love you, Essex," she *says*, "but your head must be removed."

4. Present "Future."

Sometimes the present and present progressive tenses are used to express future action. Note that in these situations the time word is very close.

We *leave* tomorrow.
The judge *arrives* on Sunday.
The people *vote* next week.
We *are leaving* tomorrow
The judge *is arriving* on Sunday.
The people *are voting* next week.

SELF-QUIZ 6

1. An important part of tense writing is to maintain _____.
2. When one is writing of a series of actions that happen at the same time,

   there is no reason to change the _____ of the verbs.

3. The three basic tenses are _____

   _____

4. What are the four variations in the use of the present tense? _____

   _____

5. When something that occurred in the past is described in the present tense,

   the tense is called the _____.

6. The statement, "He speaks well," is an example of the _____ present tense.

7. "My aunt leaves tomorrow," is an example of the present _____.

8. If a statement was true in the past and continues to be true today we often

write the statement in the _____.

SELF-QUIZ 7

Make whatever corrections are necessary. Do not change the meaning of any sentence.

1. Paul ate his supper and is soon asleep.
2. The thieves break into the bank, steal the money, and made a complete getaway.
3. Before he came to this country, he made his fortune in France.
4. No one was told that he arrived in Portugal the day before.
5. The teacher told them that H_2O was the formula for water.
6. Marvin dives into the lake, swims to the terrified child, grabs her under the chin, and towed her to shore.
7. Columbus helped prove that the earth was round.
8. The doctor decided to operate after he definitely diagnosed appendicitis.
9. They bathed and dressed in clean clothes before they get in the car and drive away.
10. Benjamin Franklin discovered that lightning discharged electricity.

Tense Shifts in Paragraphs

By now you probably realize how important time is in your paragraphs and how many words and phrases are affected by the time signal system. Paragraphs, of course, show this much more clearly than individual sentences. Four brief rules should help you keep your time mechanism in good working order.

1. Set your time clearly.
2. Do not change the time without good reason.
3. Keep your tenses consistent within each time period.
4. When you change the time, be sure that your change is clear.

The following paragraphs are marked to indicate each time change. Study them carefully so that you can mark other paragraphs in similar fashion.

1. This paragraph shifts tenses back and forth easily and clearly.

The teenagers who <u>dominated</u> a large part of the American scene in the 1960's <u>have grown</u> up. As young adults they <u>will have</u> a significant influence on the nation's economy	PAST PRESENT PERFECT FUTURE

in the 1970's. There are 25 million young   PRESENT
adults (20–29) in the U.S. today. By 1980
they will total about 40 million. Economists   FUTURE
now predict that the loud squawling of babies,   PRESENT
crying for bottles and balloons, will soon   FUTURE
smother the demand for Beatle-type bands.

2. When you write biographical material such as you find in the following paragraph, it is fairly easy to control your time system so that it moves logically from past to present or present to past.

When I was a child, my paternal   PAST
grandfather sometimes beat me with the
hockey stick with which he had won the
International Hockey Championship in 1882.
He had started life as a chicken farmer in
northwestern Vermont, but the chicken
ague, a disease spread by certain careless
Eastern chickens, had killed off several   PAST PERFECT
consecutive flocks. He had grown so sick of
living on hard-boiled, scrambled, and poached
eggs that he had left his wife and seventeen
remaining chickens and had set out to make
his living as a professional hockey player.
Aside from those beatings, my grandfather
was usually kind and good to me, and when
it came time to send me off to a city high
school, he pawned all of his hockey medals to   PAST
help pay the way. Grandpa died in 1942. I
have since tried to attend hockey games out   PRESENT PERFECT
of respect for the old fellow, but whenever a
player swings a stick I seem to feel it in my   PRESENT
nether parts. I have never found out what   PRESENT PERFECT
happened to my grandmother and her   PAST
seventeen chickens.

3. In writing a book report or discussing a historical document, you often have to handle multiple time periods. This calls for carefully working out the tenses in each time period. For example, in the following student's report on an essay about Frederick Douglass by Kelly Miller, there are three time periods: the student is writing in one time period; the author of the essay writes in a second period; the subject (Douglass) lived and wrote in a third. Within each period, every variety of tenses can be used, provided you keep control over your three frames of reference. For clarity, we will show the three time levels thus:

Student's by double underlining
Author's by broken underlining
Douglass' by wavy underlining

When I recently read "Frederick Douglass," an essay written by Kelly Miller, a Black mathematician and sociologist, I learned something very important about liberty. Douglass began his life as a slave. "Like Melchizedek of old," says Miller, "it is said of him that he sprang into existence without father or mother or beginning of days . . . We are told that he vied with the dogs for the crumbs that fell from his master's table. He tasted the sting of a cruel slavery and drank the cup to its very dregs. And yet he arose from this lowly and degraded estate and gained for himself a place among the illustrious names of his country." At a later point in his essay, Miller tells an ancedote about how Douglass was asked by a railroad conductor to move from a first class coach to a Jim Crow coach. When asked about how he felt, Douglass replied, "I feel as if I had been kicked by an ass." Douglass' love for liberty, says Miller, "included the whole world—black men, white men, Americans, Europeans, Asiatics, . . . liberty for the wise, liberty for the simple; liberty for the weak, liberty for the strong; liberty for all the sons and daughters of men." Douglass died in 1895. Miller wrote the article in 1908. Since that time there have been two world wars and a number of smaller wars. In most of them the question of liberty for one side or the other seems to have been one of the dominant issues. Perhaps the world will someday learn from Douglass and men like him that liberty is indivisible. It belongs to all men or to no men.

Student's PAST

Author's HISTORIC PRESENT

PAST

Student's PRESENT and PAST

Douglass' PRESENT and PAST PERFECT PRESENT, PAST

Student's PAST

PRESENT PERFECT

PRESENT
FUTURE

HISTORIC PRESENT

SELF-QUIZ 8

Analyze the time systems of the following paragraphs. Underline verbs and label the tenses. Check each one before going on to the next.

1. My sister was about ten and I nearly six when she brought home her first toad. She had found the toad on the sand near a pond that ran behind the school. The toad was a very quiet fellow who looked a little like some pictures I had seen of Winston Churchill—puffy-jowelled, plump-bellied. He was quite dry, not slippery like a frog, and when you looked close you could see

the many subtle colors that helped him blend with rocks and sand and leaves and twigs. He allowed us to pick him up, and he would hop about in the palms of our hands, wetting us only occasionally. Our friends and even some older relatives and teachers said that we would get warts, but we never did. Even today I find people who shudder when I mention toads, but I think that they are quite beautiful.

2. Air travel has come a long way from Kitty Hawk. One of the newer jet airliners seats about 500 people and is divided into six sections. Seating is arranged so that movies can be shown in each section, and each is decorated in different color combinations. There are three galleys, 14 lavatories, and closet space for clothing and handbags is available in the giant ship. In the first class section there is a spiral staircase that leads to a lounge on the flight deck. The Wright brothers' plane did not fly more than the length of a football field. Now people are flying in planes that are almost that long.

3. When I was twelve my family moved to Calcutta. My father was an officer of some kind in the American embassy there, and he spent a great deal of time at official meetings and banquets. My brother and I went to a British school. We had some troubles because of our "odd" American accents, and because we didn't always act superior to the "wogs." "Wogs" was the derogatory term used by some of the British to describe the Indians. The British youngsters sometimes called us "Yanks" in a friendly way, but more often to set us apart from them. When I was 15 we moved to Korea, and there we found some Americans who called Koreans "gooks." We couldn't understand this sort of thing until we came back to America a few years later and found that some Americans call others "kikes" and "wops" and "sheenies" and "niggers" and "pigs" and "honkies." It seems to be a way of dehumanizing others so that we can ignore their problems or make fun of them or hate them. Maybe that old saying

ought to be changed to "Sticks and stones can break your bones, but names can sometimes kill you."

.,.ll.,ll.,l,,ll.,ll.,ll.,ll.,ll.,ll.,ll.,ll.,ll.,ll.,ll.,ll.,ll.,ll.,ll.,ll.,ll.,ll.,ll.

4. The child who brings an apple to the teacher will be out of date soon. Instead, "an oil can for the teacher" will become the new byword in American education. This will happen because a large corporation is distributing a "talking" typewriter to help teach reading to students with severe reading problems. Children now testing these machines work in soundproof booths with typewriters that have colored as well as lettered keys. The child follows the directions given by a recorded voice that emanates from a loudspeaker in the booth. In a typical lesson the picture of a dog flashes on a small screen in front of the child and a voice says, "This is a dog. Type the word *dog*." Then a pointer points to the letters *d*, *o*, and *g* on the screen. The typewriter is so programmed that only the correct keys will operate and only in the correct order. Teachers monitor the system by looking into the booths through one-way windows and speaking to a child by telephone when necessary. The children work with the machines for only about 15 minutes a day. They spend the balance of their time with live teachers who prepare them for their next automated lesson. The company claims that the machine has helped children who had not previously been aided by the more usual teaching methods.

.ll.,ll.,l,,ll.,ll.,ll.,ll.,ll.,ll.,ll.,ll.,ll.,ll.,ll.,ll.,ll.,ll.,ll.,ll.,ll.,ll.-

5. Good mystery thrillers that really send shivers up the spine are hard to find. One of the best tests of a good thriller is to read it to a group of nine-year-olds around a campfire. They are among the best audiences one can find. I tried an old "chiller" during a recent camping trip and can report excellent results. "The Monkey's Paw" by W. W. Jacobs tells the story of Mr. and Mrs. White and their son Herbert who live in a somewhat isolated house somewhere in nineteenth century England. The Whites are visited by an old friend who has

recently returned from military service in India.
The friend has a monkey's paw which has the power
to grant the owner three wishes. The soldier
warns the old couple that the paw has been bad
luck to all of its owners, but when they insist on having
it, he finally sells it to them. They make their three
wishes, each with ironic-tragic results. The first wish
brings a sum of money but only as a result of Herbert
dying a horrible death. They make a second wish in
an attempt to counteract the results of the first
wish, and the last wish averts what could have been
an even worse tragedy. The story is realistic enough
to be eerie and spine-tingling, and supernatural
enough to make one wonder about the unknown
forces in the universe. It kept the boys in rapt
attention and stirred heated discussion about
what would have happened if the third wish had
not been made.

FINAL TEST

This is to see how well you can put together all you have learned about time and tense. Select any two of the following assignments and write a paragraph as directed. You may use reference books in preparing your topics.

1. Describe an activity that occurred in the recent past and compare it with something that occurred in the more distant past. For example, you might compare two ball games, two picnics, two Christmas or birthday celebrations, or family visits.

2. Tell about a historical event. Compare it with a similar but more recent occurrence.

3. Discuss the development of an invention such as the telephone or the light bulb. Compare it with the development of the computer or one of the moon rockets.

4. Tell about the experiences of three generations of a family (yours or someone else's). Start with the present, work back to the past and past perfect, and return to the present. (Be sure to have a good reason for every change of tense.)

what you have learned in chapter 9

Chapter 9 has focused on *tense* and *time words* and how to handle *regular* and *irregular verbs* in the various tenses. It has helped you form all tenses from the three principal parts of any verb. It has reviewed "switched" verbs and *ing*ed verbs, and discussed various special problems related to tense. It has also demonstrated the tense shifts in sentences and in paragraphs.

Remember that when you write, you must clearly establish the time for your reader and handle your tenses consistently so as not to confuse him. Never shift your tenses without good reason.

ı.ıı

KEY 1

(1) You should have used "time signals" like the examples in paragraph 1 of this chapter. (2) Verbs (3) Verbs, time, number, person (4) present, past, future (5) be, have (6) will (7) ing (8) present (9) present perfect progressive (10) future perfect progressive (11) past perfect (12) past perfect progressive (13) present progressive (14) future perfect (15) future (16) past

KEY 2

(1) They caution us not to go. (2) They expect you to attend the party. (3) The President invited them to the Anniversary Ball. (4) The medics carried us to the ambulance. (5) The police informed her of the accident. (6) The audience gave the actor a standing ovation. (7) A battery of spies will keep the diplomat under observation. (8) A tribe of pygmies kept my uncle prisoner. (9) The government sent "greetings" to many of them. (10) A psychiatrist saw his girlfriend.

KEY 3

(1) We do appreciate your work. (2) They did need the money. (3) He does help. (4) The Senate did appropriate the money. (5) His team did win the game.

KEY 4

(1) regular, irregular verbs (2) irregular, regular (3) regular (4) hear (5) doubling, *y* to *i* (6) tagging, tagged; begging, begged; disturbing, disturbed; calling, called; spotting, spotted, loving, loved; approaching, approached; denying, denied; hurrying, hurried; carrying, carried; ferrying, ferried; varying, varied (7) was (8) were (9) was (10) were (Other forms of *be* may also be correct for 7–10. If in doubt, check with your instructor.)

KEY 5

(1) have, had (2) has, had (3) have, had (4) have, had (5) has, had (6) have, had (7) have, had.

KEY 6

(1) consistency (2) tense (3) present, past, future (4) universal, historic, habitual, future (5) historic present (6) habitual (7) future (8) universal present

KEY 7

1. Paul *ate* his supper and *was* soon asleep. (Paul eats . . . is)
2. The thieves *break* into the bank, *steal* the money, and *make* a complete getaway. (The thieves *broke* . . . *stole* . . . *made*)
3. Before he came to this country, he *had made* his fortune in France.

4. No one was told that he *had arrived* in Portugal the day before.
5. The teacher told them that H_2O *is* the formula for water.
6. Marvin *dived* (*dove*) into the lake, *swam* to the terrified child, *grabbed* her under the chin, and *towed* her to shore. (Marvin *dives . . . swims . . . grabs . . . tows*)
7. Columbus helped prove that the earth *is* round.
8. The doctor decided to operate after he *had* definitely *diagnosed* appendicitis.
9. They *had bathed* and *dressed* in clean clothes before they *got* in the car and *drove* away.
10. Benjamin Franklin discovered that lighting *discharges* electricity.

KEY 8

1. My sister was about ten and I nearly six
when she brought home her first toad. She
had found the toad on the sand near a pond that
ran behind the school. The toad was a very quiet
fellow who looked a little like some pictures I
had seen of Winston Churchill—puffy-jowelled,

PAST
and
PAST PERFECT

plump-bellied. He was quite dry, not slippery like
a frog, and when you looked close you could see
the many subtle colors that helped him blend with
rocks and sand and leaves and twigs. He allowed
us to pick him up, and he would hop about in the
palms of our hands, wetting us only occasionally.
Our friends and even some older relatives and
teachers said that we would get warts, but we

PAST

never did. Even today I find people who shudder
when I mention toads, but I think that they are
quite beautiful.

PRESENT

2. Air travel has come a long way from Kitty

PRESENT PERFECT

Hawk. One of the newer jet airliners seats
about 500 people and is divided into six sections.
Seating is arranged so that movies can be shown
in each section, and each is decorated in different
color combinations. There are three galleys,
14 lavatories, and closet space for clothing and
handbags is available in the giant ship.
In the first class section there is a spiral
staircase that leads to a lounge on the flight

PRESENT

deck. The Wright brothers' plane did not fly

PAST

more than the length of a football field. Now
people are flying in planes that are almost that
long.

PRESENT PROG.
PRESENT

3. When I was twelve my family moved to
Calcutta. My father was an officer of some
kind in the American embassy there, and he

PAST

spent a great deal of time at official meetings and banquets. My brother and I went to a British school. We had some troubles because of our "odd" American accents, and because we didn't always act superior to the "wogs." "Wogs" was the derogatory term used by some of the British to describe the Indians. The British youngsters sometimes called us "Yanks" in a friendly way, but more often to set us apart from them. When I was 15 we moved to Korea, and there we found some Americans who called Koreans "gooks." We couldn't understand this sort of thing until we came back to America a few years later and found that some Americans call others "kikes" and "wops" and "sheenies" and "niggers" and "pigs" and "honkies." *PAST*

It seems to be a way of dehumanizing others so that we can ignore their problems or make fun of them or hate them. Maybe that old saying ought to be changed to "Sticks and stones can break your bones, but names can sometimes kill you." *PRESENT*

4. The child who brings an apple to the teacher will be out of date soon. Instead, "an oil can for the teacher" will become the new byword in American education. This will happen because a large corporation is distributing a "talking" typewriter to help teach reading to students with severe reading problems. *PRESENT / FUTURE / PRESENT PROG.*

Children now testing these machines work in soundproof booths with typewriters that have colored as well as lettered keys. The child follows the directions given by a recorded voice that emanates from a loudspeaker in the booth. In a typical lesson the picture of a dog flashes on a small screen in front of the child and a voice says, "This is a dog. Type the word *dog*." Then a pointer points to the letters *d, o,* and *g* on the screen. The typewriter is so programmed that only the correct keys will operate and only in the correct order. *PRESENT / FUTURE*

Teachers monitor the system by looking into the booths through one-way windows and speaking to a child by telephone when necessary. The children work with the machines for only about 15 minutes a day. They spend the balance of their time with *PRESENT*

live teachers who <u>prepare</u> them for their next
automated lesson. The company <u>claims</u> that the
machine <u>has helped</u> children who
<u>had</u> not previously <u>been aided</u> by the
more usual teaching methods.

} PRESENT

PRESENT PERFECT
PAST PERFECT

5. Good mystery thrillers that really <u>send</u>
shivers up the spine <u>are</u> hard to find. One
of the best tests of a good thriller <u>is</u> to
read it to a group of nine-year-olds around a
campfire. They <u>are</u> among the best audiences one
can <u>find</u>. I <u>tried</u> an old "chiller" during a
recent camping trip and <u>can report</u> excellent
results.

STORYTELLER'S
PRESENT and
PAST

"The Monkey's Paw" by W. W. Jacobs <u>tells</u>
the story of Mr. and Mrs. White and their son
Herbert who <u>live</u> in a somewhat isolated house
somewhere in nineteenth century England. The
Whites <u>are visited</u> by an old friend who <u>has</u>
recently <u>returned</u> from military service in India.
The friend <u>has</u> a monkey's paw which <u>has</u> the power
to grant the owner three wishes. The soldier
<u>warns</u> the old couple that the paw <u>has been</u> bad
luck to all of its owners, but when they <u>insist</u> on having
it, he finally <u>sells</u> it to them. They <u>make</u> their three
wishes, each with ironic-tragic results. The first wish
<u>brings</u> a sum of money but only as a result of Herbert
dying a horrible death. They <u>make</u> a second wish in
an attempt to counteract the results of the first
wish, and the last wish <u>averts</u> what <u>could have been</u>
an even worse tragedy.

STORY'S
PRESENT and
PRESENT PERFECT

The story <u>is</u> realistic enough
to be eerie and spine-tingling, and supernatural
enough to make one wonder about the unknown
forces in the universe.

STORYTELLER'S
PRESENT

It <u>kept</u> the boys in rapt
attention and <u>stirred</u> heated discussion about
what <u>would have happened</u> if the third wish <u>had</u>
not <u>been made</u>.

} PAST and
PAST PERFECT

Note: If you labeled the tenses right but used terms other than "Storyteller,"
consider yourself correct.

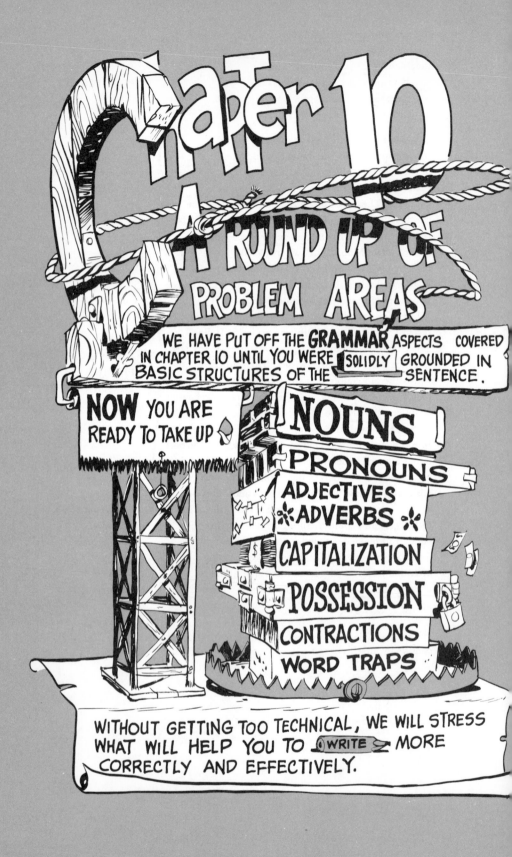

A roundup of
PROBLEM AREAS

You have learned the fundamentals of sentence construction by studying three parts of the sentence: subjects, verbs, and conjunctions. You have learned to polish the "interiors" of sentences by working with agreement of subject and verb (where you also became acquainted with prepositions), and by studying the time system. You have learned how to guide the flow of ideas with punctuation.

In this chapter we will complete the polishing process by working on certain areas which create problems for many students. These include pronouns, adjectives and adverbs, capitalization, possession, contraction, and a list of word "traps." Some of this material is already familiar to you and only requires review.

NOUNS

We have studied nouns as subjects of sentences and clauses, as objects of prepositions, and in their singular and plural forms. In this section we will examine them in relation to pronouns and adjectives. Below is a brief review of noun characteristics to help you identify them.

1. Nouns can be described by adjectives: a yellow *submarine*, the golden *rule*, the great, white *hope*, the straight and narrow *path*.

2. Most nouns can be numbered, that is, they can be singular or plural: *car, cars; pickle, pickles; nationality, nationalities*.

3. Nouns have gender. Some are masculine or feminine: *man, woman; boy, girl; hero, heroine; aviator, aviatrix; actor, actress; bull, heifer; rooster, hen*. The vast majority of English nouns are neuter: *house, song, beast, beauty*. Sometimes we use the feminine gender for inanimate things: She's quite a *ship*. She's a grand old *flag*.

4. Most nouns can show possession, and that which is possessed is also a noun: *dog's bone, aunt's gift, children's toys, man's fate, Henry's talent, life's disappointments*.

As you learned earlier in this book, words are verbs only if they function as verbs in sentences. So, too, a word is a noun only if it functions as a noun. The examples below will give you an idea of how the same word can be employed as a verb (underlined twice), an adjective (italics), or a noun (boldface).

1. They tried to <u>upright</u> the overturned car. He bought an *upright* piano. It is one of the best **uprights** on the market.

2. The sun <u>yellowed</u> the white curtains. The *yellow* color is fading. I wonder where the **yellow** went.

3. I <u>hope</u> we make it on time. That is her *hope* chest. My one **hope** is that she remain.

SELF-QUIZ 1

Underline the nouns in the following sentences.

1. She trained the dog to stay away from the train.

2. His face purpled with anger when he saw his son's purple shirt. The purple in his father's face frightened the boy.

3. The cow was cowed by the cowbell.

4. The photographer developed the pictures with the new developing fluid while we awaited developments.

5. That farm was farmed by a different farmer.

PRONOUNS

Pronouns are words that substitute for nouns. Without pronouns writing is repetitious and longwinded. For example:

"Lieutenant Berg and the Commander are going through!" The Commander's voice was like thin ice breaking. The Commander wore his full-dress uniform with the heavily braided white cap pulled down rakishly over one cold gray eye. "The Commander and Lieutenant Berg can't make it, sir. The weather is spoiling for a hurricane, if the Commander asks Lieutenant Berg." "The Commander is not asking Lieutenant Berg, Lieutenant Berg," said the Commander." "Throw on the power lights. Rev the ship up to 8,500. The Commander and Lieutenant Berg are going through!"

The same paragraph with pronouns:

"*We*'re going through!" The Commander's voice was like thin ice breaking. *He* wore his full-dress uniform with the heavily braided white cap pulled down rakishly over one cold gray eye. "*We* can't make *it*, sir. *It*'s spoiling for a hurricane, if *you* ask *me*." "*I*'m not asking *you*, Lieutenant Berg," said the Commander. "Throw on the power lights! Rev *her* up to 8,500! *We*'re going through." [From "The Secret Life of Walter Mitty" by James Thurber]

Agreement of Pronoun with its Antecedent

Pronouns must agree with their antecedents (the nouns for which they are substituting) in number, gender, and person.

NUMBER: *If the antecedent is plural, the pronoun must be plural:*

The cars were badly rusted. They had to be junked.

If the antecedent is singular, the pronoun must be singular:

The girl was so beautiful that she made the old men gasp.

Remember that the following words are considered singular and require singular pronouns: *anyone, everyone, everybody, anybody, many a, either.*

When it started to rain, almost everyone in the park donned his raincoat.

The relative pronouns *who, which,* and *that* do not change to indicate number, so it is always necessary to refer back to their antecedents to make the verbs and other pronouns agree with the antecedents. In sentences containing more than one antecedent, care must be taken to assure that each pronoun agrees with the right antecedent.

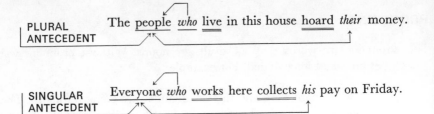

PLURAL
ANTECEDENT — The people *who* live in this house hoard *their* money.

SINGULAR
ANTECEDENT — Everyone *who* works here collects *his* pay on Friday.

Pronouns for Collective Nouns

When using a collective noun (*team, orchestra, crowd*), differentiate between referring to the group as a unit (singular) and referring to individuals in the group (plural).

> The *band* traveled to *its* destination.
> (*Band* is considered a single unit here; therefore the singular pronoun *its* is used.)

> The *band* tuned *their* instruments one at a time.
> (Here we refer to the various members of the band; therefore the plural pronoun *their* is used.)

To simplify the singular-plural problem when using collective nouns, use the word *members* when you intend that meaning.

> The club *members* were all proud of *their* donation to charity.
> *Members* of the P.T.A. raised *their* voices to ask a wide range of questions.

GENDER: Most students handle *he, she,* and *it* without trouble. They should remember, however, that the language is still slanted toward the male animal, and when they write about the human race as a whole, they must usually use the masculine gender.

> Man has a long history of conflict. *His* history is a chronicle of wars and conquests. From the time of the caveman, *he* has sought to conquer much more often than *he* has sought to compromise.

SELF-QUIZ 2

Fill in the blanks.

1. Pronouns are_____for nouns.

2. Pronouns must agree with their antecedents in_____,_____,

   and_____.
3. The noun to which the pronoun refers is called the_____.

4. Number refers to_____and_____.

5. If the_____is plural, the pronoun must be_____.

If the_____is_____the_____
must be singular.

6. The three relative pronouns are:_____.

7. Give three examples of a collective noun. _____

8. List the three kinds of gender. _____

9. _____pronouns do not indicate_____, so it

is necessary to refer back to their_____to make the

_____and other pronouns agree with the antecedent.

Underline the correct word in the parentheses.

10. Everyone in the room kept (his, their) hat on.
11. Has anyone here brought (his, their) car?
12. Either of the plans has (its, their) advantages.
13. They went to many a picnic; (each, all) was successful.
14. Everybody brought (her, their) husband.
15. Everyone who (come, comes) with us must guard (his, their) belongings carefully.
16. The trunks in the garage that (was, were) burned down (are, is) being delivered right now. (It, They) are in good condition.
17. The people who (know, knows) the answers to the questions in this letter (is, are) on vacation. (They, It) will be left with (their, his, its) secretary.
18. Everybody who (bring, brings) (her, their) husband gets a prize. (She, They) will also be given a free dinner.
19. The first group which (arrive, arrives) at the airport (is, are) greeted by a special committee. (It, They) (is, are) given the city's "super" welcome.
20. Members of the committee are working at (their, his) own homes. (They, It) will meet together on Monday. The committee is expected to make (its, their) report by Monday night.

Problems with Pronoun Reference

If there are several nouns before you get to the pronoun, you must make absolutely clear which noun you are referring to. Note the confusion as to which antecedent was intended in the following sentence taken from a student's paper:

My father and mother didn't want us to see the movies because *they* were too sexy and full of obscene ideas.

Either of the statements below can be correct, but the first one is probably what the student intended to say. Both statements, however, can now be clearly understood.

My father and mother didn't want us to see the movies because the movies were too sexy and full of obscene ideas.

(*or*)

My father and mother didn't want us to see the movies because my parents were too sexy and full of obscene ideas.

TEST 1

Edit the following so that the antecedents of all pronouns are clear. Change only the pronouns. You may have to make a choice between two possible meanings. Either can be correct, but the meaning must be *clear*.

EXAMPLE: Tom visited his dead captain's widow, and Ted took his guard duty. This was a nice gesture.
CORRECTED: Tom visited his dead captain's widow, and Ted took Tom's guard duty. The visit was a nice gesture.

1. The boy, the old man, and the dog trudged wearily up the road. They stopped for a while under the shade of a tree to rest and to eat. The boy gave the dog its food and had some too.
2. Frank told Jasper that he had become balder.
3. The child hurled the toy at the flower pot and broke it.
4. Luella told Lucinda that she had given Susie the wrong advice.
5. I hear that you are looking for a piccolo player or trumpeter, male or female. Being both, I am applying for the job.
6. In answer to your letter, I did not come down to the Bureau of Internal Revenue as you requested last week because I was married on the day that I was supposed to see you. I am sorry that I made this mistake.
7. The operation was successful although the surgeon left a sponge in the patient's stomach. This pleased the patient no end.
8. While my uncle and brother-in-law were hunting, he was taken ill.
9. Dr. Jay Tarkinson, the noted geologist, received word that his wife in Paris had sued for divorce shortly before they were caught in an avalanche. He was badly injured. This set the expedition's progress back many months.
10. Some of the ladies at the Congregational Church invited Mrs. Spongle and Mrs. Cuttle to the box lunch picnic. Mrs. Cuttle could not come at all, but Mrs. Spongle managed to get there, although she was a little late. The ladies decided that she was "uppity."

Choosing the Right Pronoun

"Me Tarzan, you Jane," is acceptable only if you are quoting or imitating the ape-man. If you find yourself wondering which is correct: *I* or *me, he* or *him, who* or *whom,* etc., you have a pronoun problem. The cure lies in learning how to use the five types of pronouns: subject, object, possessive, reflexive, and relative.[1]

Study the table below and refer back to it when working with the pages that follow.

Subject	Object	Possessive
I	me	my, mine
you	you	your, yours
he	him	his
she	her	her, hers
it	it	its
we	us	our, ours
you	you	your, yours
they	them	their, theirs
who	whom	whose

Subject Pronouns

The subject pronoun is used when pronouns are subjects of sentences or clauses or are in apposition[2] to the subjects of sentences and clauses. (Three exceptions will be discussed below.) There are simple ways of checking yourself:

Molly, Jerry, and (I—me) go there every day.

It is obvious that the pronoun is part of the subject, so there should be no question about the use of *I* rather than *me*.

Helpful hint: When a series of words which includes a pronoun causes you to question whether to use the subject or object form, read only the pronoun with the rest of the sentence. This helps to make the pronoun's function in the sentence clearer. You would not, for example, say, "Me go there every day," so you would not say, "Molly, Jerry, and me go there every day."

(We—us) students went to see the dean last week.

We is the subject of the sentence, and *students* is in apposition to we. Try the sentence without the word *students*.

who or *whom*
They all know who is here.
I do not care who thinks that I am guilty.
Who asked the question?

You can easily see that every *who* in the three above sentences is the subject of a sentence or a clause. Aside from the *be* and *than* and *as* exceptions explained below, all other sentence patterns call for *whom*.

---

[1] You have already worked with the relative pronouns (*who, which, that*) as subordinate conjunctions which also function as subjects of clauses. The pronoun *who* is included in the table because it has all three forms: subjective, objective, and possessive; *which* and *that* do not.

[2] See page 135.

the *be* exception

It is I.
It is she.
It was they.
It may be he.
It was I who ate the egg roll.
It is she who kissed the milkman.
It will be he who delivers the message.

In all of the above sentences the pronoun follows a form of the verb *be*. And in all of the above sentences the meaning of the pronoun and the subject of the sentence is the same: it—I; I—it; it—she; she—it.

The rule, then, is, when the pronoun follows a *be* verb and its antecedent is in the subjective case, the pronoun must also be in the subjective case.

Helpful hint: Now that you've learned the *be* exception, we suggest that you avoid it. It sounds rather stilted to most people, and with a little thought you can usually substitute some other phrase. You can, for example, say "I am George" or "I am the culprit" instead of "It is I."

the *who* exception

The policeman learned who he was.
The clergyman knows who Smobe is.
Many animals sense who their friends are.

This exception is essentially the same as the *be* exception. *Who*, in each of the above examples, is not the subject of the sentence or the clause, but it is written in the subjective case. The reason for this is that a *be* verb is used and that *who* and the subject are the same person or thing: in the first sentence *who—he*; in the second sentence *who—Smobe*, and in the third sentence *who—friends*.

the *than* and *as* exception

She is smarter than he.   They are wiser than she.
You are almost as beautiful as I.   They are as obnoxious as we.

A strange rule of grammar requires the use of subject pronouns following *than* and *as* in comparisons such as those above. The reasoning is that the verb is understood.

Helpful hint: You can avoid the somewhat formal, stilted effect by adding the "missing" verb. The sentences will be correct and they will also sound better:

She is smarter than he is.
They are wiser than she is.
You are almost as beautiful as I am.
They are as obnoxious as we are.

Possessive Pronouns

The possessive pronoun is used only to show possession, and it creates few, if any, problems.

That is his mother-in-law.   The money is hers.

The yacht is ours and the rowboat is yours.

Theirs is the greater problem; ours is the lesser one.

This turtle was turned on its back.

Her problems are my problems; her joys are also mine.

Object Pronouns

Once you are sure about when to use subject pronouns (bearing in mind the three exceptions and possessive pronouns which cause no difficulty), the rest is easy. All other sentence patterns require the use of object pronouns.

Give the jelly sandwich to him.

The company gave her a paid vacation.

Luella gave me a boiled onion.

The crowd gave them a wonderful reception.

Orchids were delivered to us students.

I do not know whom to blame.

Whom do we want to elect?

The "You" that Means "I"

When you go into a strange place, you often feel that everyone is looking at you. You feel a tingling in your left toe and you break out in a rash behind your right ear. Your tie seems out of kilter, your sleeves seem too long or too short, and you seem to say all the wrong things.

The paragraph above illustrates a common use of *you* instead of *I* that students should avoid. When writing about your own personal feelings or experiences, use the first person pronoun, *I*. When writing about generalizations, it is all right to use the impersonal *you* or *one*. Be consistent in the use of these pronouns, however, and don't use them when you really mean *I*.

incorrect: When *one* goes to his first job interview, *one* may feel tense and unsure of *himself*. To avoid this, *you* should dress carefully for the occasion and plan what *you* will say to the interviewer.

correct: When *you* go to *your* first job interview, *you* may feel tense and unsure of *yourself*. To avoid this, *you* should dress carefully for the occasion and plan what *you* will say to the interviewer.

or

When *one* goes to his first job interview, *one* may feel tense and unsure of *himself*. To avoid this, *one* should dress carefully for the occasion and plan what *he* will say to the interviewer. (It is permissible to alternate *one*'s and *he*'s. *He* can be substituted for all but the first *one* in this paragraph.)

Reflexive Pronouns

The reflexive pronouns are: *myself, yourself, himself, herself, itself, ourselves, yourselves, themselves*. The reflexive pronoun is used when the subject does something to himself.

I cut myself.

They isolated themselves from the crowd.

The reflexive pronoun is also used to emphasize.[1]

The little girl climbed the wall herself!

The Senator himself greeted the Cub Scouts.

The planet itself is in danger.

Avoid overusing the reflexive pronoun. Write "My wife and I went," *not* "My wife and myself went." *Theirselves* and *hisself* are not standard English. Substitute *themselves* and *himself.*

TEST 2

Underline the correct word.

1. Gwendolyn, Rosemarie, and (I, me, us) went to the dance early.
2. The hunters—Jake, Irving, and (I, me)—were caught in a storm.
3. (Who, Whom) said that?
4. (Who, Whom) delivered this package?
5. Our family doctor, the radiologist, and (I, me) agreed that she needed the treatments.
6. It is (they, them).
7. It is (she, her) (who, whom) is responsible for the accident.
8. To (who, whom) did they give the prize?
9. Bunny, Cordell, and (I, me) never got there.
10. They gave (we, us) the wrong address.
11. No one knows (who, whom) (he, they) was.
12. They are smarter than (we, us).
13. The company sent the crate of coconuts to Ed, Egbert, and (I, me).
14. It was (he, him) who caught the eagle.
15. Give the medal to (whoever, whomever) you please.
16. They are no more skillful than (we, us).
17. The ducks know (who, whom) they can trust.
18. It was (they, them) to (who, whom) the tiger was sent.
19. (We, Us) teachers are also evaluated.
20. Steve sent the invitation to his family, his club, and (I, me).
21. The house belongs to (they, them).
22. It is (their, theirs) house.
23. They built it (themselves, theirselves).
24. After seeing what they had accomplished, Frank wanted to build one (itself, himself).
25. When (you, I) meet dignified-looking adults, (I, you) feel very self-conscious.

[1] When used to emphasize, these are sometimes called *intensive* pronouns.

ADJECTIVES AND ADVERBS

Adjectives and adverbs are very closely related. In fact, you might consider an adverb as an adjective with a tail on it—the ending *ly*. But you cannot rely on the ending as a means of distinction because some adjectives end in *ly* (lovely, silly, homely, etc.), and some adverbs do not end in *ly* (too, well, quite, never, etc.). Again the distinction must be based on use, on how the word functions in the sentence.

A word is an *adjective* when it modifies a noun or a pronoun. A word is an *adverb* when it modifies a verb, an adjective, or another adverb. *Modify* means to limit or describe.

Adjectives that limit: an apple, the penguin, most people, this tree.
Adverbs that limit: very ugly, too skinny, extremely repulsive, somewhat silly.
Descriptive adjectives: tall, lean, bearded hippie; blue silk pajamas; horrible monster; mountainous waves; irreducible minimum.
Descriptive adverbs: swiftly flowing river, contagiously likeable person, deliciously flavored soup.

The Three Adjective Positions

1. Before the noun:

   The pink panther ate the purple petunias.
   The paunchy detective tried to follow the lithe youth over the rickety fence.
   Red roses and white carnations combine to make a beautiful bouquet.

2. After the noun:[1]

   Mother, lovely in her new dress, sang for the Monday Tea Club.

   Sam, worn and tired, carried the boy home.

   The dog, dirty from black nose to white tail, barked at the departing car.

3. After *be* verbs and *sensory* verbs:[2]

   The child is sensible. The egg was rotten.

---

[1] Note that the entire phrase describes the preceding noun.
[2] Examples of sensory verbs are *see, appear, smell, taste, feel*, etc.

The ship had been abandoned.   The music sounds beautiful.

The sunset looks magnificent.   The senator was very dignified.

The Three Roles of the Adverb

1. Modifying verbs:

The stream flowed rapidly up the hill.

The drunk drove directly into the telephone pole.

She carefully weighed her decisions.

2. Modifying adjectives:

She was very indiscreet.

The gorilla was exceedingly strong.

The tremendously heavy hippo sat on the tiny hornet.

3. Modifying other adverbs:

She worked quite regularly for many years.

The job was very carefully planned.

The train puffed really laboriously up the mountain.

SELF-QUIZ 3

Define the following terms:

1. adjective _____

2. adverb _____

3. modify _____

Select the correct form in the parentheses.

4. He (correct, correctly) defined the terms. The answer sounded (correct, correctly).

5. She (quick, quickly) adjusted the fees. She adapted (quick, quickly) to any situation.
6. The child's body was (perfect, perfectly) proportioned.
7. He measured the floor (exactly, exact). They proved to be (perfect, perfectly) (exact, exactly) measurements.
8. You must send the monthly payment (regular, regularly). We deal on a (strict, strictly) cash basis.
9. The horse galloped (wild, wildly) over the plains. It was, however, not a (wild, wildly) horse.
10. The stillness of the tomb was (awful, awfully). The tomb was (awful, awfully) still.
11. It was a (dangerous, dangerously) swimming hole. The man was (dangerous, dangerously) intoxicated. The gas smelled (dangerous, dangerously).
12. He was a very (sensible, sensibly) boy. He acted very (sensible, sensibly).
13. He was a very (careful, carefully) person. She worked (careful, carefully) with the retarded child.
14. She performed (magnificent, magnificently). It was a (magnificent, magnificently) beautiful drawing of the birth of a butterfly.
15. Her voice sounds (beautiful, beautifully). She sang the song (exact, exactly) as it was written. We heard it (perfect, perfectly).

Some Special Problems

"A" and "An"

Even at the college level, some students still haven't quite perfected their use of *a* and *an*. This brief review should help them to eradicate that problem.

A precedes all words that begin with consonants, with one exception: When *h* begins a word and it is not sounded, *an* is used.

a cat, a buffalo, a bingo game, a purple onion, a rotten apricot, a hair, a horrible movie, a hermit, a hornet

an honorable agreement, an honest error, an heirloom of great value

An precedes all words that begin with vowels, with one exception: When *u* makes the same sound as the *y* in *you*, *a* is used.

an eagle, an idiot, an intelligent man, an uncle, an umbilical cord, an uprising, an orgy, an egg plant, an artichoke, an opera, an up stairway

a union, a united front, a unicorn, a U.S. Flagship

"Good" and "Well"

Good is an adjective. *Well* is usually an adverb, but it is used as an adjective in reference to health.

He did a good job.	(adjective modifying a noun)
The job was well done.	(adverb modifying the verb *was done*)
He pitched well enough.	(adverb modifying another adverb)

He is well.   (adjective in reference to health)
He feels good. He looks well.   (adjective after a sensory verb)

"Most" and "Almost"

Most can be used as an adjective or a pronoun. It means the greatest number. *Almost* is an adverb which means nearly.

Most of the people polled asked for peace.   He received the most votes.
They arrived almost on time.   The rockets almost reached the moon.

The Place of "Only"

The adverb *only* modifies the word or expression that immediately follows it. Be careful to place it so to convey the meaning intended.

Only John could hope to win the 100-yard dash.
John could only hope to win the 100-yard dash.
John could hope to win only the 100-yard dash.

Don't Double the Negative

"I do *not* have *no* trouble," means that I do have trouble.

incorrect: I don't have no money.
correct: I don't have any money.
incorrect: She doesn't love nobody.
correct: She doesn't love anybody.

"Real," "Really," and "Very"

Real is an adjective. It means genuine. *Really* is an adverb used to emphasize or intensify. *Very* is usually a more apt word than *really*.

incorrect: He is a real smart man.
correct: He is a very smart man.
           He is a real fool.
           He is really (very) smart.
incorrect: It is real good story.
correct: It is a really good (very good) story.

TEST 3

Underline the correct word.

1. He ate (a, an) avocado, (a, an) aphid egg, and (a, an) apricot.
2. They came to (a, an) honorable agreement because he had made (a, an) honest error about (a, an) heirloom of great value.
3. (A, An) airfield was invaded by (a, an) influx of invaders from (a, an) unknown airbase in (a, an) United States protectorate. (A, An) union protested the invasion.
4. His voice was in (good, well) condition, so he sang very (good, well).

5. The mechanic's tools were (good, well) and he did a (good, well) job. The foreman said that his work was (good, well) done. The child was very ill. Now he is (good, well) and he feels (good, well).
6. The child had fallen down the (good, well) because the (good, well) had not been in (good, well) condition.
7. (Most, Almost) everyone who was invited attended the party. (Most, Almost) of them seemed to have a good time.
8. He worked (most, almost) of the time, but (most, almost) every Saturday he went fishing.

Rewrite the following sentences to correct the errors. Look for the placement of *only*, the use of *real* and *really*, and for double negatives. Make no change if correct.

9. He was a real fine player, but they only asked him to play once.
10. The emerald was real, but he was not a really jeweler. He only was an an apprentice. He shouldn't not have waited on her.
11. He knew that his girl wouldn't never speak to him again.
12. He only had meant to tease her.
13. She was very much in love with him, but she had been real hurt before meeting him.
14. He said that he didn't want none of that graft.
15. I wouldn't take nothing for my help.

How to Make Comparisons with Adjectives and Adverbs

Some students are unsure about when to add *-er*, *-est*, *more*, or *most* when making comparisons.

Comparing Short Adjectives. Most short adjectives (one or two syllables) add *-er* when comparing two things (comparative) and *-est* when comparing three or more things (superlative).

> She is nicer than he is. Her daughter is the nicest one in the family. This motor is hotter than mine, but Ken's is the hottest.[1] Clara is happier than Marge, but Lena is the happiest one of all.[2]

Comparing Adverbs and Longer Adjectives. Most adverbs and longer adjectives (more than two syllables) add *more* when comparing two things and *most* when comparing three or more things:

> Your floral display is more beautiful than mine, but Steve's is the most beautiful. Ken is more agile than Larry, but Ray is the most agile boy in the class.

---

[1] Be aware of some spelling problems here. The consonant doubles when added to a one-syllable word which has one vowel.

[2] The final *y* in the base word *happy* changes to *ie* in the comparative and superlative.

Irregular Comparisons. The words in the list below require special attention because they change in various ways.

bad	worse	worst
good, well	better	best
little	less	least
much, many	more	most
far	farther	farthest
	further	furthest
late	later	latest

SELF-QUIZ 4

In the blanks write the correct forms of the words indicated.

EXAMPLE: Tom's vocabulary is (highly developed) *more highly developed* than Gregg's, but Helen's vocabulary is *the most highly developed.*

1. It is a (sad)_____movie than the one we saw last week,

   but the movie we saw two weeks ago was the_____of all.

2. Doris answers questions (intelligent)_____

   than Millhouse, but Phoebe handles them_____.

3. Conditions at the women's penitentiary are (bad)_____
   than those at the Boys' Reformatory, but those at City Jail are the

   _____.

4. Company A made (little)_____profit this year than

   Company B, but Company C made the_____.

5. The Texas team played (excellent)_____, the New York

   team played_____, and the Ohio team played_____

   _____.

.ıl.ıl..ıl..ıl..ıl..ıl..ıl..ıl.ıl..ıl..ıl..ıl..ıl.ıl..ıl..ıl..ıl..ıl.ıl..ıl..ıl.ı

CAPITALIZATION

Capital letters help indicate the difference between the general and the specific.

Words that give general names to things are called common nouns. These are spelled with lower case letters. Words that give specific names are called proper nouns. These are capitalized. Study the list below.

GENERAL TERMS (common nouns)	SPECIFIC TERMS (proper nouns)
school	Branham High School
college	Cuyahoga Community College
state	Ohio, California, Georgia, Alabama
nation, continent	United States, India, Nigeria, Asia
man	Tarzan, George Smith, Mr. Jones
priest, nun, minister, rabbi	Father Thomson, Sister Josephine, Reverend Jenkins, Rabbi Gorman
doctor	Doctor Eberhardt
city	Chicago, Buffalo, Atlanta
month	July, August, September
sister	Sis
mother	Ma, Mom
father	Dad, Pa
dog, cat	Lassie, Whiskers
company	Gulch Oil Company
cigarette	Choker Specials
candy	Yummy Goo Bars
tires	General Goodwear
legislative body	Senate, House of Representatives, Iowa State Legislature
court	Supreme Court, Municipal Court, Court of Appeals
building	Empire State Building, Chrysler Building
historic period	Middle Ages, Renaissance
language	French, English, Italian, Spanish
history	History 102, Russian History 222
economics	Economics 606
department	Sociology Department, Department of Urban Affairs
president	President Hoover
king	King Louis IV
woman	Mrs. Blossom Smig

Capitalization in Titles

The first letters of the principal words of titles are capitalized. This includes books, plays, poems, magazines, short stories, articles, and the chapters of books.[1]

The Caine Mutiny
For Whom the Bell Tolls
Principles of Grammar

[1] The titles of magazines, books, newspapers, movies, and plays are usually underlined in longhand and set in italics when printed. The titles of short stories, poems, articles, and titles of chapters in books are placed in quotation marks.

"Aspects of Animal Communication: The Bees and Porpoises"
"Towards a Theory of Protest"
"The Pit and the Pendulum"
Life
The Boston Globe

Other Capitalization Rules

Capitalize the first letter of the first word of every sentence.
Capitalize the personal pronoun *I*.

Capitalize specific geographical sections but not compass directions:

He traveled northward for many days.
He lived in the South.
The children came from East Birmingham.
We will head east for two days and then turn south.

SELF-QUIZ 5

Capitalize all words that should be capitalized.

1. emily and letitia traveled north to seattle, washington, after living for many years in the east.
2. he worked at the stanton building in july and august.
3. the children read *a tale of two cities* in woodworth elementary school today.
4. stanley longstreet, the new minister, liked to call his mother "ma."
5. reverend mc allister visited the president in the california white house.
6. my brother studied spanish, business history 202, accounting 101, and he also took courses in government and sociology.
7. the old man lived on limpwillow road in southern alabama during the civil war.
8. during her trip to europe she visited the duke of edinborough, stayed at hastingden castle, and fell into lake tahootie.
9. the article, "don't eat too much turtle soup" was published in the may issue of *town and country magazine.*
10. over and over again emily screamed, "i don't believe you, henry. You are a member of the ku klux klan."

.n.n.n.n.n.n.n.n.n.n.n.n.n.n.n.n.n.n.n.n.n.n.n.n.n.n.n.n

POSSESSION

Possession may be indicated in three ways: (1) by possessive verbs, (2) by possessive pronouns, and (3) by the apostrophe.

1. Possessive verbs

He <u>has</u> a large estate.
I <u>own</u> two cars. They <u>belong</u> to us.
She <u>possesses</u> musical talent.

2. Possessive pronouns (*No apostrophes are used with these words.*)

my	your	his	whose
mine	yours	hers	her
its	our	their	
	ours	theirs	

That is *my* car. It is *mine*.   *Whose* cat is that?

This is *your* house. It is *yours*.   It is *ours*.

These are *his* shirts. They are *his*.   Where is *its* tail?

These are *her* glasses. They are *hers*.

This is *their* park. It is *theirs*.

3. Possession indicated by use of the apostrophe

Before adding the apostrophe to show ownership, you must decide whether the word is singular or plural.[1] To singular words, add the apostrophe and *s*. To plural words ending in *s*, add only the apostrophe. To plural words ending in other letters, add the apostrophe and *s*.

The boy's bicycle was broken.
The boys' clubhouse was being painted.
The woman's handbag is green.
The women's organization is fighting for equality.
The secretary's typewriter was jammed.
The secretaries' invitations were mailed today.
Mary's brother arrived yesterday.
Charles's aunt cannot attend the wedding.

Possessive Form without Ownership

A very common use of the apostrophe is to show a form of possession that does not involve ownership, as the following examples illustrate.

He did a good <u>day's</u> work.
The <u>sun's</u> rays burned through the thin parchment.
Peter did three <u>months'</u> work for one <u>month's</u> pay.
The <u>winter's</u> cold sliced through his thin jacket.
They had a full <u>night's</u> sleep.
The <u>ocean's</u> depths revealed many secrets.

SELF-QUIZ 6

Change the first words, as indicated in parentheses, to show singular or plural possession.

EXAMPLE:

he (*sing.*) He lay on *his* side.
man (*pl.*) The *men's* club held its annual meeting.

---

[1] When you are not sure of how to form the plural of certain words, turn to Chapter 4.

1. eagle (*pl.*) They found no eggs in the_____nests.

2. cliff (*sing.*) He clung tenaciously to the_____side.

3. month (*pl.*) He asked for six_____pay in advance.

4. they (*pl.*) The flood victims stood on_____roof tops.

5. citizen (*pl.*) The_____votes were not counted.

6. child (*sing.*) She did not hear her_____cries.

7. team (*sing.*) His_____clubhouse has been rebuilt.

8. people (*pl.*) The_____wishes were not taken into consideration.

9. it (*sing.*) His rusty, old wagon lay on_____side.

10. parent (*pl.*) Many interested students attended the_____ meeting.

CONTRACTIONS

A contraction combines two words into one. The apostrophe indicates that one or more letters have been omitted.

Some students confuse certain contractions with certain possessives, especially *its* with *it's* and *their* with *they're*. *Its* and *their* are possessive words without apostrophes and are used only as possessives: The car rolled on *its* side. That is *their* house. The apostrophes in *it's* and *they're* indicate only that the words are contractions: *It's* (*it is*) time to go. *They're* (*they are*) ready to leave.

Study the following common contractions:

I am ⟶ I'm
you are ⟶ you're
(he, she, it, who) is ⟶ he's, she's, it's, who's
(we, they) are ⟶ we're, they're
For the *will* contraction, use *'ll:*   I'll, you'll, they'll, we'll, etc.
For the *would* contraction, use *'d:*   I'd, you'd, they'd, we'd, etc.

Negatives

The negatives of *are, is, could, do, does, should,* and *would* are formed by combining these words with *n't*: aren't, isn't, couldn't, don't, doesn't, shouldn't, wouldn't. The two exceptions are *will not* (*won't*) and *can not* (*can't*). The negative of *I am* is *I'm not*.

Change the following into contractions and negatives.

EXAMPLE:

	Contraction	Negative
we will	*we'll*	*we won't*

1. she will

2. they are

3. it is

4. who is

5. I am

6. he will

7. it will

8. I would

9. they would

10. you are

ı.ıl.ıl.ıl.ıl.ıl.ıl.ıl.ıl.ıl.ıl.ıl.ıl.ıl.ıl.ıl.ıl.ıl.ıl.ıl.ıl.ıl.ıl.ıl.ıl.

WORD TRAPS

Listed below are words that are often confused and misused because they are similar in sound or meaning. Don't fall into these word traps. With a little effort, you can learn to make the proper distinctions.

accept (*verb*) to take something that has been offered.
   I *accept* the money with gratitude.
except (*preposition*) leaving out, excluding, other than, but.
   Everyone *except* Hudmilla was invited.

advice (*noun*) counsel.
advise (*verb*) to give advice.
   If you *advise* him not to go, he will heed your *advice*.

affect (*verb*) to influence or produce a change.
   His views *affected* my decision.
   The cloud-seeding *affected* the weather.

effect (*verb*) to bring about, cause, accomplish, produce as a result.
   The doctor *effected* a complete cure.
   The economist *effected* a change in his country's economy.

effect (*noun*) result, consequence, influence.
   The *effect* of the alcohol was immediate.
   He showed no ill *effects* from the harsh treatment.
   His discovery will have a lasting *effect*.

all ready completely prepared.
   I am *all ready* now.
   We are *all ready* to go.

already previously, beforehand.
   The meal had *already* been cooled.

all together refers to a group action in unison (never modifies another adjective or adverb).
   Try singing *all together*.

altogether wholly, entirely.
   You are *altogether* despicable.

altar raised table-like structure in a church.
   They stood before the *altar*.

alter to change.
   The company will *alter* its plan.

among used with more than two persons or things.
   We danced *among* the tombstones.

between used for two persons or things.
   They planted watermelon seeds *between* the two fig trees.

angel heavenly being.
   You are a perfect *angel*.

angle mathematical term.
   He drew a right *angle*.

angry infuriated.
   She was very *angry* with her husband.

mad insane.
   He was found to be quite *mad*.

cite (*verb*) to quote, commend, or summon.
    He *cited* long passages from the Bible.
    Letitia was *cited* for bravery.
    The defendant was *cited* for contempt of court.

site (*noun*) place or location.
    They found a beautiful *site* for their home.

sight (*noun*) view, the capacity to see; (*verb*) to catch sight of.
    It was a beautiful *sight* for his tired *sight* to behold.
    They *sighted* the planes on radar.

conscience sense of right and wrong.
    He had a guilty *conscience*.

conscious aware.
    The child was *conscious* during the operation.

council a deliberative body.
    The city *council* passed many bills.

counsel advice; attorney.
    He sought *counsel* from the lawyer.
    He is my legal *counsel*.

few (used for number).
    There were relatively *few* dropouts this year.

less (used for amount).
    Is there *less* nicotine in cigars than in cigarettes?

formal(ly) following accepted rules and regulations.
    They were *formally* presented to the president.

former(ly) previously.
    The convict had *formerly* been with the FBI.

lead (rhymes with *creed*); present tense of the verb *to lead*; (*noun*) leadership, forefront.
    We *lead* a quiet life.
    He took an early *lead*.

lead (rhymes with *bed*); (*noun*) a metal substance.
    He was hit with a *lead* pipe.

led past tense and perfect participle of the verb *to lead*.
    We have *led* a quiet life.
    The Pied Piper *led* the children into the cave.

learn to acquire knowledge, get instruction.
    He *learned* his lesson well.

teach to give knowledge or instruction.
    She *taught* the class how to swim.

let   to permit or allow someone *to do* something.
      We *let* them leave early.
      Please *let* me come in.
leave   to cause or allow someone or something *to remain* (behind).
      Don't *leave* me here alone!
      He always *left* food on his plate.

loan   (*noun*).
      He asked for a *loan*.
lend   (*verb*).
      Lend me some money.   I have already *lent* you some.

loose   (*adjective*) free, unfettered, not bound or restrained.
      They set the dog *loose*.
      I use a *loose*-leaf book.
lose   (*verb*) to mislay, become unable to find.
      I hope they don't *lose* the diamond.

past   (*adjective*) not current, gone by, ended.
      They are *past* presidents of the club.
      The *past* week has been a busy one.
passed   past tense and perfect participle of the verb *to pass*.
      The parade *passed* our house.
      The day has *passed* slowly.

principal   (*adjective*) chief; highest in rank, worth, or degree; main;
      (*noun*) the amount due on a loan; the director of a school.
      You are the *principal* character in this play.
      You paid the interest, but you still owe the *principal*.
      The *principal* spoke to the students.
principle   (*noun*) basic truth, fundamental rule.
      He stuck by his *principles*.
      The *principle* of self-determination is at stake.

quite   (*adverb*) indicates indefinite quantity depending on context.
      She is *quite* (rather) small.
      He is *quite* (very) pleasant.
      Are you *quite* (entirely) finished?
      We are *quite* (completely) alone.
quiet   (*adjective*) silent.
      The birds are *quiet* today.

their   (used only as a possessive).
      That is *their* rhinoceros.
there   (used as an adverb of place and as an expletive, see page 43).
      Put it over *there*.
      There are many ants here.
they're   (contraction for *they are*).
      They're very snobbish people.

then at that time, in that case, therefore.

    They listened to his warning; *then* they left quietly.

    They overheard the conversation; *then* they decided not to go in.

than (used for comparison).

    He is fatter *than* she.

    They have more money *than* we have.

to (*preposition;* sign of infinitive).

    He went *to* the store *to* buy supplies.

two (*number*).

    They have *two* pickles.

too (*adverb*) very, also.

    You are *too* kind.

    The dress is *too* tight.

    Glendon wants to go *too*.

SELF-QUIZ 8

Underline the correct word in the parentheses.

1. The smog (effected, affected) my ability to breathe.
2. Her singing had a strange (affect, effect) on me.
3. They were (all ready, already) here when we arrived.
4. He hit the cue ball at just the right (angel, angle).
5. She was so (angry, mad) that the doctor thought she might be (angry, mad).
6. Everyone (excepted, accepted) the invitation (accept, except) Lulu.
7. He asked you for (advise, advice). (Advise, Advice) him wisely.
8. They marched down the street (all together, altogether).
9. Don't (alter, altar) your plans at the (altar, alter).
10. They walked (between, among) the many waiting guests and then (among, between) the host and hostess.
11. My dessert has (less, fewer) starch, but yours has (less, fewer) calories.
12. Please (learn, teach) me to play guitar so that I can (teach, learn) my brother. He is eager to (teach, learn).
13. Will you (leave, let) us (leave, let) our books in your locker?
14. He has a lot of (lose, loose) change in his pocket. I hope he doesn't (loose, lose) any of it.
15. That is the first time he has asked for a (lend, loan). (Loan, Lend) him the money.

SELF-QUIZ 9

Underline the correct word in the parentheses.

1. We bought land on a lovely, mountain (cite, sight, site).
2. The view to the east was a (sight, cite, site) to behold.

3. The judge (sited, sighted, cited) the landlord for negligence.
4. Brady's (council, counsel) sat in on the (counsel, council) meeting.
5. Does your (conscience, conscious) bother you?
6. He (lead, led) the band with a (lead, led) pipe. Barbara will (lead, led) it tomorrow.
7. The (formal, former) secretary was invited to the (former, formal) party.
8. He remembered his (passed, past) weekends as he (passed, past) the house.
9. The (principle, principal) attacked the delegation's (principle, principal) point.
10. It was (quiet, quite) a (quite, quiet) day.
11. First we will hike; (than, then) we will swim.
12. She is more beautiful (then, than) her mother.
13. (Their, They're, There) arriving tonight.
14. Put (they're, their, there) clothes and food over (their, they're, there).
15. Give the (two, to, too) chops (too, to, two) the hungry child (to, two, too).

TEST 4

Write sentences using the words in parentheses correctly.

1. (affect)_____

2. (all ready)_____

3. (angle)_____

4. (accept)_____

5. (alter)_____

6. (among)_____

7. (mad)_____

8. (advise)_____

9. (learn)_____

10. (loose)_____

11. (let)_____

12. (loan)_____

13. (cite)_____

14. (quite)_____

15. (principle)_____

16. (they're)_____

17. (than)_____

18. (passed)_____

19. (too)_____

20. (counsel)_____

what you have learned in chapter 10

This chapter has centered on a few problem areas. These are the finer points which require your attention once your basic sentence is written. Do not expect to remember all that you have learned. Refer back to the various sections when questions arise, and you will gradually reinforce your knowledge.

KEY 1

(1) dog, train   (2) face, anger, son's, shirt, purple, father's, face, boy   (3) cow, cowbell   (4) photographer, pictures, fluid, developments   (5) farm, farmer.

KEY 2

(1) substitutes   (2) number, gender, person   (3) antecedent   (4) singular, plural   (5) antecedent, plural, antecedent, singular, pronoun   (6) who, which, that   (7) band, club, team   (8) feminine, masculine, neuter   (9) relative, number, antecedents, verb   (10) his   (11) his   (12) its   (13) each   (14) her   (15) comes, his   (16) was, are, They   (17) know, are, It, their   (18) brings, her, She   (19) arrives, is, It, is   (20) their, They, its.

KEY 3

(1) Adjectives modify nouns or pronouns.   (2) Adverbs modify adjectives, verbs, and other adverbs   (3) *Modify* means to limit or describe.   (4) correctly, correct   (5) quickly, quickly   (6) perfectly   (7) exactly, perfectly, exact   (8) regularly, strictly   (9) wildly, wild   (10) awful, awfully   (11) dangerous, dangerously, dangerous   (12) sensible, sensibly   (13) careful, carefully,   (14) magnificently, magnificently   (15) beautiful, exactly, perfectly.

KEY 4

(1) sadder, saddest   (2) more intelligently, most intelligently   (3) worse, worst   (4) less, least   (5) excellently, more excellently, most excellently.

KEY 5

(1) Emily, Letitia, Seattle, Washington, East   (2) He, Stanton Building, July, August   (3) The, A Tale, Two Cities, Woodworth Elementary School   (4) Stanley Longstreet, Ma   (5) Reverend McAllister, President, California White House

(6) My, Spanish, Business History 202, Accounting 101   (7) The, Limpwillow Road, Alabama, Civil War   (8) During, Europe, Duke of Edinborough, Hastingden Castle, Lake Tahootie   (9) The, "Don't Eat Turtle Soup," May, Town, Country Magazine   (10) Over, Emily, I, Henry, Ku Klux Klan.

KEY 6

(1) eagles'   (2) cliff's   (3) months'   (4) their   (5) citizens'   (6) child's   (7) team's   (8) people's   (9) its   (10) parents'

KEY 7

(1) she'll, she won't   (2) they're, they aren't   (3) it's, it isn't   (4) who's, who isn't   (5) I'm, I'm not   (6) he'll, he won't   (7) it'll, it won't   (8) I'd, I wouldn't (9) they'd, they wouldn't   (10) you're, you aren't.

KEY 8

(1) affected   (2) effect   (3) already   (4) angle   (5) angry, mad   (6) accepted, except   (7) advice, advise   (8) all together   (9) alter, altar   (10) among, between   (11) less, fewer   (12) teach, teach, learn   (13) let, leave   (14) loose, lose   (15) loan, lend.

KEY 9

(1) site   (2) sight   (3) cited   (4) counsel, council   (5) conscience   (6) led, lead, lead   (7) former, formal   (8) past, passed   (9) principal, principal   (10) quite, quiet   (11) then   (12) than   (13) They're   (14) their, there   (15) two, to, too.

PART **IV**

YOU HAVE already been asked to write a number of papers, but very little has been said about how to organize and develop them. The earlier assignments gave you practice in writing sentences in context. The next chapter will teach you how to write good paragraphs and short themes. This should help you with preparing term papers and all your

expository

writing...

CHAPTER 11

Writing

PARAGRAPHS AND THEMES

WHAT IS EXPOSITORY WRITING?

We will limit our study to expository writing because it is the most widely used and practical of the various forms of writing. It is used in business-letter writing, in scientific and industrial reports, and in theme writing for college courses. It is easily identified by its standardized, three-part form:

INTRODUCTION: presents the main idea. It may be comprised of one or more sentences in a paragraph and one or more paragraphs in a theme. It must include a *topic sentence*, which clearly states the main idea.

BODY: develops the main idea. It includes such elements as arguments, examples, and details aimed at explaining, describing, or proving the main idea as stated in the topic sentence. It may consist of just a few sentences in a paragraph or of many paragraphs in a theme.

CONCLUSION: summarizes, emphasizes, or dramatizes the main idea or otherwise gives the paper a sense of completeness. It, too, can be one sentence in a paragraph or one or more paragraphs in a theme.

WHAT IS A PARAGRAPH? WHAT IS A THEME?

Many experts define a paragraph as a group of sentences which develops a particular idea. According to this definition, paragraphs can be comprised of hundreds of sentences or of one sentence.

In recent years, however, many writers and editors have broken long paragraphs into shorter segments because it is easier to read the shorter segments, and a page with many paragraph indentations looks more inviting than one of solid print. Others have questioned the possibility of accurately judging where one idea ends and the next begins.

For these reasons, the difference between a long paragraph and a short theme becomes somewhat blurred. However, if they are expository, they each contain an introduction, a body, and a conclusion.[1] This form of writing helps the writer to formulate his ideas clearly and to arrange them in a logical manner; similarly, it helps the reader to get the message because of the carefully structured organization.

The paragraphs and themes below illustrate the three-part structure of expository paragraphs and themes.

Paragraph

The Real Hippies

INTRODUCTION   In the eyes of most of the members of the general public, the so-called "silent majority," all hippies are alike. The news media tend to present them as oddball collections of bearded, bathless, pot-smoking young people who seem to believe in peace and violent revolution at the same time.

BODY   Closer to the truth would be an appraisal of these young people which identifies some as being politically oriented, some as being inward oriented, and some as being mere imitators. There is, of course, much overlapping of these categories, and the real truth about each hippie can be found only

CONCLUSION   by asking her or him individually.

In the theme below, the words of the original paragraph above are shown in italics. You can see how the basic structure was retained, and the expansion was made by adding additional information about the three types of hippies, making each type into a separate paragraph. The conclusion uses the same idea as the original but expands on it.

[1] Although a single paragraph should contain the three parts, a paragraph within a theme may not. It may serve only to introduce, to conclude, or to act as a transition between other paragraphs. Also, because of the blurred distinction between long paragraphs and short themes, the term *topic sentence*, as used in this chapter, coincides with the term *thesis statement*.

The Real Hippies

In the eyes of most of the members of the general public, the so-called "silent majority," all hippies are alike. The news media tend to present them as oddball collections of bearded, bathless, pot-smoking young people who seem to believe in peace and violent revolution at the same time. Closer to the truth would be an appraisal which identifies some as being [1] *politically oriented,* the "New Left," [2] *some as being inward oriented,* the "druggies," *and* [3] *some as being mere imitators,* the "plastic" ones.

[1] The politically oriented hippies grow beards and long hair and wear the off-beat clothing as part of their protest against a culture which appears overly materialistic, inhuman, and militaristic. They seek life-styles that are harmonious, cooperative, and close to nature rather than competitive, polluted, and overcrowded urban life-styles. They work within and outside the political system, urging the country toward peace, racial amity, and an end to poverty and pollution. The political hippies may do these things by joining communes or just by the way they relate to other people and live each day in college and at home. They may or may not take drugs. An offshoot of the peaceful political group is the violent one, comprised of those who believe that peaceful political change is no longer possible in the United States. They have resorted to violence to achieve their political goals. Some of them have gone underground. Some are being hunted by the police.

[2] The second major group consists of those who have turned inward—to drugs, various ascetic religions, and communes. Some live this way because it is the life-style they really desire; some use it as an escape from a society which they do not like and can not change. Many of them can be found in the peace movement and in organizations that fight for other reforms.

[3] The third group consists of those who merely mimic the hair styles, clothing, and language of the hippies. They may well have conservative political views and be employed in regular jobs. In college they may be "straight" students and may participate in no peace or reform activities. They may or may not take drugs.

CONCLUSION
There is, of course, much overlapping of these categories. Individual differences are as great among hippies as they are among the general population. If you want to know what one feels or thinks, ask her or him.

In the next paragraph-to-theme example, note how the introduction and conclusion of the theme are broadened to fit the added subject matter.

Paragraph

Major Occupations

INTRODUCTION

According to the *Dictionary of Occupational Titles*, there are more than 24,000 separate occupations in the United States. They run the gamut from able seaman to zoologist. [1] The largest group includes professionals, managers, clerks, and sales people. [2] The second largest group is comprised of manual workers. This includes craftsmen, operatives, and laborers. [3] The third largest group encompasses the service occupations, such as police and firemen, barbers and beauticians, household workers, and institutional workers such as janitors, waiters, elevator operators, and ushers. These occupational groups employ about 95 per cent of the total work force.

BODY

CONCLUSION

Theme

Want a Job?

INTRODUCTION

According to the Dictionary of Occupational Titles, *there are more than 24,000 separate occupations in the United States. They run the gamut from able seaman to zoologist.* White collar workers are the largest, manual workers the second largest, and service workers the third largest group. Below is a sampling of the kinds of occupations in each area and an indication of the training necessary for some of the jobs.

BODY

[1] *White collar occupations include the professions, management, and clerical and sales people.* Scores of new professions have come into being in recent years. They include such diverse fields as oceanography, astrophysics, and cybernetics, and the more familiar professions such as medicine, teaching, and social work. All of these take years of training, a minimum of four and as much as seven and more years of college. Managerial workers are found in industry, commerce, and government. Some are self-employed in their own stores or businesses, but most are employed by others. Many of them, espe-

cially those in higher positions, must have a college education. Most clerical and sales people learn their work in high school and receive further training on the job.

[2] *Manual workers fall roughly into three categories: craftsmen, operatives, and laborers.* The craftsmen include bricklayers, electricians, carpenters, tool and die makers, pattern-makers, leadmen, layout men, setup men. Most of them are trained through apprenticeship programs set up by their unions. Operatives are used largely in mass production industry to carry out one separate operation such as drilling, cutting, sanding, or polishing. They are usually trained on the job.

[3] *The service occupations encompass* a field that ranges from *police and firemen* to *barbers and beauticians,* short order cooks, and parking lot attendants. Many of these jobs require little or no training, but some such as police and fire protection are becoming more specialized and require increasing amounts of training. Barbers and beauty operators must also attend special schools.

These occupational groups employ about 95 per cent of the total work force. Of necessity, this paper has touched on only a few of the vast number of occupations available in each group. As society becomes more complex and more scientific, discoveries are made, new fields open. There should be one that interests you.

for discussion

What new but related subject was added to the above theme? What other changes have been made? Why?

HOW DIFFICULT IS WRITING?

Many students get discouraged when they work hard on a theme only to have it returned by the teacher, bruised and tattered. They've been writing all their lives. Shouldn't it be a simple task to throw together a short theme?

No. Writing, as stated at the beginning of this book, is one of the most difficult skills that human beings learn. It does not get easier as one gets older because as one grows older he must deal with more difficult problems. These problems are, of course, reflected in his writing assignments. Only by hard work can he manage to keep his writing skills in line with his maturing thoughts.

The teacher assigns an in-class theme at the beginning of the period. The student has fifty minutes in which to plan, execute, and proofread his theme. Is it possible to do a good job under such conditions? Yes. Is it easy? No. Can most students expect to write a well-organized paper with a minimum of mechanical errors in one rapidly written draft? No. A few top students can

ASSIGNMENT: Write a paper about birth control.

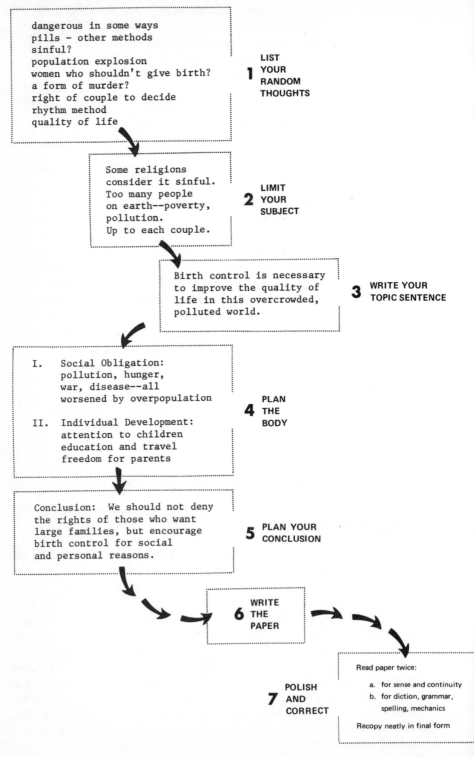

dangerous in some ways
pills - other methods
sinful?
population explosion
women who shouldn't give birth?
a form of murder?
right of couple to decide
rhythm method
quality of life

1 LIST
YOUR
RANDOM
THOUGHTS

Some religions
consider it sinful.
Too many people
on earth--poverty,
pollution.
Up to each couple.

2 LIMIT
YOUR
SUBJECT

Birth control is necessary
to improve the quality of
life in this overcrowded,
polluted world.

3 WRITE YOUR
TOPIC SENTENCE

I.   Social Obligation:
      pollution, hunger,
      war, disease--all
      worsened by overpopulation

II.   Individual Development:
      attention to children
      education and travel
      freedom for parents

4 PLAN
THE
BODY

Conclusion: We should not deny
the rights of those who want
large families, but encourage
birth control for social
and personal reasons.

5 PLAN YOUR
CONCLUSION

6 WRITE
THE
PAPER

Read paper twice:

a. for sense and continuity
b. for diction, grammar,
   spelling, mechanics

Recopy neatly in final form

7 POLISH
AND
CORRECT

do it occasionally if the subject is right, if their mood is receptive, and if all other conditions are "go."

How then does one go about writing a good paper in a short period of time? The suggestions that follow should help you tackle any writing assignment.

PRE-PREPARATION

Most class assignments are short (200 to 300 words) and based on common knowledge or assigned reading. If you have not done the assigned reading, you are probably out of luck. If you know that your instructor is likely to assign a theme based on the reading, think through some of the things you might write about the subject before you go to class.

A 7-STEP WRITING FORMULA

Once you have received an assignment in class, follow the 7-step formula described below, and illustrated by the diagram.[1]

STEP 1: **List Your Random Thoughts.** As soon as you know the subject of your assignment, zero in on it by making a list of every related idea that comes to mind in any order. Some of your thoughts may not even make sense, but writing them down helps you get started. It will help you avoid wasting time, sitting and wondering what to write about.

STEP 2: **Limit Your Subject.** Your random thoughts may take you in many different directions even if most of the ideas are related, but you must limit the subject so that your theme can be made unified and coherent and can be written in the allotted time and with the allotted number of words.

STEP 3: **Write Your Topic Sentence.** If you are like many other students, you will not immediately hit upon the exact subject that you want to develop. By the time you have finished limiting your subject, however, you should be prepared to write a topic sentence containing your main idea. It can serve as your complete introduction, or you may wish to embellish it with a few other sentences. In either case it serves as a guide for the organization and development of the balance of your paper. *Writing a good topic sentence is probably the most important single factor in the writing of a good paper.* When you write your topic sentence at the very beginning of the process, it means that you probably have gone through the first two steps mentally, and you are ready to start step 4.

STEP 4: **Plan the Body.** Write (in outline form) the major points you will use in explaining your main idea. Decide on the best order in which to present them. Now, consider how you are going to support those points. Each point must be explained, described, or proved as fully as possible. Just to say, for example, that the United Nations is a great organization does not mean any more than to say that it is a rotten organization.

[1] This formula can also be followed to good advantage in writing longer themes and papers assigned for homework. Since more time is available for such themes, however, you are expected to do a certain amount of research on your topic and a very careful job of correcting and polishing the final draft. Work done at home should be as mechanically perfect as you can make it. You should take the time to check the spelling, grammar, and mechanics, and to recopy the paper before handing it in.

Your reasons, examples, and detailed descriptions are vital to the development of a good paper. (This step is explained more fully later.)

STEP 5: **Plan Your Conclusion.** Ideas for your conclusion should come easily at this juncture. Jot them down. Your conclusion should develop naturally, as an outgrowth of the introduction and body, not as something new and different. A good test is to read the conclusion and then the introduction. Do they complement each other? Do they seem to be part of the same package? They should.

STEP 6: **Write the Paper.** This should be a relatively simple task if you have followed the formula to this point. You have already done the more difficult work. You have limited your subject and written your topic sentence. You have planned the organization and development of the body of your paper and jotted down ideas for your conclusion. The result is a rough draft of your finished product. You need only flesh it out with carefully worded sentences.

STEP 7: **Polish and Correct.** Try to save at least five minutes for this chore. Read the paper twice, once to see whether your ideas hold together, and a second time to correct the diction, spelling, grammar, and mechanics. Diction refers to your choice of words. You are asked to be aware of it at this point because, as students write longer papers, they tend to become wordy and repetitious. Use words carefully and economically. Do not repeat unnecessarily. If you have time, recopy the paper neatly.

Applying the 7-Step Formula

Let's follow a student writer as he uses the formula in a typical assignment.

ASSIGNMENT: React to the cartoon below in a theme of about 300 words.

Step 1: *He jots down his random thoughts.* Then, going back over the list, he checks those items that seem to be related.

Obviously something about the generation gap. ✓
You can't talk to older people at all.
People live longer than ever before.
Young people have new ideas. ✓
Old people start wars and young people fight. ✓
Young people brought the peace movement to life. ✓
Some older people are nice. ✓
Young people are helping the ecology movement. ✓
All older people are not in favor of war. ✓
Some of my young friends are very conservative. ✓
My grandparents were very pleasant and understanding people.
All young people are not necessarily wise or good. ✓
Some young people believe in pot and violence. ✓
Some older people drink too much and are violent. ✓
Should eighteen-year-olds have the vote?
Is there a generation gap? ✓
Can we bridge it? ✓

Step 2: *He limits his subject.* Examining the items he has checked, the writer begins to see some general ideas emerging.

(a) We can't beat the generation gap because old people are all too square.

(b) We can't beat the generation gap because too many young people are violent and smoke pot.

(c) There is good and bad in both groups. Maybe there isn't as much of a gap as we think.

(d) Younger people tend to be more idealistic than older people. That is why there's a generation gap.

One could write a paper about any of the above ideas, but the writer chooses (d), the fourth idea. (The first two ideas are weak because they overgeneralize.)

Step 3: *He writes his topic sentence.*

There is a generation gap because young people tend to be more idealistic than older people. (*He will develop his introduction more fully when he writes the paper.*)

Step 4: *He organizes and develops the body of the theme.* He lists the major points with which he will support his topic sentence (main idea), and then he jots down ideas under each point which he will develop further as he writes the paper.

1. Young people can see weaknesses and errors of adults.

| family arguments | poverty | pollution |
| war | weaknesses in schools | graft |

2. Unlike older people, the younger generation does not have to try to defend its position.

They don't have mortgages or debts.
They don't own stocks and bonds.
no jobs to hold on to

(*Later, the writer decides to eliminate this point because it is too much like point four.*)

That Good Old Generation Gap

There is a generation gap because young people are ~~always~~ *usually* more idealistic
than older people. This situation has existed ~~for hundreds of generations~~ as long
as man has existed. Some tree people, for example, were dissatisfied with living
in trees, ~~and~~ so they protested against the establishment people who ~~wanted to~~ *insisted on staying.*
~~keep on living there.~~

A cartoon from the <u>Saturday Review</u> of January 11, 1969, depicts three generations of the same family: the grandfather ~~had~~ *has* long hair and a moustache, the father
(vintage 1948) is clean shaven and short haired, the grandson (vintage 1968) has
long hair and a moustache.* The generation gap does not seem to be anything new
or different. Maybe it is basically a good thing.

Young people, after all, are in a good position to see the weaknesses, ~~erors,~~
~~and mistakes~~ *and errors* of adults. They see ~~there~~ *their* parents argue, they note weaknesses in
the school system, *and* they find pollution, graft, *and* crime, ~~poor schools~~ in the cities,
and war and poverty in the world.

Members of the older generation try to justify ~~and explain~~ what ~~have~~ *they* have accomplished in a hard and difficult world in order to ~~live and~~ survive and to help
their children survive. They sometimes do not admit their mistakes because ~~their~~ *they are*
afraid that changes will be made, *and* they will lose all that they have gained.

Young people are freer and more flexible. They do not have to make mortgage
payments or borrow money to send their children to college. They are not worried
about the world changing too much because they do not like it as it is. They have
not become cynical, callous, and hard-headed from unpleasant experiences. They have
more faith in the possibility of improving men and the world.

This does not mean that all old people are bad and all young people are pure *of heart.*
It does mean that young people are more flexible, optimistic, and eager for change.
Hopefully, their children, *too,* ~~to~~ will find improvements to make.

*If you mention the picture, poem, or other source of your idea, be sure to describe or sum-
marize it so that anyone reading your theme knows what you are talking about. Your paper
should be self-explanatory to any reader, not only your teacher.

3. Members of the older generation try to justify what they have done and to hold on to what they have worked for.

worked hard
afraid of change
don't want to admit errors

4. Young people are freer to act and are more flexible.

don't have mortgages   not so cynical, callous
don't have to send kids to college   more love, more faith

Step 5: *Some ideas for a conclusion come to him at this point, so he jots them down.*
not all older people are bad
natural for young to find fault
not all young are good
optimistic

Step 6: *He writes the theme, leaving ample space for his corrections.*

Step 7: *He polishes and corrects the theme.* First he reads the whole paper through to see if it makes sense, is logical, and does not contradict itself. (The paper is not likely to be contradictory if he did steps 1–4 carefully.) Then he corrects for diction (choice of words), mechanics, spelling, and grammar. Notice especially how the paper was improved by changing inexact words and deleting unnecessary words.

The sample paper shown here is the final, edited draft, ready to be recopied neatly for handing in. There may not be time to do this when themes are written in class, but themes should always be recopied when they are written at home.

ORGANIZING AND DEVELOPING THE BODY OF YOUR THEME

Thus far we have concentrated on the organization of the theme as a whole. Since the body of your theme, however, constitutes the largest part, special attention must be paid to its organization and development. You should focus on this problem when you reach step 4 in the writing formula.

Types of Organization

In some paragraphs and themes the order in which you place your ideas makes little or no difference. In others the order is very important. Five basic types of order are:

1. *Spatial:* Used in descriptions of persons, places, things, and processes, this kind of order helps the reader picture the situation in his mind as he reads. The description usually takes the reader from the general to the particular, helping the person to visualize the object as a whole first and then describing the parts in an orderly fashion, from top to bottom, left to right, north to south, clockwise, etc.

2. *Chronological:* When time is an important factor, you must give your reader an orderly sense of backward or forward movement. First, you make clear what your starting point in time is: present, past, or future; then, by using time words and tense, you move backward or forward in time.

3. *Process:* A combination of spatial and chronological order, process order is used to tell people how to do things in a very precise manner. For greatest effectiveness, it is often accompanied by an illustration.

4. *Logical:* Logic is an ingredient in all types of order, but its primary use is in themes dealing with reasoning. In arguing for or against something, you must usually present your ideas in a step-by-step fashion, each step laying the groundwork for the next.

5. *Emphatic* and *Dramatic:* You must often decide whether your most important point will be more effective if placed first or last. Similarly, when you wish to get an emotional response, you must carefully plan the order of your ideas.

Methods of Development

There are many means by which you can develop the body of your theme. Five of the most useful methods are *description, comparison, classification, example,* and *argument* (reason). When you are writing a theme, however, you do not say, "I will develop this theme by description," or "I will develop it by comparison." Having written your random thoughts, limited your subject, and decided on your topic sentence, you then choose the method or methods which will best support your topic sentence. Most papers are developed by a combination of methods.

Development by Description

In a sense, all writing consists of collecting and organizing descriptive details. Attention to detail becomes of primary importance in descriptions of people, places, or things, or when describing a process, or in enumerating facts.

Describing a place

The room in which I found myself was very large and lofty. The windows were long, narrow, and pointed, and at so vast a distance from the black oaken floor as to be altogether inaccessible from within. Feeble gleams of encrimsoned light made their way through the trellised panes, and served to render sufficiently distinct the more prominent objects around. The eye, however, struggled in vain to reach the remoter angles of the chamber or the recesses of the vaulted and fretted ceiling. Dark draperies hung upon the walls. The general furniture was profuse, comfortless, antique, and tattered. Many books and musical instruments lay scattered about, but failed to give any vitality to the scene. I felt that I breathed an atmosphere of sorrow. An air of stern, deep, and irredeemable gloom hung over and pervaded all.

From "The Fall of the House of Usher" by Edger Allan Poe.

Describing a person

It was Miss Murdstone who was arrived, and a gloomy-looking lady she was; dark, like her brother, whom she greatly resembled in face and voice; and with very heavy eyebrows, nearly meeting over her large nose, as if, being disabled by the wrongs of her sex from wearing whiskers, she had carried them to that account. She brought with her two uncompromising hard black boxes, with her initials on the lids in hard brass nails. When she paid the coachman she took her money out of a hard steel purse, and she kept the purse in a very jail of a bag which hung upon her arm by a heavy chain, and shut up like a bite. I had never, at that time, seen such a metallic lady altogether as Miss Murdstone was.

From *David Copperfield* by Charles Dickens.

Enumerating facts

By May of 1971 the Indochina war had taken a terrible toll in men and wealth. A combined total of more than 280,000 men from the United States, France, and South Vietnam had been killed there. France lost 92,000 men in its eight year battle against Nationalist and Communist forces, and the United States, which had gradually moved in after France's defeat in 1954, by mid-1971 had suffered over 54,000 dead and more than 150,000 wounded. South Vietnam had lost more than 129,000 men, and South Korea, Australia, New Zealand, the Philippines, and Thailand had lost more than 4,500. The war had cost the French almost six billion dollars and the United States over 135 billion dollars.

Describing a process

A process description can be as short and simple as a recipe for macaroni and cheese or as long and complicated as Herman Melville's description of how to make tappa. Descriptions of mathematical, scientific, or mechanical techniques are usually quite lengthy and involved. In describing a process, it is important that you take nothing for granted. Your reader may know nothing whatsoever about the process, and the omission of a single step (for example, how long to cook the macaroni) may mean failure for him.

Making Tappa

In the manufacture of the beautiful white tappa generally worn on the Marquesan Islands, the preliminary operation consists in gathering a certain quantity of the young branches of the cloth-tree. The exterior green bark being pulled off as worthless, there remains a slender fibrous substance, which is carefully stripped from the stick, to which it closely adheres. When a sufficient quantity of it has been collected, the various strips are enveloped in a covering of large leaves, which the natives use precisely as we do wrapping-paper, and which are secured by a few turns of a line passed round them. The package is then laid in the bed of some running stream, with a heavy stone placed over it, to prevent its being swept away. After it has remained for two or three days in this state, it is drawn out, and exposed, for a short time, to the action of the air, every distinct piece being attentively inspected, with a view of ascertaining whether it has yet been sufficiently affected by the operation. This is repeated again and again, until the desired result is obtained.

When the substance is in a proper state for the next process, it betrays evidences of incipient decomposition; the fibres are relaxed and softened, and rendered perfectly malleable. The different strips are now extended, one by one, in successive layers, upon some smooth surface—generally the prostrate trunk of a cocoa-nut tree—and the heap thus formed is subjected, at every new increase, to a moderate beating, with a sort of wooden mallet, leisurely applied. The mallet is made of a hard heavy wood resembling ebony, is about twelve inches in length, and perhaps two in breadth, with a rounded handle at one end, and in shape is the exact counterpart of one of our four-sided razor-strops. The flat surfaces of the implement are marked with shallow parallel indentations, varying in depth on the different sides, so as to be adapted to the several stages of the operation. These marks produce the corduroy sort of stripes discernible in the tappa in its finished state. After being beaten in the manner I have described, the material soon becomes blended in one mass, which, moistened occasionally with water, is at intervals hammered out, by a kind of gold-beating process, to any degree of thinness required. In this way the cloth is easily made to vary in strength and thickness, so as to suit the numerous purposes to which it is applied.

When the operation last described has been concluded, the new-made tappa is spread out on the grass to bleach and dry, and soon becomes of a dazzling whiteness. Sometimes, in the first stages of the manufacture, the substance is impregnated with a vegetable juice, which gives it a permanent color. A rich brown and a bright yellow are occasionally seen, but the simple taste of the Typee people inclines them to prefer the natural tint.

From *Typee* by Herman Melville.

for discussion

In the passages quoted, are Poe and Dickens more interested in exact descriptions or in creating certain impressions? Do they succeed? Would you add or subtract any words? Have certain words lost their meanings for the modern reader? What words might be substituted?

for writing

1. Describe, step-by-step, a rather simple job that you do. Be sure to describe it so carefully that someone who has never done that job can follow your directions.
2. Describe a familiar person, place, or thing in great detail.
3. Try writing an interesting description of something very simple, like a pencil, an apple, or a chair.

Development by Comparison

Comparison papers require careful planning. Is it more effective to compare sentence by sentence, in alternating paragraphs, or in larger units? You may often have to experiment to find the best method. In more complicated papers, you must plan the order of your points very carefully. For example, if you are to compare the climate, topography, and population distribution of Brazil and Venezuela, which of the two plans below is best? In writing your paper you may find that one form is more cumbersome and requires needless repetition. The other form may help you highlight the differences and similarities in a more effective manner.

I. Brazil
   A. Climate
   B. Topography
   C. Population distribution
II. Venezuela
   A. Climate
   B. Topography
   C. Population distribution

(or)

I. Climate
   A. Brazil
   B. Venezuela
II. Topography
   A. Brazil
   B. Venezuela
III. Population distribution
   A. Brazil
   B. Venezuela

Sentence-by-sentence comparison

Jim was loud and boisterous, gay and gregarious; his brother Jed was quiet, solemn, thoughtful. Jim was active, pushy, aggressive, bold; Jed was methodical, careful, steady. When Jed was killed in a barroom brawl, his surprised brother became pensive and thoughtful.

Paragraph-by-paragraph comparison

Grant and Lee met in the parlor of a modest farmhouse in Appomattox, Virginia, on an April Sunday in 1865. It is doubtful whether any two Americans could have been more different. Probably their only similarities lay in that they were both men and generals.

Lee was tall, handsome, imposing, dressed in a fine uniform with a sword at his side. He was an American aristocrat, representative of the leisure class, still dreaming dreams of knighthood and the Age of Chivalry. He stood for family, culture, tradition. He represented the landed gentry with their love for order and their determination to maintain the status quo. They were dignified, arrogant, ambitious. They owned vast tracts of land and thousands of slaves. Lee was noble in defeat, yet tragic in that he represented that which could no longer survive.

Grant, the son of a tanner on the Western frontier, was rough, undersized, dressed in working clothes and mud-spattered boots. He wore a private's blue coat and was swordless. He was representative of the restless, creative, vibrant frontiersmen who had, barehanded, conquered and planted and built. Now they were ready to assert themselves in helping to direct the affairs of the nation. A wild cross-section of ragamuffin democrats with a small "d," they cared little for the traditions of the past, but they saw a great new, powerful country, ruled by the people who would dare to build it.

They were more than two generals signing a peace treaty. They were the past and the future.

for writing

1. Compare the physical appearance, mannerisms, and personality of a person you like with those of a person you dislike.
2. Compare the teaching ability and personalities of two favorite teachers.
3. Compare two cars, two jobs, or two favorite meals.

Development by Examples

It is often easier to explain things by means of examples than in any other way. This method is used in the following student theme.

Lost: Three Young Men

There is a great deal of talk about "alienated" youth, and many adults tend to think of them strictly as young people who are completely opposed to the values of present day society. Research shows, however, that there are many different kinds of alienated youth.

Michael G. is a very unhappy Yale freshman who does nothing for hours because he is interested in nothing. He hates to get up in the morning because he has nothing to look forward to. He has no girlfriends and few male companions. He reads a great deal but gets bored and may sit for hours without doing anything. He takes drugs, but even they don't "turn him on" after a time. He blames his alienation on the fact that his parents were too liberal. They never forced him to do anything, not even to go to church. Thus, "I have nothing to believe in," he says.

Not yet twenty, Henry M., a high school dropout from Harlem, has already been in prison for auto theft and armed robbery. He steals because it is his way of getting along in a society in which he is not accepted as a full-fledged member. Stealing is, for him, the only way to make a living. He doesn't hate White society, and he hasn't joined the Black opposition. He wouldn't join the army because he doesn't want to fight for Whitey, but he doesn't join the Black Panthers because "They ain't gonna get no place." He shrugs off the idea of being caught again. Jail is something that he has to face if he doesn't do his job right.

Raised as a practicing Christian, George F., a junior at OSU and a member of the New Left, was a youth leader in his church in a small southern town. He was "turned off" because he came to feel that Christianity is hypocritical. He plans to spend his life struggling against war, poverty, and racism, and to do this he believes that he must reject the values he was raised with.

None of these young men fit the stereotypes that many adults seem to have drawn.

Why is it often unfair to support arguments only with examples? For instance, can you make a valid argument against increased welfare allotments merely by citing a case or two of welfare cheating that you have observed? If you know some 18-year-olds who are irresponsible, would this be a strong enough argument against supporting the vote for 18-year-olds? What other kinds of evidence should one use in situations like these?

for writing

1. Describe friends or acquaintances who might fit into the three classifications of hippies on page 209 or those similar to the alienated youth described on page 222.
2. Give examples of adults you know who bridge the generation gap.
3. Write a paper in which you give examples of incompetence among doctors, dentists, lawyers, social workers, or garage mechanics; then write a counter-paragraph in which you give examples of competence in the same classification.

Development by Classification

To classify is to arrange in groups or categories. It is an important method of organizing material so that it is easier to follow and to understand.

Psychopaths, Sexual Deviants, and Alcoholics

Many mental health problems affect social relations. Three of the most prevalent are psychopathic behavior, sexual deviancy, and alcoholism.

For the psychopathic personality, acts of violence are means of gratifying deep-seated impulses often created because of a childhood failure to find firm and dependable objects of love. Psychopaths commit hostile acts without regard for the consequences to themselves or to others. They may maim or kill despite the fact that they realize they will be punished, but they are unable to control their impulses.

One who seeks satisfaction for his sexual drives in ways not usually considered normal for his particular social group or with a person not considered a proper mate is called a sexual deviant. Normalcy is defined differently by various social groups, but deviancy is usually associated with methods of achieving orgasm outside of sexual intercourse. Among the factors believed to be the most common causes of abnormal sexual behavior are childhood frustrations, fears, and guilt feelings related to sex.

Alcoholism is one of the most common health problems affecting social relationships. Since drinking is acceptable in most social situations, it is not always easy to identify the point at which one becomes an alcoholic. Generally speaking, however, one has become an alcoholic when he takes a drink in order to face an unpleasant situation, or when he knows that he should refrain. The person who operates his automobile in an unsafe condition, who blacks out during social affairs, or who becomes obnoxious "while under the influence" has become an alcoholic. Alcoholism is not considered a disease in itself but a response to various personality weaknesses that may range from the neurotic to the psychotic. Treatment depends on a close analysis of the problems of the individual.

In judging whether or not people have mental health problems, the question is not whether an outsider considers the person capable or incapable, but whether the person himself is functioning well in his own environment.

for writing

1. Classify your friends and relatives into groups according to their social behavior.
2. Classify your interests, your activities, or your personal problems.
3. Classify some well known politicians, athletes, or movie stars.

Development by Arguments (Reasons)

At the college level your reasons for taking a position on an issue are often questioned. Unlike the neighborhood gossip or the armchair general, the college student is expected to study informed sources before arriving at opinions, and he is expected to back up his opinions with sound reasons. He should be aware of the political leanings and/or the professional reputation of his sources, and his reasoning should show an awareness of the opposing arguments.

Execute Them[1]

A vocal minority in this country has been fighting for many years to outlaw capital punishment. This would be a very serious mistake, according to an article written for the *Police Chief* in June, 1960, by Edward J. Allen, chief of police, Santa Ana, California.

"Some governors, prison wardens, criminologists, religious leaders, and defense attorneys have advanced the idea that capital punishment does not deter crime, but 'how can they possibly know how many people are not on death row because of their fear of the death penalty?' says Allen. Too often these softhearted types see the killers only after the memories of the hacked and broken victims have faded into the past, and the criminal, safely locked up, looks pathetic and helpless."

Other critics of the death penalty criticize it because the rich and powerful escape through legal loopholes while the killer who has no money is most often executed. The answer, according to Allen, is not to free the penniless killer, but to improve the system so that rich and poor are meted out the same fate.

Those who advocate the abolition of the death penalty point out that nine states have abolished capital punishment, but they often ignore the fact that eight other states which once abolished it, have since restored the penalty.

Finally, there are those who say that the state should not kill because officially sanctioned killing brutalizes human nature. Is it capital punish-

[1] Compare the opinons in this theme with those in the two articles on capital punishment in Chapter 12.

ment that brutalizes human nature, or is it coddling criminals that does it? To allow callous criminals to escape the death penalty would, indeed, make ours a barbaric society.

"All of the erudition, wisdom, experience, and knowledge of history reveals that the death penalty is morally and legally just," concludes Chief Allen. "For the just man or nation this should be sufficient."

for discussion

Is there sufficient information in the above article for you to make a decision to support capital punishment? Would you consider the source biased or unbiased? What other sources might you turn to before making your decision?

for writing

Give reasons for or against a subject about which you feel strongly. Support your reasons with as much evidence and authority as you can muster. Suggested subjects: abortion, pacifism, world government, belief in God, chastity before marriage.

WRITING IS A TWO-WAY ROAD

As you develop your ideas with the 7-step formula, remember to keep checking back to your topic sentence to be sure that you are staying on the subject. When you write the final copy, you may get new ideas and want to add additional points or even change your basic idea. This means that you have to change your topic sentence. Any changes in your original plan, in fact, require you to recheck your whole paper to be sure that you aren't getting off the subject or contradicting yourself. Your finished product should be a unified whole with all parts working together.

what you have learned in chapter 11

In expository writing the writer attempts to express his ideas as clearly as possible. To achieve this he must first *limit* his subject so that it can be expressed well in the space and time allotted.

When he has clearly stated the main idea of his work, he must *organize* his paper so that it has a definite introduction, body, and conclusion; then he must *develop* the body so that it supports the main idea fully and effectively. This usually requires the writer to use description, examples, arguments, comparisons, classification, and other such developmental methods. The conclusion should tie the idea together so as to add a sense of unity and completeness to the work.

YOU WRITE to *communicate.* Knowledge of grammar, spelling, and mechanics, and the ability to limit, organize, and develop ideas help you to communicate more effectively, but you must have *ideas.* As in chapter one, the last chapter is comprised of articles, pictures, cartoons, and poems to stimulate your thinking. How well you write papers at this stage will demonstrate how much improvement you have derived from "treatment." As you do the assignments, keep applying what you have learned and reviewing what you have forgotten. Show that you are ready to

PART

check

out of

the clinic...

CHAPTER 12

Final
DIAGNOSIS

In diagnosing your final papers, your instructor will look for the same qualities which he sought in your first papers: good grammar, spelling, and mechanics. In addition, he is likely to check your diction.

You are not asked to remember technical grammatical terms or to identify various grammatical structures. You are merely asked to write correctly enough so that your form does not interfere with your content to any marked degree.

The main focus of your attention should remain on the form of your writing, but your instructor will undoubtedly pay more attention to the organization and development of your ideas at this point than he did at the beginning of the course.

When your writing is unplanned and meandering, when your ideas are overlapping and repetitious, you have more of a tendency to lose control over your sentences and to write run-ons and fragments. When your writing is carefully planned and organized, it is easier to develop clear and correct sentences.

WRITING SUGGESTIONS

1. Read the directions for each assignment carefully.

2. Since all of the assignments provide choices, choose those which you know most about or feel most strongly about.

3. Use the 7-step formula (chapter 11) to help you write the paper.

Check Points for Polishing Your Paper

When you get to step 7, check your paper against the key problem areas listed below. Pay special attention to those areas in which you know yourself to be weak. Consult the page references where you need help.

sentence structure: Is each group of words punctuated as a sentence *actually* a sentence? (109–119)

agreement of subject and verb (57–73)

agreement of pronoun and antecedent (179)

tenses: Are they consistent? Do you change them only for a definite reason? Do you add *ed*'s when necessary? (164–168, 157)

number: Do you handle singularity and plurality correctly? Do you add *s*'s to plurals when necessary? (58–62)

spelling and usage: Check the dictionary for definitions and spelling. Refer to pages 189–190, 197–201 of this book to check on words you tend to confuse (like *there* and *their*, *it's* and *its*, *to* and *too*).

possession and contraction: Don't confuse one with the other. Place your apostrophes correctly. Do not use apostrophes in possessive words like *theirs, its, ours*. (194–197)

punctuation: Is your end punctuation correct? Does your internal punctuation help make the meaning of your sentences clearer? Are words grouped together or separated in a meaningful manner? (127–138)

capitalization: (192–193)

ASSIGNMENT 1: React to Essays

Write a paper of 200 to 300 words in which you develop a subject based on one of the essays in this section. The selections are grouped into three categories: (1) articles dealing with capital punishment, (2) articles about the state of America, and (3) articles written in a humorous vein.

Select a subject in which you are interested, read the articles, and write your paper. More specific suggestions are given for each category.

About Capital Punishment

This is a subject which has haunted the civilized world for many years. The two articles that follow are especially interesting because one was written by an American in New York, and the other by an Englishman in Burma. Both articles were written during the same decade. One author had witnessed an execution by electric chair and the other by hanging. Compare their reactions.

"Murder in the First Degree" is an example of expository writing, the kind of writing you are being asked to do. Broun states at the beginning of his article that he is opposed to capital punishment; he develops a series of arguments against it, and he concludes with his strongest argument—a religious one.

"A Hanging" is written in narrative style, and you do not learn the author's opinion of executions until about half way through the narrative.

Murder in the First Degree

—HEYWOOD BROUN

The jury came in with a verdict of murder in the first degree. It so happens that I am thinking of a particular case, but it will serve as a text chiefly because it was a trial not animated by any touch of the unusual. There was no news in the conviction or the inevitable sentence. This was simply a run-of-the-mill sort of murder. A man with a bad record stabbed an enemy. Nobody could question the guilt of the defendant or the justice of the penalty.

That is, nobody who believes in capital punishment.

But I saw the man stand up as he looked upon the jury and the jurors looked upon him. I sat far back and could not tell with what twitch of the features he received the verdict. He had his hands clasped behind him, and all he did was to lock his fingers a little tighter as they told him he was guilty. That could hardly have been a surprise.

He knew it all along. Nevertheless, the fingernails bit into his flesh. And as the fingers tightened, it was possible to notice the play of muscles across his back.

"What a magnificent body!" I thought to myself. And then I remembered that those same muscles would flex and tighten once more as the community carried out its intention to flick him away like a burned-out stub. It seemed to me a pity. It still seems a pity.

A lot of energy and time and vegetative planning went into the creation of those shoulder blades and the delicate mechanism of nerve and tissue. I could not keep from thinking of this John Doe as some sort of flowering shrub, because his individuality and his personal quirks and whimsicalities were not discussed during the trial. He killed a man and therefore must die.

There is a nice shiny surface of logic in the rule which holds that repayment for an eye must be in kind. A life for a life. It sounds like an algebraic equation. There is a sense of perfect balance. But the fiber of the reasoning is marred by a flaw. It does not constitute a literal transcript of the circumstances.

"Why," people often ask, "is there always sympathy for the criminal and none for his victim?"

The answer is easy. The dead lay beyond our pity. By quelling the heart-beat of the assassin we do not set up a rhythm in the breast of the one who was stabbed. And if we pluck out the eye of an offender there does not exist a socket into which it may fit with any utility.

And so what we are really saying is not "A life for a life," but "A death for a death." We deal in depreciated currency. Nobody profits either in a spiritual or a material sense by the transaction.

Sometimes the victim of the knife or the bullet leaves behind him sons and daughters destitute by reason of his death. The killer owes them something very specific. And it seems to me that no very material adjust-ment has been made when the community comes to the bereaved ones to say:

"The man who killed your father has paid the price. He was electro-cuted at six o'clock this morning."

In all reason, just what has he paid which is in any way tangible? Far from paying, he has been allowed—even compelled—to welsh out of a settlement. His crime constitutes an offense against certain individuals and against the community, and by all means, I would have him pay. But the payment will have to be by service. Instead of being made to die he should be compelled to sweat.

Some few exist whose potentialities for social conduct are dim, but this does not hold for the majority of criminals. There is stuff there, even in spite of flaws and marks which mar them. The human body itself is not so much kindling wood to be lightly tossed upon the slag pile. I can think of no one to whom I would deny the chance for regeneration.

Possibly I am a little romantic, but when the dramatic moment came in Cuba for the decisive yellow fever tests, I think it would have been eminently fitting to pass the call for volunteers along the corridor of some death house. In that event, the code of "a life for life" would have had some meaning. Only under such circumstances can we justly say:

"This man who killed another now has his chance to pay the price."

You see, the fault lies so close to our own home. The failure of the crim-inal is always a joint stock enterprise. We mark him as unfit to live among civilized human beings, but it follows logically that we were inept in fitting this cog into the machine we built.

Repair shops have been built for motors, but we scrap men.

If it were compulsory for every citizen to attend an execution once a year we would be done with capital punishment. We—and I mean all of us—are content to be hangmen because we walk softly and do not talk of rope at our parties. We neither see nor hear nor feel, damn our eyes! And damn our hearts and heads and the life force within us, too!

Out of the all but eternal ages comes a human being delicately knit. Even though moronic, there is the wisdom of the centuries in his spinal column. God has joined together cell and muscle, and this we tear asunder. And I have come to think that perhaps I have at last identified that mys-terious crime which worried me when I was a child. This supreme impu-dence of conduct may well be the sin against the Holy Ghost.

A Hanging

—GEORGE ORWELL

It was in Burma, a sodden morning of the rains. A sickly light, like yellow tinfoil, was slanting over the high walls into the jail yard. We were waiting outside the condemned cells, a row of sheds fronted with double bars, like small animal cages. Each cell measured about ten feet by ten and was quite bare within except for a plank bed and a pot for drinking water. In some of them brown silent men were squatting at the inner bars, with their blankets draped round them. These were the condemned men, due to be hanged within the next week or two.

One prisoner had been brought out of his cell. He was a Hindu, a puny wisp of a man, with a shaven head and vague liquid eyes. He had a thick, sprouting moustache, absurdly too big for his body, rather like the moustache of a comic man on the films. Six tall Indian warders were guarding him and getting him ready for the gallows. Two of them stood by with rifles and fixed bayonets, while the others handcuffed him, passed a chain through his handcuffs and fixed it to their belts, and lashed his arms tight to his sides. They crowded very close about him, with their hands always on him in a careful, caressing grip, as though all the while feeling him to make sure he was there. It was like men handling a fish which is still alive and may jump back into the water. But he stood quite unresisting, yielding his arms limply to the ropes as though he hardly noticed what was happening. . . .

. . . It was about forty yards to the gallows. I watched the bare brown back of the prisoner marching in front of me. He walked clumsily with his bound arms, but quite steadily, with that bobbing gait of the Indian who never straightens his knees. At each step his muscles slid neatly into place, the lock of hair on his scalp danced up and down, his feet printed themselves on the wet gravel. And once, in spite of the men who gripped him by each shoulder, he stepped slightly aside to avoid a puddle on the path.

It is curious, but till that moment I had never realized what it means to destroy a healthy, conscious man. When I saw the prisoner step aside to avoid the puddle I saw the mystery, the unspeakable wrongness, of cutting a life short when it is in full tide. This man was not dying, he was alive just as we are alive. All the organs of his body were working— bowels digesting food, skin renewing itself, nails growing, tissues forming— all toiling away in solemn foolery. His nails would still be growing when he stood on the drop, when he was falling through the air with a tenth-of-a-second to live. His eyes saw the yellow gravel and the grey walls, and his brain still remembered, foresaw, reasoned—reasoned even about puddles. He and we were a party of men walking together, seeing, hearing, feeling, understanding the same world; and in two minutes, with a sudden snap, one of us would be gone—one mind less, one world less.

The gallows stood in a small yard, separate from the main grounds of the prison, and overgrown with tall prickly weeds. It was a brick erection like three sides of a shed, with planking on top, and above that two beams and a crossbar with the rope dangling. The hangman, a grey-haired convict in the white uniform of the prison, was waiting beside his machine. He greeted us with a servile crouch as we entered. At a word from Francis the two warders, gripping the prisoner more closely than ever, half led half pushed him to the gallows and helped him clumsily up the ladder. Then the hangman climbed up and fixed the rope round the prisoner's neck.

We stood waiting, five yards away. The warders had formed in a rough circle round the gallows. And then, when the noose was fixed, the prisoner began crying out to his god. It was a high, reiterated cry of "Ram! Ram! Ram! Ram!" not urgent and fearful like a prayer or cry for help, but steady, rhythmical, almost like the tolling of a bell . . . The hangman, still standing on the gallows, produced a small cotton bag like a flour bag and drew it down over the prisoner's face. But the sound, muffled by the cloth, still persisted, over and over again: "Ram! Ram! Ram! Ram!"

The hangman climbed down and stood ready, holding the lever. Minutes seemed to pass. The steady, muffled crying from the prisoner went on and on, "Ram! Ram! Ram!" never faltering for an instant. The superintendent, his head on his chest, was slowly poking the ground with his stick; perhaps he was counting the cries, allowing the prisoner a fixed number—fifty, perhaps, or a hundred. Everyone had changed color. The Indians had gone grey like bad coffee, and one or two of the bayonets were wavering. We looked at the lashed, hooded man on the drop, and listened to his cries—each cry another second of life; the same thought was in all our minds: oh, kill him quickly, get it over, stop that abominable noise!

Suddenly the superintendent made up his mind. Throwing up his head he made a swift motion with his stick, "Chalo!" he shouted almost fiercely.

There was a clanking noise, and then dead silence. The prisoner had vanished, and the rope was twisting on itself. . . . We went round the gallows to inspect the prisoner's body. He was dangling with his toes pointed straight downwards, very slowly revolving, as dead as a stone.

The superintendent reached out with his stick and poked the bare brown body; it oscillated slightly. "*He's* all right," said the superintendent. He backed out from under the gallows, and blew out a deep breath. The moody look had gone out of his face quite suddenly. He glanced at his wristwatch. "Eight minutes past eight. Well, that's all for this morning, thank God."

for discussion

After reading the articles by Broun and Orwell, pose their ideas against those of the theme favoring capital punishment (see "Execute Them" on page 224). Have your ideas been changed or reenforced? Do you now have enough information to make an intelligent decision regarding the issue? What other sources might you seek?

for writing

Support or oppose the following statements:

The state must kill murderers.
We must exact an eye for an eye.
We should turn the other cheek.
Broun's solution—making killers work for the victim's survivors—is best.
Electrocutions don't frighten would-be murderers. They teach people to kill.
Capital punishment distorts the idea that life is sacred.

On the State of America

All five articles in this section discuss the moral condition of the United States. The first three see much good in the state of affairs; the last two are critical. The writers represent a broad spectrum of American opinion: a college president, a deceased United States president, a conservative newspaper columnist, a southern newspaper editor, a famous playwright. The articles are written in various expository styles.

Read what all five have to say; then come to your own conclusion. Respond to one or more of the opinions expressed. Writing suggestions follow the last selection.

We Have Not Failed Our Youth

—ERIC A. WALKER

This ceremony marks the completion of an important phase of your life. It is an occasion in which all who know you can share in your sense of pride and accomplishment. But no one has more pride in your accomplishment than the older generation.

But I am not going to tell that older generation how bright you are. Nor am I going to say we have made a mess of things and you—the younger ones—are the hope of mankind. I would like to reverse that process.

For if you of the graduating class will look into the bleachers, I will re-introduce you to representatives of some of the most remarkable people ever to walk the earth. People you might want to thank on this graduation day.

These are people you already know as your parents and grandparents. And I think you will agree that a remarkable people they are indeed. Let me tell you about them.

These—your parents and grandparents—are the people who within just five decades have by their work increased your life expectancy by approximately 50%—who, while cutting the working day by a third, have more than doubled per capita output.

These are the people who have given you a healthier world than they found. And because of this you no longer have to fear epidemics of flu, typhus, diphtheria, small pox, scarlet fever, measles or mumps that they

Speech delivered September 11, 1969 to the graduating class at Pennsylvania State University. Reprinted by permission of the author. Dr. Walker is President Emeritus of Pennsylvania State University.

knew in their youth. And the dreaded polio is no longer a medical factor, while TB is almost unheard of.

Let me remind you that these remarkable people lived through history's greatest depression. Many of these people know what it is to be poor, what it is to be hungry and cold. And because of this, they determined that it would not happen to you—that you would have a better life, you would have food to eat, milk to drink, vitamins to nourish you, a warm home, better schools and greater opportunities to succeed than they had.

Because they gave you the best, you are the tallest, healthiest, brightest and probably best looking generation to inhabit the land. . . .

These are also the people who fought man's grisliest war. They are the people who defeated the tyranny of Hitler and who, when it was all over, had the compassion to spend billions of dollars to help their former enemies rebuild their homelands. . . .

It was representatives of these two generations who, through the highest court of the land, fought racial discrimination at every turn to begin a new era in civil rights.

They built thousands of high schools, trained and hired tens of thousands of better teachers and at the same time made higher education a very real possibility for millions of youngsters—where once it was only the dream of a wealthy few.

And they made a start—although a late one—in healing the scars of the earth and in fighting pollution and the destruction of our natural environment.

While they have done all these things, they have had some failures. They have not yet found an alternative for war, nor for racial hatred.

Perhaps you, the members of this graduating class, will perfect the social mechanisms by which all men may follow their ambitions without the threat of force—so that the earth will no longer need police to enforce the laws, nor armies to prevent some men from trespassing against others.

But they—those generations—made more progress by the sweat of their brows than in any previous era, and don't you forget it. And if your generation can make as much progress in as many areas as these two generations have, you should be able to solve a good many of the world's remaining ills.

It is my hope, and I know the hope of these two generations, that you find the answers to many of these problems that plague mankind.

But it won't be easy. And you won't do it by negative thoughts, nor by tearing down or belittling.

You may and can do it by hard work, humility, hope, and faith in mankind. Try it.

Goodby and good luck to all of you.

NOTE: The first four paragraphs of this article are introductory.

The Miracle of America
—HERBERT HOOVER

Perhaps the time has come for Americans to take a little stock and think something good about themselves.

We could point out that our American system has perfected the greatest productivity of any nation on earth, that our standard of living is the highest in the world. We could point to our constantly improving physical health and lengthening span of life. We could mention the physical condition of our youth as indicated somewhat by our showing in the recent Olympic games.

In the government field, we could suggest that our supposedly decadent people still rely upon the miracle of the ballot and the legislative hall to settle their differences of view and not upon a secret police with slave camps.

In the cultural field, we could point out that with only about six per cent of the world's population we have more youth in high schools and institutions of higher learning, more musical and literary organizations, more libraries and probably more distribution of the printed and spoken word than all the other ninety-four per cent put together.

On the moral and spiritual side, we have more hospitals and charitable institutions than all of them. And we could suggest that we alone, of all nations, fought in two world wars and asked no indemnities, no acquisition of territory, no domination over other nations. We could point to an advancement of the spirit of Christian compassion such as the world has never seen, and prove it by the tons of food and clothes and billions of dollars we have made as gifts in saving hundreds of millions from famine and governments from collapse. . . .

America means far more than a continent bounded by two oceans. It is more than pride of military power, glory in war or in victory. It means more than vast expanses of farms, of great factories or mines, magnificent cities or millions of automobiles and radios. It is more even than the traditions of the great tide westward from Europe which pioneered the conquest of a continent. It is more than our literature, our music, our poetry. Other nations have these things also.

What we have in addition, the intangible we cannot describe, lies in the personal experience and the living of each of us rather than in phrases, however inspiring. . . .

I have seen America in contrast with many nations and races. My profession took me into many foreign lands under many kinds of government. I have worked with their great spiritual leaders and their great statesmen. I have worked in governments of free men, of tyrannies, of Socialists, and of Communists. I have met with princes, kings, despots, and desperados.

Excerpts from "The Miracle of America," in *The Woman's Home Companion*, 1947. Reprinted by permission of The Herbert Hoover Foundation, Inc.

I have seen the squalor of Asia, the frozen class barriers of Europe. I was not a tourist. I was associated in their working lives and problems. I had to deal with their social systems and their governments. And outstanding everywhere to these great masses of people there was a hallowed word—*America*. To them it was the hope of the world.

Every homecoming was for me a reaffirmation of the glory of America. Each time my soul was washed by the relief from the grinding poverty of other nations, by the greater kindliness and frankness which comes from acceptance of equality and wide-open opportunity to all who want a chance. It is more than that. It is a land of self-respect born alone of free men.

for discussion

"The Miracle of America" was published in 1947. Do you believe that conditions in the United States were much better then than they are now, or was Mr. Hoover too uncritical in his appraisal?

What Is Right with America?

—HENRY J. TAYLOR

. . . The nation's heart is restless and millions are unsure. But our great country was built on faith, not fear, and this is its very foundation. . . .

Sometimes in our difficulties it is good to look on our blessings, and where we have done all right.

Everything that is good in America didn't happen one day out of nothing. It sits square on the shoulders of everything good that came before it. These goods are the product of our forebears all across America who faced what they found in life and in our country and tried to make it better. The result is a warming display of what can happen. For they knew that when people put a limit on what they can do they put a limit on what they will do. . . .

. . . It is the same at the national level. When a nation thinks there is no more great work it should do, and that the purpose of its life is to hang on and stay put, such a nation begins to die. But in our American outlook we have preserved our great principles and guides.

Beneath the surface we are a land of wonderful people—good people, dear people, decent, warmhearted, courageous, energetic, hard-working, fun-loving people!—but people ready to give their all when the need arises.

We believe that when human beings become intelligent enough to fight nature's forces instead of fighting one another, battles against disease, winds and sand will be far more important than any war ever fought.

We know, of course, that men are products of different races and of particular cultures, but they are also men, more and more caught up in shared dilemma. And beyond this we believe in mankind not as fated, but in mankind as struggling.

© 1971 United Feature Syndicate, Inc. Reprinted by permission.

Blessings be, our national strife springs not from our permanent nature, not from the land or heritage we inherit, not from our national homestead. Our strife pertains to ourselves. It can and must, without convulsion, be corrected. For the fundamental belief on which our country was founded, and which still stands, is that men need not be victims.

Here life, freedom, security and a better living for all are problems to be mastered. This is a heritage which all Americans under our great, broad, star-spangled sky may share with joy and hope—the liberty, dignity, the productivity and the general welfare of each individual citizen.

We stand also for peace beyond our shores. We everlastingly resist history's verdict that fratricide, which is the true definition of war, is mankind's permanent condition.

The great hope of mighty America is that the people of the world can live together in a smaller world, at a higher level of prosperity, without wars.

No nation, we believe, should be an aggressor against any other nation or people. We believe every people should be left free to determine its own way of development—unhindered, unthreatened, unafraid—the small along with the powerful.

To that objective our country has given more and asked less than any nation in the history of the world. This is another reason why we can be proud we are Americans. And in this continuing intention there is a high national purpose and spirit, and we have it.

And, finally, behind the scenes of discord, defeatism and agony a broad, deep tide of national fidelity bears us forward. We love this country. The deep patriotism of a great people guards this nation, maintained and cherished from generation to generation for the advancement of the public good and the glory of Almighty God.

for discussion

Mr. Taylor also gives a rosy view of America. Read the next two articles; then return to this one. Which are the more constructive approaches, the complimentary or the critical? Why? Would you say that any of the writers are more patriotic than the others?

The Shame of America

—EDITORIAL

An injured dog, unable to move and bleeding, remained on a St. Petersburg street for nearly 12 hours last week before he was taken to a veterinarian.

In the Queens area of New York City Sunday, an 8-year-old boy ran frantically from house to house trying to call the police because his friend was buried under 20 feet of sand. The boy was forced to run all the way home to use a telephone. When his friend was dug out of the sand after this 30-minute delay, he was dead.

From the *St. Petersburg Evening Independent,* March 12, 1968. Reprinted by permission.

We commit a half million of our young men to get involved in a war in Southeast Asia, but we refuse to get involved in our own neighborhoods.

We ignore and stand by idly while elderly women have their purses snatched, while accident victims cry in pain, while women are knifed and raped, while children are beaten and while cashiers are pistol-whipped.

We are aloof to calls of help from people drowning. We walk around an ill person who has fallen to the sidewalk. We encourage disturbed people to jump when they stand on window ledges of tall buildings.

We root for the bad guy. We applaud the person who gets away with something. We cheat on our income tax. We make a mockery of marriage vows. We scorn religion. We laugh at the good guy and call him "square."

We refuse to yield the right-of-way to emergency vehicles. We don't vote—or, if we do, we too often do it blindly. We respect only affluence.

We shut our eyes to racial prejudice. We shut our ears to the pleas of the poor. We shut our mouths when it is time to say a kind word. We shut our hearts when we are called on for a warm thought.

This is the decay of America.

An insensitivity of man for his fellow man is a sign of a nation's decay. A nation can be no better than that nation's people.

We adults must change. Our children are emulating us.

The quivering, small, brown and white dog lay in the street so cars had to change lanes to avoid hitting it again. Children in the neighborhood walked past the helpless animal, looked and resumed their play.

Even our children refused to get involved with this bleeding, pathetic animal.

This is the shame of America.

The preceding article does not have the usual expository-type introduction. The title serves that purpose. (As a general rule, it is best to state your main idea in your opening paragraph even if it is stated in the title.) Notice the effective use of repetition in the final sentence and in the references to the little dog.

On the Shooting of Robert Kennedy

—ARTHUR MILLER

Is it not time to take a long look at ourselves, at the way we live and the way we think, and to face the fact that the violence in our streets is the violence in our hearts, that with all our accomplishments, our spires and mines and clean, glistening packages, our charities and gods, we are what we were—a people of violence?

Lincoln, Garfield, McKinley, John F. Kennedy, Martin Luther King, Medgar Evers—plus the line going into a sad infinity of lynched men, of men beaten to death in police cells, of Indians expropriated by knife and gun, of the Negro people held in slavery for a century by a thousand small armies dubbed chivalrous by themselves who long ago enchained black labor and kept black mankind from walking in freedom—Robert Kennedy's brain received only the latest fragment of a barrage as old as this country.

Here is a Congress literally face to face with an army of poor people pleading for some relief of their misery—a Congress whose reply is a sneer, a smirk and a warning to keep order.

Here is a people that would rather clutch hatred to its heart than stretch out a hand in brotherhood to the black man and the poor man. That is why there is violence. It is murderous to tell a man he cannot live where he wishes to live. It is murderous to tell a woman that because she has borne a child out of wedlock that she cannot eat, nor the child either.

There is violence because we have daily honored violence. Any half-educated man in a good suit can make his fortune by concocting a television show whose brutality is photographed in sufficiently monstrous detail. Who produces these shows, who pays to sponsor them, who is honored for acting in them? Are these people delinquent psychopaths slinking along tenement streets? No, they are the pillars of society, our honored men, our exemplars of success and social attainment.

We must begin to feel the shame and contrition we have earned before we can begin to sensibly construct a peaceful society, let alone a peaceful world. A country where people cannot walk safely in their own streets has not earned the right to tell any other people how to govern itself, let alone to bomb and burn that people.

What must be done? A decent humility, not cynicism. Our best cards are finally being called. Thomas Jefferson, a slaveholder, wrote the promise he could not keep himself and we must now keep it. "Life, Liberty and the Pursuit of Happiness." The pursuit of happiness is impossible for millions of Americans.

Let us take the $30 billion from the war, and let us devote the same energy and ingenuity we have given to war and apply it to wiping out the disgrace of poverty in this richest of all nations. Let us feel that disgrace, let us feel it for what it is, a personal affront to each of us that cannot be permitted to stand.

We are 200,000,000 now. Either we begin to construct a civilization, which means a common consciousness of social responsibility, or the predator within us will devour us all.

It must be faced now that we are afraid of the Negro because we have denied him social justice and we do not know how to stop denying him.

We are afraid of the poor because we know that there is enough to go around, that we have not made it our first order of business to literally create the jobs that can and must be created.

We are afraid of other countries because we fear that they know better how to satisfy the demands of poor people and colored people.

We are afraid of ourselves because we have advertised and promoted and sloganized ourselves into a state of contentment, when we know that desperate people surround us everywhere and we do not know how to break out of our contentment.

We are at war not only with Vietnamese but with Americans. Stop both. We are rich enough to wipe out every slum and to open a world of hope to the poor. What keeps us? Do we want peace in Vietnam? Then make peace. Do we want hope in our cities and towns? Then stop denying any man his birthright.

Because America has been bigger on promises than any other country, she must be bigger by far on deliveries. Maybe we have only one promise left in the bag, the promise of social justice for every man regardless of his color or condition.

Between the promise and its denial—there stands the man with the gun. Between the promise and its denial stands a man holding them apart—the American. Either he recognizes what he is doing, or he will take the final, fatal step to suppress the violence he has called up.

Only justice will overcome the nightmare. The American Dream is ours to evoke.

for writing

America: Love It or Leave It

America: If You Love It, Help Improve It

America Must Have a Moral Rebirth

Our Parents Were Wrong

Our Parents Were Right

Critics Are Communists

Constructive Critics Are Real Patriots

Articles Written with a Lighter Touch

Read the three humorous articles below and then decide on a subject of your own.

After reading "The Grown-Up Problem," you may wish to take off on adults in your own humorous way—or pick on parents, aunts and uncles, baby brothers, or dogs.

How dirty are "dirty words?" Do you agree with Wallace Stegner that they should be saved for special occasions, or do you feel that they should be banned altogether? What else would you censor? Whatever it is, have funny reasons.

"Draw One Concentrated Beer" may inspire you to write about your own experiences with or your views of alcoholic beverages, non-alcoholic beverages, or food. Do you see terrible dangers ahead for the human race because of the use of concentrates, frozen foods, and such? If so, write something funny about the dangers you foresee.

The Grown-Up Problem

—ART BUCHWALD

There has been so much discussion about teen-age problems that the grown-up problem is practically being ignored. And yet if you pick up a newspaper, you realize grown-ups are responsible for some of the most serious problems this country has ever faced.

Reprinted by permission of G. P. Putnam's Sons from *Son of the Great Society* by Art Buchwald. Copyright © 1965, 1966 by Art Buchwald.

For example, 60 percent of all crime in the United States is committed by grown-ups.

The birth rate among grown-up women is four times that of teen-agers. The divorce rate is double.

The purchasing power of grown-ups almost exceeds that of teen-agers.

Grown-ups are responsible for more daytime accidents than any other age group.

The source of these statistics is sociology Prof. Heinrich Applebaum, B.A., M.S., LL.D., Y.E.H., Y.E.H., Y.E.H., who told me in an exclusive interview that his studies showed grown-ups were drifting farther away from society all the time.

"The average grown-up," Prof. Applebaum said, "feels his children don't understand him. The more time he spends with them, the less they communicate with him. So the adult feels isolated, insecure, and misunderstood. In defense he seeks out other grown-ups who feel the same way he does. Pretty soon they form gangs, go to the theater together, hold cocktail parties and dances, and before you know it you have a complete breakdown of the family."

"Why do you think grown-ups are constantly rebelling against their children, Professor?"

"I guess it's an age-old old-age problem. You have parents wanting to break away and yet not having the nerve to cut the ties completely. Grown-ups are afraid to stand up to their children, so they rebel against society instead."

"Do you think teen-agers could in some way be responsible for the behavior of their parents?"

"I definitely do," the Professor said. "Grown-ups try to emulate teen-agers. They want to do exactly what teen-agers do, which is to drink, smoke, and drive fast cars. If teen-agers didn't do these things, their parents wouldn't. For every bad adult in America, I'm sure you'll find a bad teen-ager somewhere in the background."

"Where do you think the trouble starts?"

"In the home. Teen-agers are too rough on their parents. They're always criticizing them for listening to Frank Sinatra records and reading *Holiday* magazine. Teen-agers don't have any patience with their mothers and fathers. They can't understand why their parents like Doris Day and Rock Hudson movies or what they see in Cary Grant. If teen-agers spent more time with grown-ups and tried to understand them, I don't think you'd have half the trouble that you have in the United States today."

"Do you mean teen-agers should spend more time at home with their parents?"

"Of course. Grown-ups need security. They want to know where their children are. They want the feeling they belong. Only teen-agers can give grown-ups this feeling."

"Professor, have you found any homes where grown-ups are leading healthy, normal, secure lives, thanks to the attention they've received from their loving teen-age children?"

"We haven't yet. But we've been looking only a year. These surveys take time."

Good-Bye to all T - - t!

—WALLACE STEGNER

Not everyone who laments what contemporary novelists have done to the sex act objects to the act itself, or to its mention. Some want it valued higher than fiction seems to value it; they want the word "climax" to retain some of its literary meaning. Likewise, not everyone who has come to doubt the contemporary freedom of language objects to strong language in itself. Some of us object precisely because we value it.

I acknowledge that I have used four-letter words familiarly all my life, and have put them into books with some sense that I was insisting on the proper freedom of the artist. I have applauded the extinction of those d——d emasculations of the Genteel Tradition and the intrusion into serious fiction of honest words with honest meanings and emphasis. I have wished, with D. H. Lawrence, for the courage to say shit before a lady, and have sometimes had my wish.

Words are not obscene: naming things is a legitimate verbal act. And "frank" does not mean "vulgar," any more than "improper" means "dirty." What vulgar does mean is "common"; what improper means is "unsuitable." Under the right circumstances, any word is proper. But when any sort of word, especially a word hitherto taboo and therefore noticeable, is scattered across a page like chocolate chips through a toll-house cookie, a real impropriety occurs. The sin is not the use of an "obscene" word; it is the use of a loaded word in the wrong place or in the wrong quantity. It is the sin of false emphasis, which is not a moral but a literary lapse, related to sentimentality. It is the sin of advertisers who so plaster a highway with neon signs that you can't find the bar or liquor store you're looking for. Like any excess, it quickly becomes comic.

If I habitually say shit before a lady, what do I say before a flat tire at the rush hour in Times Square or on the San Francisco Bay Bridge? What do I say before a revelation of the inequity of the universe? And what if the lady takes the bit in her teeth and says shit before *me*? . . .

. . . Some acts, like some words, were never meant to be casual. That is why houses contain bedrooms and bathrooms. Profanity and so-called obscenities are literary resources, verbal ways of rendering strong emotion. They are not meant to occur every ten seconds, any more than—Norman Mailer to the contrary notwithstanding—orgasms are.

So I am not going to say shit before any more ladies. I am going to hunt words that have not lost their sting, and it may be I shall have to go back to gentility to find them. Pleasant though it is to know that finally a writer can make use of any word that fits his occasion, I am going to investigate the possibilities latent in restraint.

I remember my uncle, a farmer who had used four-letter words ten to the sentence ever since he learned to talk. One day he came too near the circular saw and cut half his fingers off. While we stared in horror, he stood watching the bright arterial blood pump from his ruined hand. Then he spoke, and he did not speak loud. "Aw, the dickens," he said.

I think he understood, better than some sophomore girls and better than some novelists, the nature of emphasis.

From the *Atlantic Monthly*, March 1965. Reprinted by permission of Wallace Stegner.

Draw One Concentrated Beer

—HERBERT MITGANG

At the Third Avenue-type saloon on Eighth Avenue a couple of the regulars were discussing a subject close to hand—namely, beer. A rumor flew up and down the long mahogany bar that next month automation was going to hit the kegs. Or, rather, a first cousin of automation called concentration. The United States Treasury Department has approved the concentration and reconstitution of the stuff with a label saying: BEER— MADE FROM BEER CONCENTRATES. How the Feds get into the act is that the Alcohol and Tobacco Tax Division puts the arm on beer and thus on the gargler himself.

Anyway, the barflies wondered, was this another blow to those who believed in beer for beer's sake? Here it was four o'clock in the afternoon, perfect beer-drinking time—too late to go back to work after lunch and too early to go home to dinner—and how many such hours of quiet wonder remained? It was bad enough when they took down the El on Third Avenue, pouring in light that could blind a man, put up all those fancy buildings and let anybody into the saloons, turning them into public instead of private places. Now the search for anonymity drove these honest beer drinkers west to Eighth and Ninth. If the saloons served up a concentrate, would the bartender pass you a jigger of beer mix if you asked him to draw one?

Not likely. For 6,000 years beer has been the brew that made some places famous. It has survived voting beauty contests, baseball announcers, Prohibition's 3.2, warnings 'alfway through a pub pint of, "Time, gentlemen, please," bottles, cans and tab tops. It will survive concentration, too.

Beer concentrate is noncarbonated with about 75 percent of the water removed; it is reconstituted by adding the water and carbon dioxide.

But beer isn't just beer. It's place and mystique, too. The delicate balance of the beer drinkers pressed against the bars of the country depends on certain constants. It begins with a size-up of bartender or barmaid and ends in silence or conversation. But not plain silence: bar silence. A man at the four o'clock bar isn't kidding. If his glass hits bottom, it is refilled without a word, before a look of terror crosses his eyes.

And what about those hard-boiled eggs, stacked like cannon balls, behind the bartender? They are a vital part of the ritual, for the man who drinks his lunch of beer, to put a little lining on his insides. Beer or beer concentrate, that hardboiled artillery has got to stay.

The approach to the concentrate raised an interesting point. Would it be possible to do some do-it-yourself mixing? For example, take a nip of concentrate, follow with half a glass of seltzer, then jump up and down in place for two minutes. Would the result meet a brewmaster's delicate proportions? Might the stomach be used as a lager tank, with leftover yeast added to the wort, and occasional ice bags applied to cool the hops?

Anyway, there might be an immediate advantage: no more of those Coney Island heads. The strange bartender who shot the beer into the glass so quickly that the top half became slowly sinking foam might not be able to pull his fast ones any longer. On the other hand, would it still be possible to enlist the sympathy of a friendly bartender filling the request, "Put a little head on it"? Meaning, "I've run out of money, so fill the top half of the glass and I'll be able to make it home better."

What it all added up to, said one of the four o'clock barflies, was the synthetic way things were going all over. Zip codes. Frozen orange juice. Digit dialing. Pre-crinkle-cut French fries. Instant coffee. Checks that talk back: "Do not fold, spindle or mutilate." Prerecorded answering services. Artificial flowers. Powdered eggs.

"You name it," said the talkative man to the bartender, peeling his second hard-boiled, or supper egg, "they got it."

His silent companion nodded, repeated his favorite phrase, "Draw one," then added, "unconcentrated."

ASSIGNMENT 2: React to Cartoons

Write a 200 to 300-word paper in which you develop a subject based on one of the cartoons in this section.

No further writing suggestions are given. From now on you are on your own.

"This is progress?"

© 1959 St. Louis Post-Dispatch. Reproduced by courtesy of Bill Mauldin.

"You mean there's no other way to
keep them from going Communist?"

© 1959 St. Louis Post-Dispatch. Reproduced by
courtesy of Bill Mauldin.

Lee Lorenz © 1965 Saturday Review, Inc.

"Good heavens! Look what's moved in next door."

"... and I ask, gentlemen, if this is the face of a villain, a cheat and a parasite?"

© PUNCH, London.

ASSIGNMENT 3: React to Poems

Write a 200 to 300-word paper in which you develop a subject based on one or more of the poems in this section.

Sea-Fever

——JOHN MASEFIELD

I must down to the seas again, to the lonely sea and the sky,
And all I ask is a tall ship and a star to steer her by,
And the wheel's kick and the wind's song and the white sail's shaking,
And a gray mist on the sea's face and a gray dawn breaking.

I must down to the seas again, for the call of the running tide
Is a wild call and a clear call that may not be denied;
And all I ask is a windy day with the white clouds flying,
And the flung spray and the blown spume and the sea-gulls crying.

I must down to the seas again to the vagrant gypsy life,
To the gull's way and the whale's way where the wind's like a whetted
knife;
And all I ask is a merry yarn from a laughing fellow-rover,
And quiet sleep and a sweet dream when the long trick's over.

The Heroes

—LOUIS SIMPSON

I dreamed of war-heroes, of wounded war-heroes
With just enough of their charms shot away
To make them more handsome. The women moved nearer
To touch their brave wounds and their hair streaked with gray.

I saw them in long ranks ascending the gang-planks;
The girls with the doughnuts were cheerful and gay.
They minded their manners and muttered their thanks;
The Chaplain advised them to watch and to pray.

They shipped these rapscallions, these sea-sick battalions
To a patriotic and picturesque spot;
They gave them new bibles and marksmen's medallions,
Compasses, maps, and committed the lot.

A fine dust has settled on all that scrap metal.
The heroes were packaged and sent home in parts
To pluck at a poppy and sew on a petal
And count the long night by the stroke of their hearts.

"The Heroes" (Copyright 1950 Louis Simpson) is reprinted by permission
of Charles Scribner's Sons from *Good News of Death and Other Poems* by
Louis Simpson (POETS OF TODAY II).

The Man He Killed

—THOMAS HARDY

Had he and I but met
By some old ancient inn,
We should have sat us down to wet
Right many a nipperkin!

But ranged as infantry
And staring face to face,
I shot at him as he at me,
And killed him in his place.

I shot him dead because—
Because he was my foe,
Just so: my foe of course he was;
That's clear enough; although

He thought he'd 'list, perhaps
Off-hand-like—just as I—
Was out of work—had sold his traps—
No other reason why.

Yes; quaint and curious war is!
You shoot a fellow down
You'd treat if met where any bar is,
Or help to half-a-crown.

This Excellent Machine

—JOHN LEHMANN

This excellent machine is neatly planned,
A child, a half-wit would not feel perplexed:
No chance to err, you simply press the button—
At once each cog in motion moves the next,
The whole revolves, and anything that lives
Is quickly sucked towards the running band,
Where, shot between the automatic knives,
It's guaranteed to finish dead as mutton.

This excellent machine will illustrate
The modern world divided into nations:
So neatly planned, that if you merely tap it
The armaments will start their devastations,
And though we're for it, though we're all convinced
Some fool will press the button soon or late,
We stand and stare, expecting to be minced—
And very few are asking *Why not scrap it?*

Men

—DOROTHY PARKER

They hail you as their morning star
Because you are the way you are.
If you return the sentiment,
They'll try to make you different;
And once they have you, safe and sound,
They want to change you all around.
Your moods and ways they put a curse on;
They'd make of you another person.
They cannot let you go your gait;
They influence and educate.
They'd alter all that they admired.
They make me sick, they make me tired.

Love

—ANONYMOUS

There's the wonderful love of a beautiful maid,
    And the love of a staunch true man,
And the love of a baby that's unafraid—
    All have existed since time began.
But the most wonderful love, the Love of all loves,
    Even greater than the love for Mother,
Is the infinite, tenderest, passionate love
    Of one dead drunk for another.

Unsatisfied Yearning

—R. K. MUNKITTRICK

Down in the silent hallway
    Scampers the dog about,
And whines, and barks, and scratches,
    In order to get out.

Once in the glittering starlight,
    He straightway doth begin
To set up a doleful howling
    In order to get in!

ASSIGNMENT 4: React to Pictures

Write a 200 to 300-word paper in which you develop a subject based on one of the pictures in this section.

Courtesy Equitable Life Assurance Society

Courtesy The Council on Human Relations, Cleveland

Hubert LeCampion, LIFE Magazine © Time Inc.

Courtesy Denver Public Library

Photo by Martha Swope

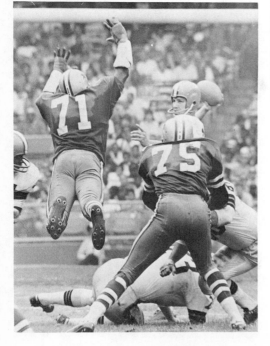

Photos by Tony Tomsic

IT IS SAID that a truly intelligent person will not remember everything that he has studied, but he will know where to look for the answers. Now that you are acquainted with this "clinic," use its facilities whenever you are unsure of yourself. It should be referred to for grammar and mechanical problems in the same way that you refer to a dictionary for spelling problems. So, good writing, and remember to

INDEX

come back

for

checkups...

INDEX

Adverbs (*continued*)
  modifying adjectives, 188
  modifying other adverbs, 188
  modifying verbs, 188
  most | almost, 180
  no | not, 190
  only, position of, in a sentence, 190
  really | very, 190
  well | good, 189–90
Advice | advise, 198
Affect | effect, 198
Agreement:
  of pronouns with antecedents, 179–80, 181–82
  of subject with verb, 25*n*, 27, *57–73*
  See also Subject-verb agreement
All ready | already, 198
All together | altogether, 198
Altar | alter, 198
Am | are | is, to form present progressive tense, 145
Among | between, 198
And:
  as coordinate conjunction, 79, 80
  to separate coordinate adjectives, 133
  to start a sentence, 104
And-but pattern, in compound sentences, 78–79
Angel | angle, 198
Angry | mad, 198
Antecedents, agreement of pronouns with, 179–80
Anyone, anybody, singular verb with, 179
Appositives, 135–36
  of pronouns with subjects, 183
  punctuation of, 135–36
  restrictive, 135–36
Apostrophe:
  in contractions, 196
  to form possessives, 195
Arguments (reasons), development by, in expository writing, 224–25
Auxiliary verbs, 32–34
  am | are | is, to form present progressive tense, 145
  do, as an emphatic, 155
  errors of omitting, 157
  had, to form past perfect tense, 147, 149
  had been, to form past perfect progressive tense, 147–48
  have | has | has been, to form present tenses, 145
  with *-ing* verbs, 161–62
  modal auxiliaries, 32–34
  in past tenses, 66–67
  placement of, in questions, 42
  regular auxiliaries, 33–34

Auxiliary (*continued*)
  with tenses of verbs, 145–48
  was | were, to form past progressive tense, 147
  will (have) (be) (have been), to form future tenses, 146

B

Be verbs:
  with adjectives, 187–88
  defined, 27
  past tense forms, 66–67
  present tense forms, 63, 145
  in present progressive tense, 145
  as regular auxiliaries, 33
  subjective case of pronouns with, 183
  in the subjunctive mode, 156
BROUN, Heywood, 231–32
BUCHWALD, Art, 242–43
But:
  as a coordinate conjunction, 79, 80
  to start a sentence, 104

C

Can | could, 32
Capitalization, 192–94
  of compass directions, 194
  of first words, 194
  of geographical sections, 194
  of proper nouns, 192–93
  of titles, 193–94
Chronological organization, in expository writing, 217
Cite | site | sight, 199
Classification, development by, in expository writing, 223–24
Clauses:
  distinguished from phrases, 90
  main, in compound sentences, 45*n*, 78
  non-restrictive, 136
  subordinate, *88–89*, 93–94
  restrictive, 136
  in series, comma with, 133
Collective nouns:
  list of, 60
  pronouns with, 180
  singular or plural, 180
Colon, 130–31
  function of, 130
  before a list, 131
  before a quotation, 131
  after the salutation of a letter, 131
  before a series of directions, 131
Comma, 132–37
  in addresses, 137
  with adjectives in a series, 133

Comma (*continued*)
with appositives, 135–36
comma splice, *82*, 113
in complex sentences, 93, 94, 99*n*, 137
in compound sentences, 111, 137
with conjunctive adverbs, 81*n*
with coordinate adjectives, 133
with coordinate conjunctions, 78–79
with dates, 136–37
before direct quotations, 137
function of, 132–33
with interjections, 135
with non-restrictive appositives, 135–36
with nouns of address, 25–26, 134
omission of, before non-coordinate adjectives, 133
with parenthetical expressions, 135
with phrases, 52*n*
to prevent misreading, 134
before quotations, 137
with restrictive appositive, not used, 135–36
in salutations, 137
to separate words out of their usual order, 135
in series, 133
with semicolon in series, 133
to separate words out of their usual order, 135
in series, 133
Commands:
with present tense, 144
and the subjunctive use of *be*, 156
with "you understood," 25–26
Comma splice, *82*, 113
Common nouns, 192
Comparative degree, when used, 191–92
Comparison, development by, in expository writing, 220–22
paragraph-by-paragraph, 221–22
sentence-by-sentence, 221
Comparison of adjectives and adverbs, 191–92
Compass directions, capitalization of, 194
Complex sentences, *87–195*, 111–12
commas in, 137
introductory phrases in, 96
patterns of, 93–94
punctuation of, 93–94
subjects and verbs, patterns of, 98–99
subordinate conjunctions in, *88–89*, 93–94, 99
review of, 111–12
Compound sentences, 77–84
and-but pattern, 78–79
commas in, 137
comma splices in, 82

Compound senteeces (*continued*)
conjunctive adverbs in, 81*n*
coordinate conjunction-semicolon pattern, 79
coordinate conjunctions in, 78, 81
either . . . or pattern, 79
main clauses in, 78
patterns of, 78–80
review of, 110–11
run-on sentences, 82
semicolon in, 78, 79, 131
Conclusion of theme, in expository writing, 207–208, 210–11, 214, 217
"*Conformity of Young Rebels*" (Preston), 15
Conjunctive adverbs:
defined, 81*n*
as introductory words of a new sentence, 131*n*
semicolon before, 131
Conjunctions:
and or *but*, to start a sentence, 104
coordinate conjunctions, 78–81
punctuation with, 78
subordinate conjunctions, *88–89*, 93–94
Connectives. *See* Conjunctions
Conscience / conscious, 199
Consequently, as a coordinate conjunction, 81
Consonants, doubling of:
in comparison of one-syllable adjectives, 191*n*
to form past tense, 144*n*, 157
Contractions, 196
Coordinate adjectives, commas with, 133
Coordinate conjunctions, 78–81
omission of, in compound sentences, 79, 111
semicolon before, 131
to start a sentence, 104
with words or phrases, 78*n*
Coordinate conjunction-semicolon pattern, in compound sentences, 79
Council / counsel, 199
CULLEN, Countee, 10

D

-d or *-ed*:
errors of omitting, 157
with past tense of verbs, 144, *147*
Dash, 137–38
for emphasis, 137–38
for parenthetical remarks, 138
for a series using commas, 137
Dates, commas with, 136–37

Nouns (*continued*)
    as objects of prepositions, 69–71
    plurals of, 58–60
    proper nouns, 58, 192–93
    properties of, 178
    as singulars or plurals, 60
Nouns of address, not subjects of a
    sentence, 25–26
Number:
    of nouns, 58–60
    of verbs, 62–64
    of words with only one form, 59
Numbers, in series, parentheses with,
    138

O

Object of the preposition, 69–71
Object pronouns, 185
One, as an impersonal pronoun, 185
Only, position of, in a sentence, 190
"*On the Shooting of Robert Kennedy*"
    (Miller), 240–42
Organization, types of, in expository
    writing, 217–18
    chronological, 217
    emphatic and dramatic, 218
    logical, 218
    process, 218
    spatial, 217
ORWELL, George, 233–34
Otherwise, as a coordinate conjunction,
    81
Ought to, as a verb, 33*n*

P

Paragraph-by-paragraph comparison,
    in expository writing, 221–22
Paragraphs. *See* Expository writing
Parentheses, 138
Parenthetical expressions:
    commas with, 135
    dash with, 138
PARKER, Dorothy, 250
Participle, perfect (past), 145*n*, *149–52*,
    157
Passive voice, 154
Past / passed, 200
Past participle, with perfect tenses,
    145*n*, 149–52, 157
Past perfect progressive tense, 147–48
Past perfect tense, 147
Past progressive tense, 147
Past tense:
    of *be*, 66–67
    irregular verbs, 149–52
    and perfect tense, in writing, 164

Past tense (*continued*)
    regular verbs, 147–48
Perfect (past) participles, with perfect
    tenses, 145*n*, *149–52*, 157
Perfect tenses, and past tenses, in
    writing, 164
Period, 128–29
    with abbreviations, 129
    after a declarative sentence, 128
    in dialogue, 128–29
    with ellipsis points, 129
    in rhetorical questions, 129
    in sentences introduced by a
        conjunctive adverb, 131*n*
Person, of verbs, 62–63
Persons, description of, in expository
    writing, 218–19
Phrases:
    distinguished from clauses, 90
    introductory adverbial phrases, 44
    introductory phrases, in complex
        sentences, 96
    prepositional phrases, 69–71
    in series, commas with, 133
    verbs phrases, 32–34
Places, description of, in expository
    writing, 218
Plurals:
    of collective nouns, 60
    formed by change of vowel, 59
    on nouns, 58–60
    possessive forms of, 195
    of proper nouns, 59
POE, Edgar Allen, 218
Possessives, 194–95
    apostrophe in, 195
    forms of, without ownership, 195
    of nouns, 178
    of pronouns, 184–85, 195
    verbs, 28, 33, 194
"*Potter's Field*" (Styron), 16–17
Prepositional phrases, 69–71
Prepositions, 69–71
    list of, 70
    with subordinate conjunctions, 97*n*
Present "future" tense, 165
Present perfect progressive tense, 145
Present perfect tense, 145, 149
Present progressive tense:
    defined, 145
    to express future action, 165
Present tense, 144–52
    of *be*, 63, 66–67
    habitual present tense, 165
    historic present tense, 165
    of irregular verbs, 149–52
    present "future" tense, 165
    of regular verbs, 144–45

NOTES

NOTES